Verbal Workout for the

GMAT®

4th Edition

By Doug French and the Staff of The Princeton Review

PrincetonReview.com

Penguin
Random
House

The Princeton Review
24 Prime Parkway, Suite 201
Natick, MA 01760
E-mail: editorialsupport@review.com

Published in the United States by Penguin Random House LLC,
New York, and in Canada by Random House of Canada,
a division of Penguin Random House Ltd., Toronto.

ISBN: 978-1-101-88165-1
eBook ISBN: 978-1-101-88171-2
ISSN: 2163-6060

Editor: Colleen Day
Production Editor: Jim Melloan
Production Artist: Keren Peysakh

Printed in the United States of America on partially recycled paper.

10 9 8 7 6 5 4 3 2 1

4th Edition

Editorial

Rob Franek, Senior VP, Publisher
Casey Cornelius, VP Content Development
Mary Beth Garrick, Director of Production
Selena Coppock, Managing Editor
Calvin Cato, Editor
Colleen Day, Editor
Aaron Riccio, Editor
Meave Shelton, Editor
Orion McBean, Editorial Assistant

Random House Publishing Team

Tom Russell, Publisher
Alison Stoltzfus, Publishing Manager
Melinda Ackell, Associate Managing Editor
Ellen Reed, Production Manager
Kristin Lindner, Production Supervisor
Andrea Lau, Designer

Acknowledgments

I'm especially indebted to John Fulmer, Jack Schieffer, and Rob Tallia, who have supervised almost all of the GMAT course development work that I've done for The Princeton Review. Thanks for the work, boys.

Thanks also to Elia Zashin, Dave Ragsdale, Patricia Dublin, Stephanie Martin, and Suzanne Markert, who helped in revising this book.

Thanks as well to the many hundreds of GMAT students I've helped over the years, all of whom have helped me become a better instructor. My most challenging and satisfying teaching experience was the three-month course I taught at Samsung in South Korea, where my students were gluttons for homework. Much of this book derives from my experiences during that course; thanks for teaching me that the best weapons against the GMAT are diligence and patience.

Special thanks to Adam Robinson, who conceived of and perfected the Joe Bloggs approach to standardized tests and many other techniques used in this book.

The Princeton Review would also like to thank John Fulmer and Kyle Fox for their work on this edition.

Contents

Part I
Introduction

THE IMPORTANCE OF BEING VERBAL

Welcome to The Princeton Review's *Verbal Workout for the GMAT*. If you've just purchased this book (or you're just casually browsing while you throw back your third cup of coffee), you probably fall into one of the following three categories:

1. You're about to take the GMAT and you feel okay about the math section, but you need to brush up on your verbal skills so that you can get the best score possible;

2. You're about to take the GMAT, you're petrified that you'll bomb it, and you've made it your goal to get the best test-prep guide to ensure that you will avoid utter humiliation;

3. You have no plans to take the GMAT, but you're just one of those people who digs books about grammar and wants to learn to read more efficiently.

More Great Books!

Check out *The Best Business Schools,* our survey-driven guide to the top business schools in the country.

If your circumstances match any of those above, you've found the right book. Sure, there are many prep guides for taking the GMAT, but this one is especially designed to concentrate *only on your verbal skills*. If you want to follow a test-prep book that reviews all aspects of the GMAT, check out The Princeton Review's *Cracking the GMAT*. For further, specific review of the Quantitative, or Math, section of the GMAT, The Princeton Review's *Math Workout for the GMAT* is an excellent resource.

Having strong verbal skills extends beyond increasing your appreciation of proper grammar and learning how to deconstruct arguments. Applying to business school is a decidedly verbal process, during which you will be judged by how well you assimilate information and how well you express yourself. If you doubt this, just look at all of the essays on Harvard's business school application. Most applicants don't get into business school because they know the Pythagorean theorem or can calculate π to the 1,000th decimal place. Most students gain admission because their essays eloquently tell admissions committees about themselves and indicate how well they can share ideas with others.

This book's purpose is twofold. First and foremost, the goal of this book is to teach you how to improve your score on the GMAT's Verbal section. But we're also going to look at the bigger picture; by learning to read actively and write expressively, you'll build skills that will serve you long after you gleefully descend the podium while clutching your MBA diploma.

Granted, our goal is not to turn you into James Joyce. It's just that in the business world, too often verbal skills are overlooked. If you can master the skills discussed herein, applying to business school and succeeding once you are there will be a lot easier.

WHAT IS THE PRINCETON REVIEW?

The Princeton Review is a test-preparation company founded in New York City, with branches in more than 50 cities across the country and abroad. The Princeton Review's techniques are unique and effective, and they were developed after a study of thousands of real GMAT questions—which is why they work. The Princeton Review's strategies for beating the GMAT Verbal section will help you improve your scores by teaching you to

- think like a test writer

- take advantage of the computer-adaptive algorithms upon which the GMAT is based

- use Process of Elimination (POE) and other strategies to find answers to questions you may not understand

- avoid traps set by the test writers

By learning and using our strategies, you'll be on your way to your best verbal score.

A LITTLE ABOUT THE GMAT

The GMAT is published and administered by a private company called the Graduate Management Admission Council, or GMAC. The exam is 3.5 hours long and offered on a computer. Here's a rough breakdown of how these 3.5 hours will be spent:

- One 30-minute essay, to be written on the computer using a generic word processing program

- A 30-minute, 12-question Integrated Reasoning section. This section is multiple choice and some questions may have multiple parts.

- (Optional break)

- A 75-minute Math section consisting of 37 questions

- (Optional break)

- A 75-minute Verbal section consisting of 41 questions

About 25 percent of the questions you encounter in the Math and Verbal sections are experimental and, therefore, will not count towards your score.

How to Register

Important Website!
To register for the GMAT, go to **www.mba.com**.

You can take the GMAT year-round, on almost any day, and as of this writing, it will cost you $250. You can take the GMAT once every 31 calendar days and a maximum of five times in a year. The easiest way to register is online. If you check out GMAC's GMAT website at **www.mba.com**, you can find information on all sorts of topics, including the following:

- the latest GMAT information, including upcoming MBA forums

- practice test questions

- Analytical Writing Assessment (AWA) essay topics

- testing sites and phone numbers

- links to hundreds of business schools

- financial aid information

How the Computer-Adaptive GMAT Sections Work

To understand how to beat the computer-adaptive sections of the exam (Math and Verbal), you should first understand how they work. Unlike paper-based standardized tests that begin with an easy question and get progressively more difficult, computer-adaptive sections on the GMAT begin with a question of medium difficulty. If you get it right, you'll see a question that's a little harder; if you get it wrong, your next question will be easier. If you get a lot of questions wrong on the outset, the computer will give you slightly easier questions. The idea is that the computer will zero in on your exact level of ability very quickly and thus make a more finely honed assessment of your abilities.

That's why it's important to take a lot of time on the early questions while the computer is still finding out about you. As the section progresses, a right or wrong answer has less of an impact on your overall score. In fact, the computer has a pretty good idea what your verbal score will be when the section is about half over.

Another important feature of computer-adaptive sections is that you can't skip any questions. On a paper-and-pencil test, if you don't like a question, you can move on and find something else you like better. But the computer doesn't know what to give you until you answer the question in front of you. That's the whole point of an adaptive test: It takes your earlier responses into account when deciding what to give you next. So you have no choice but to answer the questions on the GMAT in the order it gives them to you.

Finally, not only can you not skip any questions, but you also can't go back and change anything after you select an answer. Once you finish a question, it's gone. Keep focused on the question in front of you, and don't worry about the ones before and after it.

The Good and the Bad of the Computer-Adaptive Test

At first some students react negatively to the computer format because it's unfamiliar, and different types of questions arrive in rapid-fire order. Plus, using the mouse to click on an answer can seem disconcerting when you're trying to eliminate wrong answers because you can't cross 'em out.

When you think about it, though, there really isn't much to be upset about. The questions themselves are pretty much the same. Like anything, the computer format has good points and bad points. Let's get the brief rundown out of the way now.

The Bad

- You can't skip any questions, and you can't go back to them later.

- You can't cross off answer choices on the page, write on the problems, or underline passages like you can on a paper-and-pencil test.

- You have to know how to type in order to write the essay.

- The test costs about four times as much as it used to.

The Good

- There are generally a lot fewer questions on computer-adaptive tests than on paper-based tests, and you have more time per question.

- You don't have to worry about mis-bubbling answers or desperately filling in your answer sheet at the last minute.

- You get your scores for the Math and Verbal sections right away—no more waiting.

THE STRUCTURE OF THE GMAT

When you take the GMAT, you'll spend about four hours in front of a computer screen. Your experience will go something like this:

- **Check-In:** You show your ID, sign some paperwork, and have a photograph taken. Before you go into the testing room, you have to put your belongings into a small locker. You aren't allowed to take anything with you into the testing room. The test center provides you with scratch paper and pens.

- **Essay:** The AWA consists of one essay: Analysis of an Argument. You will have 30 minutes to write this essay, and it is scored on a scale of 1 to 6. This score is not factored into your three-digit GMAT score. You get a separate essay score when you receive your official score report from the Graduate Management Admission Council (GMAC).

- **Integrated Reasoning:** You get 30 minutes to answer 12 questions of four different types—table analysis, graphics interpretation, multi-source reasoning, and two-part analysis. Each of the 12 questions has multiple parts, and there may be more than one answer that is correct.

- **Optional Break #1:** Drink some water, do some jumping jacks, whatever makes you happy and keeps you alert, but be prompt. The break is 8 minutes long and timed on your computer, and it will start the next section with or without you.

- **Math Section:** You get 75 minutes to answer 37 multiple-choice questions. Approximately 25% (or around 9) of the questions are experimental.

- **Optional Break #2**

- **Verbal Section:** You get 75 minutes to answer 41 multiple-choice questions. Approximately 25% (or around 11) are experimental. The three types of questions—sentence correction, argument, and reading comprehension—are interspersed throughout the section.

- **Scores Delivered:** In 2014 GMAC announced that test takers will now be able to preview their unofficial scores for Math, Verbal, and Integrated Reasoning before deciding whether to report them to schools or to cancel them. Under this new process, you will have two minutes after you finish the exam to decide if you want to accept or cancel the scores. Your scores will be automatically canceled if you do not make a choice within the two-minute time frame. If you decide to cancel the scores at the test center but then change your mind, you have the option of reinstating them within 60 days of the test date for a $100 fee. After 60 days, this option is no longer available. Also note that you will not see your Analytical Writing Assessment score at the test center; this score will be included on the official score report, which is available to view online within 20 days of the test date.

THE GMAT AND BUSINESS SCHOOL ADMISSIONS

Students think too much about the importance of GMAT scores. Sure, they're required, but there are many other factors involved. These include the following:

- your grade point average (GPA) in college

- the school at which you earned your GPA

- how long you've been out of college

- what you've done since college

- what your superiors think of what you've done since college (which will be expressed in their recommendations)

- your application essays

- your interview, if you have one

Admissions officers look at your GMAT verbal score as a broad indicator of your verbal skills. It's not the best indicator of your abilities, but it's the best they've got. More importantly, though, business schools want to discern two important things from the vast quantity of verbal work you submit to them: They want to know that your command of English is sufficient to keep up with the lectures in class, and they prefer applicants who can communicate ideas eloquently.

These two considerations are especially important if you're a foreign student hoping to attend business school in the United States. The number of business school applicants from overseas has ballooned greatly over the past decade, and entrance into the top programs has become much more competitive. If you are a foreign student, be sure to ask the programs in which you are interested about their requirements for the Test of English as a Foreign Language (TOEFL) or the Test of English in Conversation (TOEIC).

You can find a lot more information about the application process on The Princeton Review's website, **www.PrincetonReview.com**. Our online bookstore carries a large number of titles regarding business vocabulary, internships, careers, interviewing, networking, creating résumés and cover letters, and hunting for the perfect job. The site's Internship Search tool provides access to thousands of internships worldwide.

HOW TO USE THIS BOOK

This book is a "workout" because it focuses solely on the Verbal portion of the GMAT. We've covered the nuts and bolts of the Verbal section by devoting a chapter to each of the three types of multiple-choice questions—Sentence Correction, Critical Reasoning, and Reading Comprehension. There is also a chapter on how to write the best essay for the Analytical Writing Assessment, and we've added a chapter that gives you the basics on the Integrated Reasoning section.

Train Yourself

With practice, you can become a skilled reader, writer, and communicator—which will take you far!

Because this book focuses only on the Verbal section, however, we've tried to explore the less tangible concepts that every test taker should consider, such as assessing your strengths and weaknesses as a communicator and processing information. Use this book to help develop a more basic appreciation for your verbal skills. Among the topics we discuss is the idea of "active reading," which is quite different from the reading most adults do in their daily lives but is essential to improving your scores on the Reading Comprehension and Critical Reasoning sections. In addition, training yourself to be a better writer (and anyone can do it with practice) will improve the quality not only of your application essays but also of anything you write that someone else will read.

Identify Wrong Answers

As we'll discuss later in this book, one of the most useful skills you'll develop is the ability to determine why an answer choice is *wrong*. When the test writers create GMAT questions, there are several tricks they use to get you to pick the wrong answer. Each section will outline several common trap answer choices the test writers use to distract you, so you'll learn to recognize and eliminate them.

Note: The answer choices on the actual GMAT don't have letters assigned to them. Instead, you select your response by clicking on an adjacent oval. For the sake of clarity and brevity, we'll refer to the five answer choices as (A), (B), (C), (D), and (E).

Use Scratch Paper to Practice

One of the great things about a paper-and-pencil test is that you can mark up your test booklet—especially while you're using Process of Elimination to get rid of answer choices. Because the computer monitor doesn't afford you this option, you want to avoid the urge to mark up this book and get used to working solely with scratch paper. Get some loose-leaf paper (preferably as part of a notebook, so you can refer to it as often as you need) and leave the problems alone. It will feel a little odd, but getting used to it will help on test day. We discuss the use of scratch paper in greater detail on page 13.

Practice, Practice, Practice!

We've included drills and practice questions to help you absorb and apply the techniques you'll learn and there's a practice GMAT Verbal section in Part IV, complete with answers and explanations. For the best results, you should work on as many problems as possible. This means getting the most recent edition of GMAC's *Official Guide for GMAT® Review*, which has hundreds more questions, and working through them until these techniques become second nature. You can find more practice questions (and get accustomed to the computer interface) by using the GMATPrep® software that GMAC will send to you when you register for the test. (It's also available as a free download at **www.mba.com**.)

As you do the work, both on paper and on the computer screen, look for patterns in the questions you answer correctly and those you keep getting wrong. This will help you pinpoint your strengths and weaknesses and guide you to the areas in which you need more practice. It will also help you make the most of your study time—which, for adults holding down demanding jobs, can be quite limited.

EXPAND YOUR VOCABULARY

Suppose you or someone you know is expecting a baby. You buy one of those baby care books, and you read the following sentence in the introduction:

> Opinions of parenthood vary from couple to couple, but most parents agree that raising children can be an enervating experience.

If you don't know what *enervating* means (and let's face it—it isn't a word that you come across often), are you likely to look up the word? Or will you just assume that you can figure out the word's meaning using the context of the sentence?

If you fall into the latter category, you might come to the conclusion that *enervating* means "exhilarating" or "life-affirming." And you would be incorrect: *enervate* means to "lessen the vitality or strength" of something!

Fall Back in Love with the Written Word!

One of the most powerful ways to improve your verbal skills is to redevelop an appreciation for the English language. We see written words all the time, so we tend to take them for granted. If you sit back and think about the many ways we weave them together to make prose, you'll see how versatile they are. And you'll also see how awful it is that we confine ourselves to the same small fraction of the verbal spectrum in our daily dialogue.

You were probably first told to learn new words when you started scribbling the meanings of big words on index cards as you prepared for the SAT. Right now, you're probably thinking to yourself, "Exactly. That's what kids do." As it happens,

Look It Up!

If you come across an unfamiliar vocabulary word, brush off that dictionary (or open up a dictionary app on your smart phone) and look it up. You'll be a wordsmith before you know it.

you're never too old to expand your lexicon, especially because you're going to spend the next several months writing essays both on the GMAT and for your business school applications.

So don't be so contumacious. Avoid recalcitrance and nescience. As you're reading whatever you're reading, take note of any words you haven't seen before. Don't just get a feeling for the word using the context of the sentence. Instead, follow these simple instructions:

- Get up.

- Go find a dictionary (every GMAT student should have one) and blow the dust off it. Alternatively, you can use an online dictionary, such as **www.Merriam-Webster.com**, or a dictionary app, which are available for most tablets and smart phones.

- Look the word up. It's very simple. For your convenience, all the words in the dictionary are in alphabetical order.

Get in the habit of learning at least ten new words per week. You'll be surprised how fast your appreciation for language improves.

Embrace the Bumps in the Road

Most importantly, keep in mind that no course of test preparation is perfect. You're about to learn several new techniques that might seem difficult to use at first, and your practice scores might dip downward as a result. Don't be discouraged by this because it's quite normal. Preparing for the GMAT involves a little tearing down of your old methods in order for these new techniques to take root. You're bound to make mistakes, and that's perfectly fine—mistakes teach you a lot more about yourself.

It usually takes a while for the techniques to sink in, so when you try the practice problems, be sure to apply what you've learned as much as possible. Keep practicing, and stay focused. Good luck!

Part II
General
Test-Taking
Tips

HAVE NO FEAR

Do you consider yourself a good test taker? Or does the thought of all this rigidly timed mayhem reduce you to heart palpitations and night sweats?

The GMAT can seem like an intimidating impediment to your acceptance to business school. After all, the GMAT doesn't exist to help you get into school; it's mostly used as a reason to keep you out. But the experience doesn't have to be as intimidating as you might make it out to be. This chapter is devoted to helping you get over whatever neuroses about the exam you might harbor deep down, and it will reveal a few basic elements of test taking that will help you increase your score.

PACE YOURSELF!

Keeping your brain revved up to full power for four hours is a strenuous undertaking. Therefore, it's probably helpful for you to know that you don't have to stay in fifth gear during the entire exam. Working at a steady pace that's comfortable for you is actually better than racing through the entire section. Time is your most valuable asset on the GMAT, so learn to use it wisely.

As we discussed in the Introduction, the computer-adaptive test reacts to how well you're doing so far. In the early part of each section, the computer is still getting a feel for your level of ability, so it's best to make a good first impression. For this reason, it's best to linger on the early questions and take your time to ensure your best effort. Once you've answered twenty questions or so, the computer has made up its mind about you for the most part.

Thus, it makes sense to take extra time to answer the early questions because they have a much greater impact on your score than the later ones do.

Pacing Guidelines

It is very important that you answer every question on the GMAT. If you don't, you will be heavily penalized. However, that doesn't mean that you have to give every question your maximum effort. Pace yourself with these guidelines in mind:

Don't Linger!

If you don't know the answer to a question, it's better to make an educated guess and move on rather than get stuck trying to figure it out.

- Work slowly and deliberately on the first twenty or so questions of each section.

- Speed up gradually, keeping aware of the time remaining.

- When time winds down, you may have to stop working on questions and just click through the remaining ones to ensure that you answer them all.

- Don't linger on questions if you think they're just plain impossible. Staring at a question rarely results in the "lightbulb moment" you're hoping for. Make an educated guess (we'll show you how in upcoming chapters), and move on.

POE Shall Set You Free

Process of Elimination (POE) is a valuable tool that will come up a lot in this book. POE involves eliminate wrong answer choices to reveal the correct one.

> If you've narrowed your choices down to two, don't look for reasons why one is better than the other. Instead, find reasons why one is *worse* than the other.

In many circumstances, you don't have to know why the correct answer is correct. All you have to realize is that the other four are definitely wrong. The only answer choice left is correct by default. Each chapter will discuss what makes wrong answers wrong in greater detail. For now, just recognize that POE is one of the biggest weapons in your arsenal. If you work methodically and learn to recognize the patterns that wrong answers fall into, you can increase your score by making educated guesses that reduce the number of possibilities you have to choose from.

Use Your Scratch Paper

Even though you can't cross off answer choices on a computer-based test, the test center will provide you with a blank 10-page booklet and a fine-tipped black marker for scratch work. The pages are laminated and have a grid pattern so that you can draw math diagrams. You can always request more scratch paper if you run out, but you'll have to hold your hand in the air and wait for a proctor to bring it in to you. So it's in your best interests to make your booklet last for an entire section; you can re-stock your supply during the break.

For every verbal question, you should list A, B, C, D, and E vertically on your scratch paper so that you can cross wrong answers off as you apply the Process of Elimination. You may also find it helpful to use your scratch paper for other purposes such as making notes about reading comprehension passages or identifying the assumptions of arguments. The most important thing, however, is using your scratch paper to apply POE.

Using this technique, you can keep track of the answer choices you've eliminated more easily. With all that's going through your head during the exam, it pays to keep things as simple and direct as possible.

A LITTLE ZEN

Speaking of making things easier, here's a point that few test-prep guides bring up. Scoring well on standardized tests requires two important and different skills. Of course, you need to prepare for the exam by practicing techniques on practice material so that you know how to match up subjects and verbs and how to calculate percentages. But the second skill, which is just as important as the first, is the ability to be a better test taker. Your eloquence and facility with the English language might put Churchill to shame, but if you stress out when the computer launches your test, you won't get far.

Don't Stress

We know it's easier said than done, but it's important to stay focused on doing your best rather than panicking about the possible consequences of the exam.

Test stress occurs when you think too much about the consequences of the exam you're taking. Few would argue that taking a standardized test is a pleasant, stress-free experience. In truth, most find it to be a real pain. You're stuck in a room with a computer terminal staring at you mockingly. You know you need a good GMAT score to get into the top-echelon program of your choice.

Many students who have planned to attend business school for a long time become obsessed with the subtleties of the application process. They preoccupy themselves with questions such as "How important is the GMAT to my overall application?" and "What if my GPA is too low?"

These are valid questions, but you have no way of ascertaining their answers. We would all like to think that we know exactly what admissions folks want, but in truth, we don't. The precise process by which applications are considered is too subjective and too unpredictable to obsess over. So don't.

Stay Focused on the Task at Hand

The best way to approach a standardized exam is to live in the present. Don't think about your application, your interview, or the impact that your GMAT score will have on your chances for admission. Just accept the idea that you will give it your best shot and see if the admissions gurus think you would be a good fit for their program.

The same is true for the test itself. When you're working on a problem, try concentrating on that problem and nothing else. You can't skip it, so you might as well do your best and make your best guess. Whether you think you're doing well or poorly, don't dwell on it. The past is gone, and fortunes can change rapidly.

You can't change any of the responses you've already given, and you can't possibly predict the questions that lie ahead. Don't worry about things over which you have no control. Just give each question the best of your attention and see what happens.

If you can't help but concentrate on the long-term significance of this test, remember this: To be a doctor, you have to attend medical school and you must take the MCAT. To be a lawyer, you have to attend law school and take the LSAT.

To pursue any other postgraduate degree, you have to attend graduate school and take the GRE. But the GMAT is the only exam you take as an option to advance in the world of business—it's not absolutely necessary to have your MBA.

Think about it. There are lots of incredibly successful businesspeople who have never attended business school. It's true, of course, that an MBA carries a lot of weight in the business world, but it is not essential to your success. Remember that. If the absolute worst outcome is that you don't end up getting your MBA, it will not be the end of the world. Once you face down the fear of failure and realize that your world won't end if you don't do well, it won't gnaw at you as much and you'll be able to concentrate on the test at hand.

Patience, Grasshopper

Finally, there is the value of patience. As we mentioned in the Introduction, a few of these techniques will seem strange at first. You're probably not accustomed to working backward using the answer choices the test provides. You also probably haven't worked much on your grammar, logic, or reading skills in a while.

Learning these techniques is like learning to ski for the first time. When you first clamp on those skis and head out of the lodge, your friends might encourage you to head to the top of a triple black diamond and work out the kinks on the way down. As many people who now walk with a limp will attest, this technique doesn't work. Let yourself learn GMAT skills without a time limit at first—that is, head for the bunny slope and learn such mundane skills as turning and stopping. As you get better, the speed will come naturally, and you'll be able to handle the moguls, the ice, and those slow bratty kids who cut you off as they snowplow into the shrubbery.

Of course, the real stuff you're looking for in this book is the best way to ace the GMAT, shoot off to business school, and get on with the rest of your life. So let's get to it.

Part III
Content and Strategy Review

Chapter 1
Sentence
Correction

Grammar Gaffes

If you love someone, set them free. —Sting

Aha. Pronoun trouble. —Daffy Duck

You're about to find out the degree to which most Americans butcher the English language—especially in songs. Case in point: the lyrics above. Sting may have mastered the art of songwriting, but he's got some work ahead before he gets into Wharton. The grammar is off because the noun *someone*, which is singular, doesn't agree with the pronoun *them*, which is plural. The proper sentence could be rewritten correctly two ways:

If you love someone, set **him or her** free.

OR

If you love **more than one person,** set them free.

Of course, had Sting bothered to achieve grammatical perfection, he would have messed up the meter of the song. Picture his backup singers chanting:

Free, free. Set him or her free.

Free, free. Set him or her free.

The supreme irony in all this is that before his musical career took off with The Police in the early 1980s, Sting worked as a primary school English teacher near Newcastle, England.

WHY GRAMMAR?

You may wonder why a little more than one-third of the verbal questions you'll see on the GMAT involve proper sentence construction, or why grammar could have the slightest impact on your business school education. You have a valid point; the odds are heavily against the possibility that your finance professor will ask you to conjugate a list of verbs for homework. For the sake of the GMAT, however, it is absolutely essential that you develop a grasp of what the test writers consider to be proper grammar.

Learning the test writers' grammar rules often provides students with the easiest way to improve their verbal scores because the grammar questions don't rely as much on reading comprehension skills, which are often more difficult (but not impossible) to improve. To do well on the Sentence Correction section, you don't have to learn to read faster and with greater comprehension (which we'll discuss at length in later chapters); all you have to do is familiarize yourself with a basic core of grammar rules that most sentence correction questions incorporate.

Don't be intimidated by the sentences that the GMAT throws at you. The questions might seem complicated, but the rules can be as basic as making sure the subject agrees with the verb. In this chapter we'll outline most of the basic grammar errors you should be able to recognize, and you'll have the chance to practice on questions both here and in the Verbal Practice Test in Part IV.

THE DIRECTIONS

When you see your first sentence correction question, directions that look something like this will pop up:

> **Sentence Correction Directions:** Each of the <u>sentence correction</u> questions presents a sentence, part or all of which is underlined. Beneath the sentence you will find five ways of phrasing the underlined part. The first of these repeats the original; the other four are different. Follow the requirements of standard written English to choose your answer, paying attention to grammar, word choice, and sentence construction. Select the answer that produces the most effective sentence; your answer should make the sentence clear, exact, and free of grammatical errors. It should also minimize awkwardness, ambiguity, and redundancy.

Once you're through with this chapter, you won't need to waste valuable time on the actual test reading these directions. It suffices to say that you want to find the answer choice that employs the best use of GMAT grammar.

Don't Look for Perfection

It's important to make the distinction between the "best" answer and what you might perceive to be the "correct" answer. If you consider yourself someone who has a rather strong grasp of English usage, your quest for the perfect sentence may be stymied. Not all correct answers (which GMAC refers to as "credited responses") reword the sentence as you might. In effect, you need to remember that it's the test writers' sentence. Your job is to find and cross off errors. Fixing the sentence, if you can call it that, is the job of the test writers.

> Choosing your response to a question can be akin to voting for an elected official; you select the one that stinks the least.

This leads us to the importance of Process of Elimination. As we'll emphasize later in this chapter and throughout the book, the best way to improve your sentence correction skills is to differentiate the grammar the test writers like from the grammar they do not like. Many times you'll end up choosing the right answer by default.

Use Your Scratch Paper

This piece of advice is worth repeating. As mentioned in Part II, you will receive a blank 10-page booklet for scratch work when you begin the test. For every verbal question, you should list A, B, C, D, and E vertically on your scratch paper so that you can cross wrong answers off as you apply POE. You can keep track of the answer choices you've eliminated by putting an X in their corresponding boxes. Given the stress of the exam, it's important to make POE as foolproof and jitter-proof as possible so that you can focus your concentration on the questions.

Don't Get Hung Up on "Difficulty"

Because the computer gives you questions based on its perception of how well you're doing, you might be compelled to look at a question and ask yourself, "Is this a hard one?" Of the three types of questions in the Verbal section, sentence corrections are the toughest to gauge in terms of difficulty. A grammatical construction that seems impossible to you might be a piece of cake for someone else, and vice versa. So if you find yourself trying to assess the difficulty of a sentence correction question, don't bother; it's just misdirected energy.

Worrying Is a Waste
If a question seems difficult to you, it's difficult. Don't waste your time worrying about it.

Of course, there is an upside to coming across a difficult question. If you've done a lot of preparation for the GMAT, then questions that seem difficult to you will also be deemed difficult by the test writers. If you see a difficult question, then one of the following two things is true:

- The computer "thinks" that you're doing very well so far, and it's giving you more difficult questions to work on.

- The question is experimental, and it doesn't count.

WHAT SENTENCE CORRECTION QUESTIONS LOOK LIKE

Each sentence correction question consists of one sentence, and part or all of that sentence is underlined:

> <u>To attempt at curbing the water hyacinth, an ornamental plant which was infesting Lake Victoria and was native of</u> the Brazilian rain forest, ecologists are introducing weevils and fungi into the lake's ecosystem.

- ○ To attempt at curbing the water hyacinth, an ornamental plant which was infesting Lake Victoria and was native of
- ○ The attempt at curbing the infesting of Lake Victoria of the water hyacinth, an ornamental plant which is a native to
- ○ In an attempt to curb the water hyacinth, an ornamental plant which had been infesting Lake Victoria and had been native to
- ○ In an attempt to curb the infestation of Lake Victoria by the water hyacinth, an ornamental plant native to
- ○ By attempting to curb Lake Victoria's infestation of the water hyacinth, an ornamental plant native in

If you think the sentence is correct as it is written, choose choice (A) which always repeats the underlined portion word for word. If you can detect a flaw in the sentence, you can eliminate (A) and concern yourself with the other four answer choices, which provide alternative ways to write the sentence.

THE FIVE STEPS TO SENTENCE SUPREMACY

Consider, though, that the best answer in your mind might not match the best answer on the page. This brings us to the first of our five guidelines for grammatical glory:

> 1. **Whatever you do, DO NOT rewrite the sentence in your head and look for a match among the choices.**

This will grow to be a very common first impulse for you—especially if you feel as though your grammar chops are strong. If you've practiced sentence correction for a while, you might start to think that you can anticipate what the correct answer should look like. This might sound cool at first, but it's actually not very productive (as you'll see in subsequent examples). If you visualize the correct answer and then fail to find it among the answers (a situation that tends to happen more often than not), you're likely to get rattled and lose your equilibrium.

If you detect a flaw in the original sentence, there are myriad ways to fix it. Your universe, however, is restricted to the four other choices you've been given. The key to success, as always, is Process of Elimination. You'll have much more success if you learn to recognize the incorrect stuff and cross it off.

2. Train yourself to find grammatical mistakes.

Overall, it's more important (and a lot easier) to recognize rotten grammar than to defend proper grammar. Dedicate yourself to scrutinizing each answer choice and looking for questions. The moment you find one, give the answer choice the thumbs-down and move on.

In the following pages, we'll show you the seven most common errors that appear in sentence correction questions. Once you learn them, you need to keep an eye out for them. You'll learn, for example, that verb tense and subject-verb agreement are important issues. Therefore, you should always check any underlined verbs to make sure everything is kosher with those two issues. You want to learn to actively seek out the common errors rather than passively reading the sentence and just hoping to notice what's wrong.

Let's take another look at that sentence about the hyacinth:

> To attempt at curbing the water hyacinth, an ornamental plant which was infesting Lake Victoria and was native of the Brazilian rain forest, ecologists are introducing weevils and fungi into the lake's ecosystem.

If you're not positive the sentence is written incorrectly, assume that choice (A) is correct for the time being and move on to the other four answer choices. (Think of making an answer choice in terms of dating; you keep the one you like until something better comes along.) With lots of practice (and a little bit of luck), you'll start to recognize grammatical flaws right away. They'll stand out like this:

> To **attempt at** curbing the water hyacinth, an ornamental plant which was infesting Lake Victoria and was native of the Brazilian rain forest, ecologists are introducing weevils and fungi into the lake's ecosystem.

"Hey!" you'll say to yourself. "Those two words—attempt and at—don't go together! That's wrong! I'm gonna cross it out!" (We emphasize again that you should keep these epiphanies to yourself. Yelling out loud like that during the GMAT will elicit some choice dirty words from your test-taking brethren and sistren.)

You've found something wrong with the sentence (in this case it's an issue of idioms which, you will learn shortly, are Common Grammar Goof #7). You've crossed off (A). Now what?

3. Get rid of the choices that have the same grammatical flaw as the original sentence.

Put yourself in the test writer's wingtips for a second. Anyone who has written thousands of these questions can tell you that it's relatively easy to write a grammatically correct sentence. The tough part is creating four decoy answer choices that are attractive enough to trick someone into choosing one of them yet are decisively incorrect. One of the ways the test writers create distractors (wrong answers) is by repeating an error that appears in the original sentence and changing another part of the underlined portion. This is somewhat akin to taking your car in for an oil change and getting it back with new shock absorbers instead.

Here are the answer choices for the hyacinth question again:

○ To attempt at curbing the water hyacinth, an ornamental plant which was infesting Lake Victoria and was native of
○ The attempt at curbing the infesting of Lake Victoria of the water hyacinth, an ornamental plant which is a native to
○ In an attempt to curb the water hyacinth, an ornamental plant which had been infesting Lake Victoria and had been native to
○ In an attempt to curb the infestation of Lake Victoria by the water hyacinth, an ornamental plant native to
○ By attempting to curb Lake Victoria's infestation of the water hyacinth, an ornamental plant native in

True to form, choice (B) has the same problem, so you can cross it off as well. The other three choices use the correct idiom *attempt to*. Before you know it, your chances of choosing the correct answer have jumped from one in five to one in three.

Lather, Rinse, Repeat

Try this process again and look for any new mistakes among the remaining choices. There are three choices left. What's wrong with any of the remainders?

○ In an attempt to curb the water hyacinth, an ornamental plant which had been infesting Lake Victoria and had been **native to**
○ In an attempt to curb the infestation of Lake Victoria by the water hyacinth, an ornamental plant **native to**
○ By attempting to curb Lake Victoria's infestation of the water hyacinth, an ornamental plant **native in**

Aha! Another gaffe! There are two ways to use the word *native*:

The gibbon is *native* to southeastern Asia.

John Cleese is *a native* of England.

Native in is not idiomatic, so you can kill (E). If you didn't know this idiom before, check out the Idiom List (Appendix C) in Part V. Now you have two choices left—and your odds are improving.

4. Use Process of Elimination (POE) to play the answer choices off each other.

Suppose you read the sentence and you can't find a mistake. (Hey, it happens.) You're not out of options. The right answer is right there in front of you, hidden among the five choices. Compare them to each other and see how they differ.

Poker fans recognize a "full house" as a five-card hand in which you have three of one type of card and two of another. Many sentence correction questions are created in a similar fashion.

> If you look at the five answer choices and three choices phrase the answer one way and the other two phrase it a different way, there is a high probability that one of those two ways has to be grammatically correct and the other incorrect. Determine which is correct, and then eliminate the choices that go the wrong way.

Never assume that the majority rules. You can't determine that one option is better than the other just because it appears more times in the answer choices. If you see a two/three split, be sure to judge each possibility on its own merit, not by its superior numbers. One grammar usage can appear in three choices and be wrong each time.

If you didn't see the faulty idiom in the previous sentence, you could have compared the answer choices like this:

○ To attempt *at* curbing the water hyacinth, an ornamental plant which was infesting Lake Victoria and was native of

○ The attempt *at* curbing the infesting of Lake Victoria of the water hyacinth, an ornamental plant which is a native to

○ In an attempt *to* curb the water hyacinth, an ornamental plant which had been infesting Lake Victoria and had been native to

○ In an attempt *to* curb the infestation of Lake Victoria by the water hyacinth, an ornamental plant native to

○ By attempting *to* curb Lake Victoria's infestation of the water hyacinth, an ornamental plant native in

See the two/three split? Two choices say *at*, and the other three say *to*; it has to be one or the other. At this point, you consult your mental idiom Rolodex, realize that the proper idiom is *attempt to*, and eliminate (A) and (B).

In many cases, there are patterns of difference in the answer choices of sentence correction questions, including a fair number of two/three splits. However, you'll often find that these two/three splits are not perfectly aligned the way the one in our example is. But being on the lookout for patterns of difference in the answer choices is an invaluable POE tool on sentence correction questions. (Reference *The Official Guide for GMAT Review* to see some examples. You can find this book in most bookstores or at **www.mba.com**.)

5. If you're down to two choices, find the flaw in the wrong one.

Now comes the final showdown. If you're likte most people, eliminating the first three choices is a lot easier than knocking off the fourth. How many times have you narrowed down your choices to two and then picked the wrong one?

Let's revisit the hyacinth question and the two remaining answer choices:

> To attempt at curbing the water hyacinth, an orna-
> mental plant which was infesting Lake Victoria and
> was native of the Brazilian rain forest, ecologists
> are introducing weevils and fungi into the lake's
> ecosystem.

○ In an attempt to curb the water hyacinth, an ornamental plant which had been infesting Lake Victoria and had been native to

○ In an attempt to curb the infestation of Lake Victoria by the water hyacinth, an ornamental plant native to

Both choices pass the idiom tests and seem plausibly correct. Ask yourself this: How are they different? The top choice uses the past perfect verb tense (*had been infesting* and *had been native*), and the other choice is in the present tense. Which do you use?

Look at the sentence's main clause, which is not underlined (and thus must be grammatically correct): *ecologists **are introducing** weevils and fungi into the lake's ecosystem*. This is written in the present tense, and the verb tense of the underlined portion should match. Therefore, (C) doesn't match, and the best answer is (D).

That's the best process to follow. Succinctly put, it's easier to point out why an answer choice is wrong than to defend why an answer choice is right. So make things easier for yourself and learn to spot the flaws.

Note: If any of those grammar terms flew over your head (like "main clause" or "past perfect verb tense"), don't sweat it. Refer to the Grammar Review section on page 29, and check out Appendix B: Grammar Glossary in Part V.

Look for Differences

If you've narrowed it down to two answer choices and both seem correct, ask yourself: How are they different?

MEANING AND STYLE

Two final points before we jump headfirst into grammar. Unquestionably, the most important part of applying POE to sentence correction questions is checking for grammar errors. But it's not the only thing. Once you've looked for grammar errors, there are two other things you should consider.

Meaning

Applying POE

When using POE, you should look for more than grammar errors. Also pay attention to meaning and style.

The meaning of a properly constructed sentence should always be clear. Thus, a lack of clarity in a sentence—if you can't figure out what a sentence is supposed to say—can be a reason to eliminate it.

Furthermore, the meaning of the corrected sentence should be the same as the original meaning. An *unnecessary* change in meaning indicates a wrong answer. Many answer choices can be eliminated because they change the original meaning of the sentence.

Style

You can have an answer choice in a sentence correction question that is perfectly grammatical, and means the same thing as the original sentence, but is nevertheless the wrong answer. How can this be? Because there may be another answer choice that uses proper grammar, preserves the meaning of the original sentence, and is stylistically preferred.

The most important style point is that the GMAT likes answer choices that are concise. The rule is to keep it short and sweet. If you have a choice between two answer choices, many times simply picking the shorter one will be the right choice. Long, wordy, convoluted, verbose answer choices are bad. Simple, direct, clear answer choices are good.

This is the last thing you should look at, so always make sure that grammar and meaning are correct before you worry about style. But definitely remember to check for it. When using POE, you want every tool that can help to be in your toolbox.

GRAMMAR REVIEW

First thing first: This book is not a comprehensive English grammar textbook. If you want to learn how a gerund differs from a present participle, scan the grammar textbook section of one of those tremendous bookstore websites. With few exceptions, this book details only the basic grammar principles that the GMAT bothers to test. We'll start out with basic sentence construction from its most simple to the rather complex. Other rules will reveal themselves as we discuss the test writers' favorite mistakes later in the chapter.

The Simple Sentence

If you hitch any *noun* (for anyone who's never seen *Schoolhouse Rock*, a noun is a person, place, or thing) to any verb (which denotes action), you get a simple sentence:

Noun	Verb
Bill	ate.
Cleveland	rocks.
Speed	kills.

The subject noun commits the action in a sentence, and you can add another noun—the object noun—to receive action.

Fuad kicked **the ball**.

Mandy married **her boyfriend**.

Types of Modifiers

As far as proper sentence structure is concerned, the rest is all fluff and modifiers. The key is making sure that none of the modifying stuff compromises the sentence structure:

> Hoping to keep her wedding out of the newspapers, Mandy, a brilliant brain surgeon, secretly married her boyfriend, Max, in a small church on the property of a huge farming combine in Michigan.

Notice that even though you know a lot more about Mandy and her boyfriend, the original simple sentence—"Mandy married her boyfriend"—remains intact. The main types of modifiers that appear on the GMAT are:

- **Adjectives:** An adjective is a word that describes (modifies) a noun. What kind of church was it? A *small* church. What kind of brain surgeon was she? A *brilliant* brain surgeon. You get the idea.

- **Adverbs:** An adverb is a word that modifies a verb (or, less commonly, an adjective or another adverb) and usually ends in *-ly*. How did Max and Mandy marry? They married *secretly*. The adverb *secretly* modifies the verb *married*.

- **Adjectival phrases:** Don't let the name scare you. An adjectival phrase is simply a phrase that modifies a noun, just like an ordinary adjective does. They usually appear at the beginning of sentences. Here, the phrase *hoping to keep her wedding out of the newspapers* serves to modify *Mandy*.

- **Prepositional phrases:** A prepositional phrase starts with a preposition (such as in, *over, around, of, with, to, on,* and so on), and ends with a noun—the object of the preposition. The prepositional phrase relates the object to another word in the sentence, modifying that other word. The most important thing about prepositional phrases is that you need to ignore them when you're trying to identify the subject of a sentence.

Here's another look at that practice sentence with all the prepositional phrases in brackets:

> Hoping to keep her wedding out [of the newspapers], Mandy, a brilliant brain surgeon, secretly married her boyfriend, Max, [in a small church] [on the property] [of a huge farming combine] [in Michigan].

Why Is It Wrong?

Now is an important moment in your GMAT-prep career. As of this moment, it is no longer adequate to cross off an answer choice because "it looks kinda strange." Every so often, the test writers like to use grammatical formats that are perfectly legal yet are seldom used in conversational English. That's how they get you. Unless you can find a tangible problem with a possible answer (such as when the subject and verb don't agree), leave the choice alone at first. It may end up to be the right choice if you find errors in the other four options.

Referring back to the practice question, (A), which was a repetition of the underlined text, has just as much of a chance of being the correct answer as the rest of the answer choices, so don't be afraid to pick it. Before you do, though, it pays to consider the other answer choices and make sure that none of them are better.

GMAC'S FAVORITE GRAMMAR MISTAKES

Sure, it's important to recognize grammatical mistakes. But the thought of memorizing every grammar rule leaves you queasy, doesn't it? You don't have to do that. Luckily, most of the errors that the test writers conjure up in its sentence correction questions fall into several clear categories. In no particular order, here are the seven most common goofs that the test writers set up for you to identify. If you can spot these, you'll be in great shape.

1. Misplaced Modifiers

There is one basic rule about words that modify, or describe, other words:

Modifiers should be next to the words they describe.

The most common example of this occurs when a sentence has an opening phrase followed by a comma, as in the following example:

Unwilling to threaten the revenue generated by the city's two airports, <u>the plan to build a third airport outside the city limits was opposed by the mayor</u>.

- ⬭ the plan to build a third airport outside the city limits was opposed by the mayor
- ⬭ the mayor opposed the plan to build a third airport outside the city limits
- ⬭ opposition to the plan to build a third airport outside the city limits was expressed by the mayor
- ⬭ it was opposed by the mayor that a third airport was planned to be built outside the city limits
- ⬭ the third airport that had been planned to be built outside the city limits was opposed by the mayor

The opening phrase *Unwilling to threaten the revenue generated by the city's two airports* is not underlined. Therefore, the first noun that appears after the comma has to be the subject that the opening phrase modifies. The way the question is written, it looks as though *the plan* was unwilling to threaten the revenue. That's obviously wrong, so you can get rid of it.

Whom does the phrase modify? The mayor! Once you realize that, this question is rather easy. The only answer choice that begins with *the mayor* is (B). Attention you skeptics out there: Some sentence corrections questions are this easy!

Drill 1: Misplaced Modifiers

Which of these sentences are correctly written, and which need to be fixed? If you find an incorrect sentence, how would you correct it? The answers are on page 49.

1. Crazed with hunger, the park ranger finally subdued the stray coyote.

2. Based on several manuscripts that date back to the Middle Ages, historians believe that Charlemagne first rose to power as a mere teenager.

3. First published at the turn of the nineteenth century, *The Literary Quarterly Review* has provided its readership with examples of the era's finest fiction.

4. Unlike executive skills, which most people can learn at any qualified business school, a person usually derives a sense of leadership from social relationships.

5. Though usually a calm person, Arthur's patience was tried more than once by his son's destructive behavior.

6. Although Bill had not driven the car in weeks, his father had no trouble starting the engine.

Another Way to Fix the Problem

Most misplaced modifier questions come down to making sure that the opening phrase modifies the noun after the comma, which is usually the subject of the sentence. There is another way, however, to fix a misplaced modifier that you should know about. As the Grammar Glossary in Part V will tell you, there is a fundamental difference between a phrase and a **clause**. A clause is a group of words that contains a subject and a verb. A **phrase** is a group of words that lacks either a subject or a verb.

Grammar Tip

On the GMAT, a phrase is usually missing a subject.

Clause: Although he looked for his glasses for hours,

Phrase: Having looked for his glasses for hours,

See the difference? If you take away *Although* from the clause, you have a complete sentence: *He looked for his glasses for hours.* The phrase, however, has no chance to stand by itself as a complete sentence. The misplaced modifier rule applies to phrases, but *not* to clauses. Therefore:

> You can change a misplaced modifier into a legal sentence by changing the opening phrase into a clause.

Here's an example:

> **Wrong:** While leaving the bank, Evelyn's purse was stolen.

> **Right:** As she was leaving the bank, Evelyn's purse was stolen.

The opening phrase is now a clause (with the subject *she* and the verb *was*), so it's okay.

How to Spot Misplaced Modifiers

- Look for a descriptive phrase set off by a comma at the beginning of the sentence.

- Look to see if the part of the sentence after the comma changes in the answer choices or if the opening phrase is changed into a clause in any of the answers.

2. Pronoun Errors

We owe pronouns a great debt. Without them, we would all have to talk like this:

> "When Janet brought Janet's car to the mechanic, the mechanic told Janet that the mechanic would call Janet after the mechanic looked at Janet's car in the mechanic's garage."

In return for all this linguistic convenience, pronouns ask that we observe two conditions. The first one is this:

Pronoun Rule 1: Each pronoun must agree with the nouns they replace.

Whoa, there. If you spotted the error in the gray box, don't worry. We made the error on purpose to see if you were on your toes. Pronoun agreement is an easy error to miss. Because *pronoun* is a singular word and *they* is a plural pronoun, the sentence is incorrect. You need to rewrite the sentence in one of two ways:

> **Each pronoun** must agree with the noun **it** replaces.

> OR

> **All pronouns** must agree with the nouns **they** replace.

If you have a singular noun, be sure to replace it with a singular pronoun. If the antecedent is plural, its pronoun must be plural.

> **Pronoun Rule 2:** Each pronoun must refer directly and unambiguously to the noun it replaces.

Assume nothing. When you're considering whether all the pronouns refer directly to the nouns they've replaced, there's no such thing as "probably." You have to be certain. Take a look at this example:

> After Victor Hugo referred to the newly crowned Emperor Napoleon as a "crayfish," **he** tried to have **him** arrested.

Upon reading this, you might assume that *he* refers to Napoleon (because he was the guy in power) and *him* refers to Hugo. It might make common sense to make this assumption, but it does not make grammatical sense. (After all, it is possible that Hugo tried to have Napoleon arrested.) Therefore, in the eyes of the GMAT grammar gurus, that sentence is incorrectly constructed.

One thing that will help you out a lot in pronoun questions is keep on eye on the words *it* and *they*. Those two words (along with their kin *its, their, and them*) are notorious for causing trouble. If you see the word *it* underlined in a sentence, make sure you know what it's referring to and that the original word is singular. Likewise, if you see the word *they* underlined, make sure it's referring to something plural, and make sure you know exactly what that is.

Drill 2: Pronoun Errors

Which of these sentences are correctly written, and which need to be fixed? If you find an incorrect sentence, how would you correct it? The answers are on pages 49–50.

1. As the melon farmers delivered their crop, they were dismayed to find that they were infested with fruit flies.

2. The Commerce Department, which usually doesn't make any fiscal announcements until after the budget is ratified, announced that their accounting practices would be overhauled next year.

3. Enrico and Simone have absolutely no idea how valuable their father's antique desk is.

4. There is a psychological difference between people who do their taxes as soon as they receive all the forms and those who wait until the very last minute.

5. Neither Alice nor Beatrix could figure out why she failed the math exam.

6. Every employee brought their softball mitt to the game.

For additional information about specific pronouns, as well as a few tips on making sure the subject pronouns agree with the object pronouns, be sure to consult Appendix A: Grammar Odds and Ends in Part V.

How to Spot Pronoun Errors

- Look for pronouns changing from singular to plural and vice versa in the answer choices.

- Pay attention to all underlined pronouns, particularly ones that show up late in the sentence.

- Watch out for *it* and *they*.

3. Verb Tense Errors

Situations when you have to change the verb tense of a sentence are pretty rare. Therefore, the tense of the verbs in a sentence usually stay the same. When in doubt, keep it as simple and consistent as possible.

> The verb tense of a sentence should remain consistent. If the tense is established somewhere in the sentence, there's rarely a need to change it.

The best way to determine the proper verb tense is to look at the portion that is not underlined because it sets the tone for the rest of the sentence.

> Every time Martin goes to the beach, <u>he will get a really bad sunburn.</u>

The first part of the sentence isn't underlined, so it isn't subject to change. Therefore, it must be correct. *Martin goes* is in the present tense, so there's no need to move into the future tense (*he will get*). The correct sentence is:

> Every time Martin goes to the beach, <u>**he gets** a really bad sunburn.</u>

The Basic Tenses

Sentence correction questions seldom stray from the three basic tenses that we use every day in ordinary conversation.

- The *past tense* indicates that something has already happened:
      Wayne **attended** the Bueller School of Business.

- The *present tense* indicates that something is currently happening:
      Wayne **attends** the Bueller School of Business.

- The *future tense* indicates that something will happen later:
      Wayne **will attend** the Bueller School of Business.

The Complex Tenses

There are also three more complicated tenses that you should know how and when to use. Don't worry about their official names; just learn to recognize when they're needed.

- The *past perfect* tense indicates that two things have happened in the past, and you have to show which one happened first. For this, you use the word *had*:

    > Wayne **had attended** business school for more than a year when he got married.

    In this example, we now know that Wayne attended school *before* he got married. The important thing to remember is that you should never use *had* unless you explicitly have to. If only one thing has happened in the past, then the use of *had* is wrong.

- The *present perfect tense* indicates that something started in the past and carries up to the present moment. For this, you use the word *has* or *have*:

    > Wayne **has attended** business school since last October.

    Now we know that Wayne started school in the past and he is still there. The best clue that you need to use the present perfect is the word *since*.

- The *future perfect tense* indicates that something will have finished happening at a certain date in the future. Here, you use the words *will have*:

    > When Wayne gets married, he **will have attended** business school for more than a year.

    At some future date, Wayne's schooling will be half over (assuming he's in a two-year business program). The future perfect is extremely rare on the GMAT, so don't get too worked up over it.

Drill 3: Verb Tense Errors

Which of these sentences are correctly written, and which need to be fixed? If you find an incorrect sentence, how would you correct it? The answers are on page 50.

1. Before the new library was built, children are playing around in the vacant lot.

2. A recent study has found that within the past decade, many lawyers not considered for partnership had chosen to quit rather than wait until the following year.

3. John is jealous of Judy because she has a nicer briefcase.

4. Fire alarms will sometimes fail to detect a fire if they haven't been cleaned recently.

5. Never before had my parents been more surprised than they had been when my sister brought home her new fiancé.

6. The old gymnasium was abandoned until a real estate consortium bought the facility and renovated it.

Note: One important issue that is worth studying for the GMAT is the subjunctive mood, which is discussed in Appendix A: Grammar Odds and Ends.

How to Spot Verb Tense Errors

• Look for verbs changing tense in the answer choices.

• Look for underlined verbs that don't share the same tense as other verbs in the sentence and that don't match time clues in the sentence.

4. Parallel Construction Errors

In the same way that verb tenses should be consistent within a correctly written sentence, parallelism is also a structural necessity on the GMAT. Parallelism involves the need for consistent word forms when you're making a list as well as for consistent tenses of all the verbs.

See how that last sentence is parallel? It sets up a nice, consistent structure by using the preposition *for* twice.

Parallelism involves the need	**for** consistent word forms when you're making a list
as well as	**for** consistent tenses of all the verbs.

> Items in a list should be parallel in form and structure.

The need for parallelism exists in its most basic form when a sentence features a list:

> The CEO attributed her company's increased revenue to higher-than-expected sales of its new product line, the expanded budget for research and development, and demand was increasing in emerging markets.

The CEO cites three factors—*sales, budget,* and *demand*—so each should appear as the same part of speech. In this case, the list is inconsistent because the third factor is not expressed in the same form as the previous two. For the sentence to be correct, the underlined portion must also be expressed as a simple noun:

> The CEO attributed her company's increased revenue to higher-than-expected sales of its new product line, the expanded budget for research and development, and <u>increased demand</u> in emerging markets.

This works the same way with verbs. As long as each verb is in the same format, the sentence is perfectly legal:

> The Alaskan sea otter spends the majority of its time <u>sunning</u> itself on offshore rock formations, <u>foraging</u> for small shellfish along the ocean floor, and <u>swimming</u> playfully with its companions.

When the test writers are feeling a little creative, they like to throw a red herring into the sentence, and you might think that this red herring is part of the list when it actually is not. Can you spot the distractor in this sentence?

> In order to change the company's image, the marketing director suggested <u>a modified strategy targeted at younger consumers, new market research for designing the new company logo, and searching</u> for well-known actors to appear in its TV commercials.

The test writers want you to think that all the items in the list should be *-ing* words, but that's wrong. They put *designing* in the second part of the list to trick you into thinking that *searching* is parallel with *designing*. In fact, the items in the list should all be nouns, and the corrected sentence looks something like this:

> In order to change the company's image, the marketing director suggested <u>a modified **strategy** (noun 1) targeted at younger consumers, new market **research** (noun 2) for designing the new company logo, and **a search** (noun 3)</u> for well-known actors to appear in its TV commercials.

Comparing the answer choices to one another is especially useful here because you can keep the answer choices that exhibit parallel construction and dump the ones that don't.

Drill 4: Parallel Construction Errors

Which of these sentences are correctly written, and which need to be fixed? If you find an incorrect sentence, how would you correct it? The answers are on pages 50–51.

1. Doctors agree that their patients should take medication within a strictly monitored regimen instead of at random times during the day.

2. When he reached the age of sixty-one, my father chose to retire over searching for another job.

3. To evaluate Internet stocks using antiquated valuation models is like competing in the Indianapolis 500 with a horse and buggy.

4. Even the most experienced teen counselor can find it difficult to distinguish attention deficit disorder, which results when a student is chemically unable to process information, from being bored.

5. Members of ant colonies have skills as diverse as protecting the queen against predators, gathering food from the surrounding area, and maintaining the fragile infrastructure of the anthill's many chambers.

6. The first task to accomplish when writing an application essay is formulating an outline that lists all the things you want to say.

How to Spot Parallel Construction Errors

- Look for items in a list.

- Be alert for inconsistencies in form and structure.

5. Comparing Apples and Oranges

Once again, the need for consistency looms overhead. (Do you see a pattern emerging here?) The concept of "apples and oranges" relates to the consistency of anything that is compared with something else.

> Whenever you make a comparison in a sentence, you have to make sure the things you compare are, in fact, comparable.

Whenever an answer choice does not make a comparison in a consistent manner (or there's any ambiguity as to the validity of a comparison), it's incorrect:

> A recent market research study revealed that the back of Michael Jordan's shaved head is more recognized than Bill Clinton, Newt Gingrich, or Jesus Christ.

This sentence is unclear, because we don't know if the author is comparing Jordan's head to the heads of the other men or to the other men themselves.

If you see a sentence like this one, scan the answer choices for one that clarifies the situation like this:

> A recent market research study revealed that the back of Michael Jordan's shaved head is more recognized than the **back of the shaved head of** Bill Clinton, Newt Gingrich, or Jesus Christ.

You can also use a pronoun in the second half of the comparison. Learn to recognize the proper use of a pronoun in these situations because the test writers almost always prefer to use a pronoun rather than sound redundant or verbose:

> A recent market research study revealed that the back of Michael Jordan's shaved head is more recognized than **that of** Bill Clinton, Newt Gingrich, or Jesus Christ.

Another possibility is the comparison of actions instead of nouns:

> French wines taste better than Australian wines.

Although this sentence might seem perfectly fine in conversation, it's incorrect as far as the test writers are concerned. The wines aren't compared; the ways the wines *taste* are compared. So a verb needs to appear in both the front and the back of the sentence, in any of these forms:

- French wines taste better than Australian wines **taste**.

- French wines taste better than Australian wines **do**.

- French wines taste better than **do** Australian wines.

Drill 5: Comparing Apples and Oranges

Which of these sentences are correctly written, and which need to be fixed? If you find an incorrect sentence, how would you correct it? The answers are on page 51.

1. The population of Asian Americans in California is almost three times as big as Missouri.

2. Ordinary people have much more trouble solving the Sunday crossword puzzle than does the average member of MENSA.

3. In New Zealand, the average sheep eats almost ten more pounds of grass annually than that of its Australian counterpart.

4. Édouard Manet's struggle for acceptance among the European art community was not unlike that of Pablo Picasso, who went on to enjoy enormous success before he died.

5. My uncle Rupert grows tomatoes that are bigger than a baby's head.

6. The New York Public Library's main branch, located on the southwest corner of Fifth Avenue and 42nd Street, is larger than any branch in Manhattan.

How to Spot Apples and Oranges Comparisons

- Look for things or actions that are compared in the sentence.

- Look for words that indicate comparisons such as *like, similar, more than, less than, as big as,* and so on.

6. Subject-Verb Agreement Errors

In their typical fashion, the test writers like to trick you. When they construct a long sentence, they like to put the subject at the beginning, the verb near the end, and a bunch of modifiers and other junk in between to distract you.

> Verbs must agree with their subjects in number. That is, singular subjects need singular verbs, and plural subjects need plural verbs.

Take a look at this exaggerated example of how the simple subject-verb connection can be lost among the muddling modifiers:

> The cross-eyed Burmese white panther, a species indigenous to the deepest jungles of Southeast Asia and sought as a trophy by wildlife poachers who hunt the massive, myopic beasts using 12-gauge shotguns and assault rifles, are rapidly nearing extinction.

See the nasty trick? The verb of the sentence is are, and the noun nearest to that verb is *rifles*, which is plural. "Rifles are" makes grammatical sense, but *rifles* isn't the subject of the sentence. When determining the subject of a sentence, ask yourself: "Who or what is this sentence about?" Answer: the panther.

> The cross-eyed Burmese white **panther**, [a species indigenous to the deepest jungles of Southeast Asia and sought as a trophy by wildlife poachers who hunt the massive, myopic beasts using 12-gauge shotguns and assault rifles,] **are** rapidly nearing extinction.

After you bracket off all of the descriptive phrases and clauses, you can see that this sentence is written incorrectly. The corrected sentence looks like this:

> The cross-eyed Burmese white panther, a species indigenous to the deepest jungles of Southeast Asia and sought as a trophy by wildlife poachers who hunt the massive, myopic beasts using 12-gauge shotguns and assault rifles, **is** rapidly nearing extinction.

Remember what we said at the beginning of this grammar review: Properly constructed sentences on the GMAT need a subject and a verb; the rest is all filler.

Drill 6: Subject-Verb Agreement Errors

Which of these sentences are correctly written, and which need to be fixed? For each of these examples, put brackets around the parts of the sentence that are not crucial to its structure and identify the subject and the verb. Then show how you would correct it. The answers are on pages 51–52.

1. Neither my pet monkey nor my sister's pet rabbit is able to drive a car.

2. All of the major food groups, including proteins, fruits and vegetables, and carbohydrates, is crucial for optimal health.

3. Of all its sea-faring relatives, the California gray seal stands out because of its winsome demeanor and shiny coat.

4. A small number of buildings that were damaged in the Great Fire of 1909 are finally about to be rebuilt with the cash of an anonymous benefactor.

5. Each of Liz Taylor's husbands—including actor Richard Burton, Virginia senator John Warner, and construction worker Larry Fortensky—have described her as a rare beauty both in body and in mind.

6. A secret cache of personal journals that were the property of Finnbar Brenneisen, the renowned and reclusive billionaire known as much for his eccentric behavior as for his extraordinary philanthropy, are about to be published.

For more information about subject-verb agreement, including lists of singular pronouns and weird plurals, take a look at Appendix A: Grammar Odds and Ends on page 227.

How to Spot Subject-Verb Agreement Errors

- Look for verbs changing from singular to plural and vice versa in the answer choices.

- Pay attention to all underlined verbs, particularly when they show up late in a sentence.

- Watch for tricky subject pronouns, particularly those that look plural but aren't.

- Ignore prepositional phrases when identifying the subject.

7. Idiom Errors

Idioms are examples of proper usage of the English language. Certain words just go together. For example, you wouldn't say, "I'm *applying at* the Darden School of Business," because *at* doesn't go with *apply*. The correct expression is, "I'm *applying to* the Darden School of Business."

No Rules
Idioms don't have rules. They just are. Make a list of idioms and learn to recognize them.

Most idioms will just sound correct to your ear because you've been using them since you first learned to speak. If you're a student whose first language is not

English, you probably have a lot of studying to do because like many things in the English language, these can be tricky. The Idiom List (Appendix C) in Part V is a terrific way to get started. Take note of proper idiomatic writing as you read. If you come across an idiom that you haven't seen before, add it to the list.

> AARP has proposed that each person carry a personal health card, which can store data ranging from background information, such as any genetic predispositions to heart disease, and the list of medications the person is currently taking.

The sentence is incorrect because *range from…and* is unidiomatic. The correct way to write this one is to replace *and* with *to*:

> AARP has proposed that each person carry a personal health card, which can store data **ranging from** background information, such as any genetic predispositions to heart disease, **to** the list of medications the person is currently taking.

Drill 7: Idiom Errors

This is a little different from the other quick quizzes. In each of these sentences, a word has been taken out that is part of an idiom. Your job is to use the right word in the blank. This quiz only covers a handful of the idioms contained in the Idiom List. The point is just to give you some familiarity with what idioms are about on the GMAT. Be sure to learn the Idiom List and work as many problems as you can. The answers are on page 52.

1. Students are prohibited _____ using school facilities without a teacher present.

2. Students are forbidden _____ go on field trips without a signed permission slip.

3. I tried to distinguish one twin _____ the other, but they truly were identical.

4. The Mona Lisa is believed _____ one of the greatest paintings in history.

5. He is not only a great guitar player, _____ a great violin player.

6. I will try _____ see you tomorrow if I can get all my work done.

How to Spot Idiom Errors

- Learn the idioms by heart and look for them.

Make Note of the Miscellaneous

Unfortunately, an exhaustive chronicling of every error that the test writers have included in every GMAT over the years won't fit in this chapter, or this whole book for that matter. The goal of this chapter is to acquaint you with the mistakes that appear on the GMAT most often, and more than 95 percent of all sentence correction questions will incorporate one or more of the errors discussed in this chapter in some way. Try as many questions as you can to determine as thorough a list as you desire. Once you do enough practice questions, the mistakes will start to leap out at you.

Comprehensive Drill: Sentence Correction

Put the collective knowledge of this behemoth chapter together and try these practice sentence correction questions. The answers and explanations begin on page 53.

1. Equestrian enthusiasts predict that the alleged abuse of anabolic steroids among horse trainers would subside as long as the testing of the animals is more random and more rigorously enforced.
   - ○ would subside as long as the testing of the animals is more random and
   - ○ would subside if the testing of the random animals were
   - ○ will have subsided when testing of the animals is more random and
   - ○ will subside if random testing of the animals were
   - ○ will subside if the random testing of the animals is

2. A representative of the Internal Revenue Service usually finds most people are willing to cooperate during an audit, yet they become agitated, defensive, and suspect computer error.
   - ○ most people are willing to cooperate during an audit, yet they become agitated, defensive, and suspect
   - ○ most people to be willingly cooperative during an audit, and they are also agitated, defensive, and they suspect
   - ○ that most people are willing to cooperate during an audit, yet they become agitated, defensive, and suspicious of
   - ○ that people are mostly willing to cooperate during an audit, and they become agitated, defensive, and suspicious of
   - ○ that most people are willingly cooperative during an audit, yet they are becoming agitated, defensive, and suspect

3. The Center for Public Integrity has discovered that drug companies obtain people's health records through the Internet either to contact them individually and suggest alternative forms of treating various illnesses or the estimation of the market of each new drug they produce.
   - ○ the estimation of
   - ○ to estimate
   - ○ for estimating
   - ○ they want to estimate
   - ○ it wants to estimate

4. Gianlorenzo Bernini should be judged not by the degree to which his sculptures and architecture are admired throughout the world, but by his Bacchanalian lifestyle, his notorious temper, and his scathing jealousy of his counterparts.
   - ○ be judged not by the degree to which his sculptures and architecture are admired throughout the world, but by
   - ○ not be judged by the degree of admiration the world has for his sculptures and architecture, and instead by
   - ○ be judged to the degree that his sculptures and architecture are admired throughout the world, and not by
   - ○ not be judged by the degree to which the world admires his sculptures and architecture, but instead
   - ○ be judged to the degree of admiration which the world has for his sculptures and architecture, not by

5. The three largest American airlines stunned the financial world by announcing a full-scale merger of their business, which created an alliance controlling more than 60 percent of all domestic air traffic.

- ⬭ business, which created an alliance controlling
- ⬭ businesses, creating an alliance that would control
- ⬭ businesses that created a controlling alliance of
- ⬭ business, and this alliance controlled
- ⬭ business that created an alliance that would control

6. Recent research revealed that roughly one-third of all Americans keep a gun in the house, and that on any given day, one out of every 50 adults carry a handgun away from home.

- ⬭ one out of every 50 adults carry
- ⬭ every one out of 50 adults carry
- ⬭ out of every 50 adults, one carries
- ⬭ each adult among 50 carries
- ⬭ one adult in 50 carries

7. The price of a bushel of corn has fallen so drastically that some farmers have found it to be more cost-effective to destroy their crops as to make the effort to get them to market.

- ⬭ have found it to be more cost-effective to destroy their crops as to make
- ⬭ found that the destruction of their crops is more cost-effective than making
- ⬭ find the destruction of their crops as more cost-effective than making
- ⬭ find it more cost-effective to destroy their crops than to make
- ⬭ are finding that the destruction of their crops is more cost-effective than the making of

8. In 1985, the California Supreme Court lifted a ban on fortune tellers, which likened them as economic prognosticators and investment counselors who also make predictions for profit.

- ⬭ which likened them as
- ⬭ who have been likened as
- ⬭ who are likened to be
- ⬭ likening them to
- ⬭ which were likened to be

9. Otto Wichterle, the Czech inventor who created the first soft contact lens, was not like most successful inventors due to his making a fortune from human vanity instead of being inspired by necessity.

- ⬭ Otto Wichterle, the Czech inventor who created the first soft contact lens, was not like most successful inventors due to his making a fortune from human vanity instead of being inspired by necessity.
- ⬭ The Czech inventor Otto Wichterle, who was not like other inventors' developments that were inspired by necessity, made his fortune from human vanity instead by creating the first soft contact lens.
- ⬭ Unlike most successful inventors, whose developments were inspired by necessity, Otto Wichterle, the Czech inventor who created the first soft contact lens, made a fortune from human vanity.
- ⬭ The first soft contact lens, which was created by Czech inventor Otto Wichterle, who made a fortune from human vanity, was unlike most successful inventors whose developments were inspired by necessity.
- ⬭ The developments of most successful inventors, which had been inspired by necessity, were unlike the first soft contact lens that was created by Czech inventor Otto Wichterle, who made a fortune from human vanity.

10. Any political figure who is intending on running for president will not succeed without a large quantity of campaign money contributed by wealthy benefactors.

   ⊙ who is intending on running
   ⊙ who has the intention of running
   ⊙ who is intent to run
   ⊙ intending on running
   ⊙ intent on running

11. The government's attempts to store chemical weapons in a rural community in Oregon, a state with a decidedly environmentalist history, have encountered massive political resistance from Oregon's state legislature.

   ⊙ have encountered massive political resistance
   ⊙ has encountered massive resistance politically
   ⊙ have politically encountered massive resistance
   ⊙ has encountered massive political resistance
   ⊙ had encountered politically massive resistance

12. The most prominent result of Professor Winick's archaeological research has been discovering that a pharaoh who had ruled in the last days of Egypt was buried with fewer artifacts than their earlier counterparts.

   ⊙ discovering that a pharaoh who had ruled in the last days of Egypt was buried with fewer artifacts than their
   ⊙ the discovery that pharaohs who had ruled in the last days of Egypt were not buried with as many artifacts as their
   ⊙ to discover that pharaohs, which ruled in the last days of Egypt, was buried with fewer artifacts than their
   ⊙ the discovery that pharaohs who ruled in the last days of Egypt were buried with fewer artifacts than were their
   ⊙ to discover that a pharaoh who ruled in the last days of Egypt was buried with fewer artifacts than were his

13. Due to his temperament being fueled by distrusting technology, Stanley Kubrick did his best to insulate himself from what he regarded as the pains of modern living.

   ⊙ Due to his temperament being fueled by distrusting
   ⊙ Because his temperament was being fueled by a distrust of
   ⊙ His temperament fueled by a distrust of
   ⊙ Due to the fact that his temperament had been fueled by a distrust in
   ⊙ Having had his temperament fueled by his lack of trust in

14. Unlike smaller apartment buildings, which have fewer than four residential units in them, each room within any residential complex must be equipped with a sprinkler system.

   ⊙ Unlike smaller apartment buildings, which have fewer than four residential units in them
   ⊙ Apart from those apartments that are in buildings that contain fewer than four residential units
   ⊙ In contrast to smaller apartment buildings that contain fewer than four residential units
   ⊙ Unless the apartment building contains fewer than four residential units
   ⊙ Excluding those apartment buildings that have fewer than four residential units in them

15. Goethe's talents as a poet, painter, and dramatist were so diverse they inspired his many fans to refer to him as the "giant of Weimar."

   ⊙ so diverse they inspired
   ⊙ so diverse as to inspire
   ⊙ as diverse as those which inspired
   ⊙ diverse enough so as to inspire
   ⊙ as diverse as to inspire

16. Since 1994, when voters in several American cities rejected plans <u>for the using of public money in building of new sports stadiums, voters in San Diego, Pittsburgh, and Denver</u> changed their minds.

- ○ for the using of public money in building of new sports stadiums, voters in San Diego, Pittsburgh, and Denver
- ○ to use public money to build new sports stadiums, voters in San Diego, Pittsburgh, and Denver have
- ○ for using public money for the building of new sports stadiums, voters in San Diego, Pittsburgh, and also in Denver
- ○ for the public use of money to build new sports stadiums, voters in San Diego, Pittsburgh, and Denver have
- ○ to use public money to build new sports stadiums in San Diego, Pittsburgh, and Denver

17. Any real estate professional will tell you that the value of a parcel of land is most directly affected by <u>the extent of its development</u> and how close it is to a major business center.

- ○ the extent of its development
- ○ whether it has been developed extensively
- ○ how extensively it has developed
- ○ the extent to which it has developed
- ○ how extensively it has been developed

18. Baseball, the only major professional sport during the Great Depression, was <u>as present as the weather, and as much discussed</u>.

- ○ as present as the weather, and as much discussed
- ○ present like the weather was, and it was also discussed as much
- ○ as present and was discussed as the weather was
- ○ so present as to be discussed like the weather
- ○ present and discussed as often as the weather was

19. Never again will sports fans suffer <u>collective grief as much as they had</u> the day that Joe DiMaggio died.

- ○ collective grief as much as they had
- ○ so much collective grief as
- ○ so much grief collectively than
- ○ as much collective grief as they did
- ○ as much grief collectively than

20. <u>Proponents of affirmative action, including most university presidents, need only cite declining minority enrollment in universities in California and Texas, the two most populous states, to support their cause.</u>

- ○ Proponents of affirmative action, including most university presidents, need only cite declining minority enrollment in universities in California and Texas, the two most populous states, to support their cause.
- ○ Most university presidents who are proponents of affirmative action need to support their cause by only citing that declining minorities are enrolling in universities in the two most populous states of California and Texas.
- ○ In order for proponents of affirmative action, which include most university presidents, to support its cause, they need only to cite the decline in minority enrollment in universities in California and Texas, the two most populous states.
- ○ Minority enrollment in universities in California and Texas, the two most populous states, are declining, and proponents of affirmative action, including most university presidents, only need to cite this fact to support their cause.
- ○ University presidents, including those in California and Texas, the two most populous states where declining minorities are enrolling in universities, should cite these facts and support their cause as proponents of affirmative action.

21. As did many other newer American cities, Atlanta doubled in size in only its first ten years of existence.

- ○ As did
- ○ As have
- ○ Like
- ○ Just like
- ○ As with

22. Accredited travel agents were not required to provide advice pertaining to hotels and entertainment when they were organizing travel packages, but many do so anyway in an attempt to secure repeat business.

- ○ were not required to provide advice pertaining to hotels and entertainment when they were organizing travel packages, but many do so
- ○ are not required to provide advice pertaining to hotels and entertainment when they organize travel packages, but many do so
- ○ were not required for providing hotel and entertainment advice when they organized travel packages, but many do it
- ○ were not required that they provide advice pertaining to hotels and entertainment when they organized travel packages, but many had been doing so
- ○ had not had the requirement for them to provide advice pertaining to hotels and entertainment when they organize travel packages, but many do it

23. In China, wages are two times more than Taiwan's are and tens of thousands of companies have shifted operations to the mainland in search of wider margins.

- ○ In China, wages are two times more than Taiwan's are and
- ○ China's wages are two times more than in Taiwan, where
- ○ In China, where wages are more than two times those in Taiwan,
- ○ China has wages that are more than two times those of Taiwan's, and
- ○ The wages of China, which are two times more than in Taiwan, are causing

24. Due to the many huge building projects that have recently broken ground, such as $3.5 billion for the Kuala Lumpur airport and $5.3 billion which was spent creating a new seat of government, the Malaysian prime minister has developed a reputation for profligacy.

- ○ such as $3.5 billion for the Kuala Lumpur airport and $5.3 billion which was spent creating a new seat of government,
- ○ such as the $3.5 billion Kuala Lumpur airport and the $5.3 billion new seat of government,
- ○ like the $3.5 billion that he spent for the Kuala Lumpur airport and the $5.3 billion to create a new seat of government,
- ○ like the Kuala Lumpur airport, which cost $3.5 billion, and the $5.3 billion spent creating a new seat of government,
- ○ like the $3.5 billion Kuala Lumpur airport and the $5.3 billion creating of a new seat of government,

25. Anger has been determined by behavioral economists to make people assess situations more optimistically, downplay risks, and overestimate potential benefits, while fear affects this in the opposite way.

- ○ Anger has been determined by behavioral economists to make people assess situations more optimistically, downplay risks, and overestimate potential benefits, while fear affects this in the opposite way.
- ○ It has been determined by behavioral economists that anger makes people assess situations more optimistically, downplay risks, and potentially overestimate the benefits, while fear is affecting them in the opposite way.
- ○ Behavioral economists have determined anger to make people assess situations more optimistically, downplaying risks and potentially overestimating benefits; fear affects them in the opposite way.
- ○ Behavioral economists have determined that anger makes people assess situations more optimistically, downplaying risks and overestimating potential benefits, and that fear has the opposite effect.
- ○ Behavioral economists have determined that anger, which makes people assess situations more optimistically, downplay risks, and potentially overestimate the benefits, has the opposite effect of fear.

DRILL ANSWERS AND EXPLANATIONS

Drill 1: Misplaced Modifiers

1. Incorrect, because the sentence suggests that the park ranger was crazed with hunger. The corrected sentence should read: *Crazed with hunger, the stray coyote was finally subdued by the park ranger.* The sentence is in the passive voice, but it's still grammatically correct.

2. Incorrect, because the sentence literally reads that historians themselves are based on several manuscripts. A corrected sentence might read: *Relying on several manuscripts that date back to the Middle Ages, historians believe that Charlemagne first rose to power as a mere teenager.*

3. Correct.

4. Incorrect, because the sentence wrongly compares *executive skills* and *a person.* (The descriptive phrase *which most people can learn at any qualified business school* is stuck in the middle to confuse you.) The corrected sentence should read: *Unlike executive skills, which most people can learn at any qualified business school, a sense of leadership is usually derived from a person's social relationships.*

5. Incorrect, because the opening phrase describes Arthur, not Arthur's patience. The corrected sentence should read: *Though usually a calm person, Arthur had his patience tried more than once by his son's destructive behavior.*

6. Correct.

Drill 2: Pronoun Errors

1. Incorrect, because in the second part of the sentence, the pronoun *they* is ambiguous—does it refer to the farmers, the crops, or the melons? A corrected sentence could read: *As the melon farmers delivered their crop, they were dismayed to find that it was infested with fruit flies.*

2. Incorrect. The Commerce Department is singular, not plural. The corrected sentence should read: *The Commerce Department, which usually doesn't make any fiscal announcements until after the budget is ratified, announced that its accounting practices would be overhauled next year.*

3. Correct.

4. Correct.

5. Incorrect. We don't know which one the *she* refers to, so it's an ambiguous pronoun. The sentence could be corrected by writing, *Neither Alice nor Beatrix could figure out why they failed the math exam,* or by writing something like, *Neither Alice nor Beatrix could figure out why Beatrix failed the math exam.* Both of those are grammatically correct (but you'd have to know the actual situation to know which sentence was accurate).

6. Incorrect, because the plural pronoun *their* does not agree with the singular pronoun *every*. The corrected sentence should read: *Every employee brought his or her softball mitt to the game.* (For more about the insidious use of *they* in conversation, refer to the "Insidious 'They'" section of Grammar Odds and Ends in Part V.)

Drill 3: Verb Tense Errors

1. Incorrect. The corrected sentence should read: *Before the new library was built, children had played around in the vacant lot.* There are two past-tense events in the sentence, so you need to use the past perfect to indicate which happened first.

2. Incorrect. The corrected sentence should read: *A recent study has found that within the past decade, many lawyers not considered for partnership have chosen to quit rather than wait until the following year.* Because there's no other past-tense event in the sentence, the past perfect is incorrect. Rather we want a verb consistent with *has found*, which is the present perfect tense. Thus, *have chosen*.

3. Correct.

4. Correct.

5. Incorrect. The corrected sentence should read: *Never before had my parents been more surprised than they were when my sister brought home her new fiancé.* The past perfect is already being used in *had...been...surprised* and you don't want to use it twice. The two things can't both have happened first. The simple past is sufficient for the verb *brought*.

6. Incorrect. The corrected sentence should read: *The old gymnasium had been abandoned until a real estate consortium bought the facility and renovated it.* There are two past-tense events in the sentence, so you need to use the past-perfect to indicate which happened first.

Drill 4: Parallel Construction Errors

1. Correct. The structure of the two prepositional phrases *within a strictly monitored regimen* and *at random times* is parallel. The sentence wouldn't be parallel if one of the prepositions was missing.

2. Incorrect, because *to retire* and *searching* are not parallel forms. The corrected sentence should read: *When he reached the age of 61, my father chose to retire rather than to search for another job.* You can also rewrite it as *When he reached the age of 61, my father chose retirement over the search for another job.* But the first one works better.

3. Incorrect, because the verb forms *to evaluate* and *competing* are not parallel. The corrected sentence should read: *Evaluating Internet stocks using antiquated valuation models is like competing in the Indianapolis 500 with a horse and buggy.*

4. Incorrect, because the two things being distinguished, *attention deficit disorder* and *being bored*, are not parallel. The corrected sentence should read: *Even the most experienced teen counselor can find it difficult to distinguish attention deficit disorder, which results when a student is chemically unable to process information, from boredom.*

5. Correct.

6. Incorrect, because *to accomplish* is not parallel with *formulating*. Parallel construction requires that you use the same word form. The corrected sentence should read: *The first task to accomplish when writing an application essay is to formulate an outline that lists all the things you want to say.*

Drill 5: Comparing Apples and Oranges

1. Incorrect, because the sentence improperly compares the *population* of Asian Americans in California to the state of Missouri itself. The corrected sentence should read: *The population of Asian Americans in California is almost three times as big as that in Missouri.*

2. Correct.

3. Incorrect, because the sentence improperly uses the word *of* and doesn't compare what the sheep eat. The corrected sentence should read: *In New Zealand, the average sheep eats almost 10 more pounds of grass annually than its Australian counterpart does.*

4. Correct.

5. Correct. You're not comparing Rupert's tomatoes to a baby's tomatoes. It's perfectly fine to compare the size of a tomato with the size of a baby's head. Grammatically fine, at least.

6. Incorrect. The corrected sentence should read: *The New York Public Library's main branch, located on the southwest corner of Fifth Avenue and 42nd Street, is larger than any other branch in Manhattan.* Without *other*, the sentence says that the main branch is bigger than itself. That would certainly be an improper comparison.

Drill 6: Subject-Verb Agreement Errors

1. Correct. The pet monkey and the pet rabbit are both singular, so the singular verb *is* is proper.

2. Incorrect, because the subject *all*, which is plural, doesn't match the singular verb tense of *is*. The corrected sentence should read: *All of the major food groups, including proteins, fruits and vegetables, and carbohydrates, are crucial for optimal health. All* can be singular or plural depending on whether we mean *All of it* or *All of them.* We would say, *All of the people **were** there,* but, *All of the cake **was** eaten.*

3. Correct. If you bracket off the prepositional phrases and unnecessary junk, you can see how the subject and verb agree. *[Of all its sea-faring relatives,] the [California gray] seal stands out [because of its winsome demeanor and shiny coat].*

4. Correct. Let's bracket the unnecessary things. *A small number [of buildings] [that were damaged] [in the Great Fire] [of 1909] are [finally] about to be rebuilt [with the cash] [of an anonymous benefactor].* The rule is that the phrase *a number* is plural but *the number* is singular. We would say *A **number** of stones **were** found on the lawn,* but *The **number** of stones found on the lawn **was** scandalous.*

5. Incorrect, because the singular pronoun *each* needs a singular verb. The corrected sentence, with unnecessary parts bracketed, should read: *Each [of Liz Taylor's husbands][—including actor Richard Burton, Virginia senator John Warner, and construction worker Larry Fortensky—] has described her [as a rare beauty] [in both body and mind].*

6. Incorrect, because the subject, *cache*, is singular; therefore, it needs the singular verb tense, *is*. The corrected sentence should read: *A secret cache [of personal journals] that were the property [of Finnbar Brenneisen], the renowned and reclusive billionaire known as much [for his eccentric behavior] as [for his extraordinary philanthropy], is about to be published.*

Drill 7: Idiom Errors

1. *Students are prohibited **from** using school facilities without a teacher present.* The correct idiom is *prohibit…from.*

2. *Students are forbidden **to** go on field trips without a signed permission slip.* The correct idiom is *forbidden…to.*

3. *I tried to distinguish one twin **from** the other, but they truly were identical.* The correct idiom is *distinguish…from.*

4. *The Mona Lisa is believed **to be** one of the greatest paintings in history.* The correct idiom is *believe… to be.*

5. *He is not only a great guitar player, **but also** a great violin player.* The correct idiom is *not only…but also.*

6. *I will try **to** see you tomorrow if I can get all my work done.* The correct idiom is *try…to.*

Comprehensive Drill: Sentence Correction

1. **E** The two/three split is about as obvious as possible—right at the beginning of the answer choices. Because the enthusiasts are predicting what will happen in the future, it makes sense to use the future tense: *will*. Eliminate (A) and (B). Choice (C) unnecessarily uses the future perfect tense with *will have subsided*. You might be inclined to keep it until you reach (E), which is better because it uses the present tense *is*, and the sentence is less verbose than (C). Choice (D) uses the subjunctive tense.

    Note on the subjunctive tense: You might be inclined to like (B) because it uses *would* and *were*, but (B) has a problem because *random* modifies the wrong word. *Random* should modify *testing*, not *animals*.

2. **C** The first idiom to recognize is *find that*. Because (A) and (B) don't contain *that*, you can eliminate them. The key to the rest of the question is parallel construction. Choice (C) is correct because it describes people with three parallel adjectives: *agitated*, *defensive*, and *suspicious*. Choice (D) is wrong because it used *mostly* to describe *willing*. Also, the two descriptions (*willing to cooperate and agitated*) are contrary thoughts; therefore, you should use *yet*, not *and*. Choice (E) does not use parallel construction—there's no need to use *are becoming*.

3. **B** Here's a subtle example of parallelism, and it relates to the word *either*. The drug companies obtain records either to contact or to estimate. Therefore, (B) is the only parallel choice. Also, (E) has pronoun trouble because the drug companies are doing the estimating. The plural noun takes *they*, not *it*.

4. **A** The correct idiom here is *not...but*, and (B) uses *not...and*, so get rid of it. Choices (C) and (E) change the meaning of the original sentence unnecessarily, plus the phrase *judged to* is not parallel with *by* at the end of these choices. Choice (D) lacks the second *by* at the end of the choice and is thus illogical in meaning and non-parallel, unlike (A).

5. **B** Note the two/three split once again. The three airlines are separate businesses that are merging, so you can eliminate (A), (D), and (E). This is an example of when the majority doesn't always rule on a two/three split. Choice (B) is better because of the comma it uses. The construction in (C), *merger of their businesses that*, suggests that the businesses created the alliance, but it was the airlines who did the creating. Also, the use of *would control* here is better because the actual control hasn't happened yet.

6. **E** Here's a stellar example of the old subject-verb sucker punch. Students are inclined to pick (A) because *adults carry* makes sense to the ear. But the subject of this latter thought is *one*, which needs to be paired up with the verb *carries*. Use the two/three split and cross off (A) and (B). The rest comes down to the proper use of the statistics cited in the sentence. Choices (C) and (D) are incorrect because they use *every* and *each*, which suggest that if you take 50 people off the street and put them in a room, exactly one will be carrying a handgun. But the point of the sentence is to establish a more general ratio: for every 49 people who don't pack heat, there is one person who does.

7. **D**   The sentence is wrong as written because *more* needs *than*. Because it uses *as* instead, you can get rid of (A). Choice (B) changes to the past tense, but the present tense *is* remains later on. There's also an improper tense shift, so (B) is gone as well. Choice (C) isn't parallel because *destruction* and *making* aren't in the same format. It might have a chance if it used *destroying* instead. And (E) is a verbose mess; there's no need to use *the making of* when *making* is just fine by itself.

8. **D**   Here's one of those obscure idioms: *liken...to*. (In case you're worried, this idiom appears in Appendix C: Idiom List.) Note that *liken to* is correct, but *liken to be* is wrong. Also, there is a construction issue here. The use of *which* in (A) suggests that the fortune-tellers likened themselves to prognosticators. (See Appendix A: Grammar Odds and Ends in Part V for clarification of the use of *which*.) Choices (B), (C), and (E) are in the passive voice, which is not considered ideal on the GMAT. When you have a choice, go with active voice.

9. **C**   These total-sentence questions can be either a real pain in the neck, or the answers can come to you right away. When you see one of these, just scan each one individually and look for errors. Choice (A) is out because it contains *being*; (B) compares Wichterle to the developments of the other inventors; and (D) compares the contact lens to the other inventors. Both are apples-and-oranges mistakes, and both must go. Choice (E) is also screwy because it suggests that the inventors had been inspired by necessity instead of by their developments. Choice (C) is correct because its modifiers all match and are in the right place.

10. **E**   Don't get these two idioms confused: *intend...to* and *intent...on*. Each is correct as is, but many students confuse the prepositions. The use of *who* in (A), (B), and (C) is fine, but (E) is better because *who* is not necessary; in this case, shortest is sweetest. Choice (D) is wrong because it should read *intending to run*.

    Note: This question does a good job of illustrating that it's better to decide among the choices rather than cook up your own answer. Many students who see this question think the right answer should be *who intends to run*. That's a correct answer, but it's not among the choices.

11. **A**   Be sure to line up your subjects and verbs! The subject of the sentence is *attempts*, so the verb needs to be *have*. Choices (B) and (D) use *has*, so they're gone. Choice (E) has a different verb problem because there's no reason to use the past perfect form of *had*. Therefore, you can knock that off as well. Once you're down to (A) and (C), the only difference is the placement of the word *political*, which should modify *resistance*. Choice (C) is wrong because it turns *political* into the adverb *politically* and makes it modify *encountered*.

12. **D** The subject of the sentence is the noun *result*. For the sake of parallelism, then, *discover* should also be in noun form (*result...has been the discovery*). Remember that basic noun forms are usually preferable to *-ing* words unless the words all end in *-ing* for the sake of parallelism. The best choices left are (B) and (D), and (D) is better because it uses the simple past tense *ruled* instead of *had ruled*, which is unnecessary. Also, (D) has an important distinction from (B) because it uses the word *were*. The best parallel tense should appear like this: *Pharaohs were buried with fewer artifacts than their successors were.* The *were* can also appear in the middle of the sentence: *Pharaohs were buried with fewer artifacts than were their successors.*

13. **C** Process of Elimination is the only way to go here because it's hard to express grammatically why (C) is superior. However, it's much easier to kill off the other choices because of their flaws. Choices (A) and (B) contain *being*, so they can go. Choice (D) is a wordy mess that contains that most odious phrase *the fact that* and also needlessly uses the past perfect tense *had been fueled*, and (E) suggests that Stanley Kubrick had his temperament fueled on purpose, as if he pulled into a gas station. That point is clearly not what the author wanted to get across.

14. **D** Time to weed out the misplaced modifiers. The beginning of the nonunderlined portion of the sentence begins with *each room*, so if the sentence wants to compare anything by using the word *Unlike*, the underlined portion should also be about rooms. Choice (A) compares smaller buildings to rooms, and so do (B) and (C), even though they replace *Unlike* with *Apart from* and *In contrast to*, respectively. A lemon painted blue is still a lemon. Choice (E) survives the first cut because it doesn't commit this error, although its construction is still awkward because it suggests that each room is *Excluding* those apartment buildings. Given the choice of (D) or (E), (D) is much more concise.

15. **B** Be sure you know the idiom *so...as to*. It's an idiom that the test writers love because it doesn't make its way into basic conversation very often, so most people are unfamiliar with it. Choice (A) flirts with the idiom *so...that* (another one you should know) but lacks the word *that*. Choices (C) and (E) change the meaning of the original sentence unnecessarily. Choice (D) uses the *so...as* to idiom correctly, but the phrase *diverse enough* changes the meaning of the sentence and makes this choice wordy and awkward.

16. **B** Again, the simple noun form *use* is better than the gerund *the using*; (A) is history. There's also a two/three split on the end of each answer choice; (B) and (D) use *have*, and (A), (C), and (E) do not. Because the sentence begins with *Since*, you need to use *have*. The construction is similar to this one: "I have eaten three dozen Oreos since breakfast." Choices (C) and (E) can join (A) on the sidelines. Choice (D) has another one of those subtle modifier problems because *public* should modify *money*, not *use*. The taxpayers aren't actually using the money; they're paying and it will be used by someone else.

17. **E** Before you give yourself migraines trying to figure out the proper use of *extent*, look instead at the need for parallelism. Because *how* appears in the nonunderlined portion at the end of the sentence, it should also appear at the beginning of the underlined portion (affected *by how...and how*). Eliminate all but (C) and (E), and then compare the remaining choices to each other. The only difference is that (E) uses *been*. Those who argue that shortest is sweetest might pick (C) at this point, but (E) is actually correct because the property hasn't developed; it has been developed by others.

    Note: Here's a good example that although "vigorous writing is concise," the shortest answer isn't automatically correct. A short answer choice could omit something very important.

18. **A** This is another toughie that is best attacked using POE. Choice (B) is long and redundant, because you don't need to say *and it was also*. Choice (C) tries to combine the two thoughts, but they're better off left apart (and there's no need to say *was* twice). Choice (D) wants to use that highfalutin idiom *so...as to*, but it suggests that *baseball* and *the weather* were actually compared to each other. Choice (E) is awkward because it suggests that the weather is sometimes not present.

19. **D** Nothing like two consecutive baseball questions to get the blood pumping, eh? Well, this one may have been a little easier for you to solve. The idiom you're looking for is *as...as...*, and (B), (C), and (E) are unidiomatic. Choice (A) is wrong because you don't need to use the past perfect tense *had*, although you do need to add the verb *did* at the end. Also, (C) and (E) change the meaning slightly; *collective* should be an adjective and modify *grief*.

20. **A** Here's another full-sentence question, and it also needs to have all of its descriptive words and phrases placed in the proper order. Choices (B) and (E) are wrong because they change the meaning; *declining minorities are enrolling* does not mean the same thing as *minority enrollment is declining*. The former suggests that minorities themselves are declining, when in fact it is their numbers that are declining. Choice (C) has pronoun problems (*support its cause?*) and (D) has a subject-verb flaw. Because enrollment is the subject, the verb should be *is*, not *are*.

21. **C** There is a straightforward comparison going on here; Atlanta is like other cities, so *like* is all you need. *Just like* is redundant, so (D) is out. The *have* in (B) and the *with* in (E) are not parallel with the rest of the sentence, and (E) is not idiomatic, so they can go, too. The use of *as* in (A), (B), and (E) is also incorrect because you use *as* to indicate that the processes are the same. Therefore, you would use *as* here only if you knew that Atlanta had expanded in exactly the same way as the other cities had. Because you don't know that for sure, *like* is the better choice.

22. **B** The verb tense should remain constant throughout a sentence unless there's a tangible reason to do otherwise. Choice (B) is the best choice because its verbs, *are not required* and *do so,* are both in the present tense. The verb tenses in (A) don't match because *were* is in the past tense. Choice (D) also uses the past tense *were* and complicates things further by using *had been doing so*, which is completely unnecessary. The same is true for (E)'s *had not had* the requirement. Choice (C) is close, but *do so* is better than *do it* because it is an ambiguous pronoun. (Remember, you can't assume anything when it comes to pronouns.)

23. **C** As written, the sentence uses an improper idiom, *two times more than*, rather than the proper construction, *more than two times*. Using *are* twice is also not necessary. In (B), (D), and (E), the construction of the comparison between wages in the two countries is not parallel. Choice (D) uses a redundant phrase, *those of Taiwan's*, and (E) adds *are causing*, which messes up the idiom of the second half of the sentence (the idiom is *cause...to*).

24. **B** There is a nice two/three split among the beginnings of the answer choices, and because the underlined portion deals with examples of huge building projects, it's proper to use *such as* rather than *like*. *Such as* means "for example" and *like* means "similar to." Eliminate (C), (D), and (E). From here, (B) is better than (A) because (A) seems to say that money is an example of a building project. It's the airport itself that is the project, for example, not the $3.5 billion. Choice (B) is also more concise, and the test writers like that.

25. **D** The sentence needs correcting because it uses an ambiguous pronoun, *this*. Choices (B) and (C) repeat this error, but the bad pronoun here is *them*, which could refer to any of the several plural nouns in the sentence. Choice (C) also misuses the idiom *determine...that*. Choice (E) scrambles the meaning of the sentence, making it seem that fear and anger being opposites is the point of the sentence. It also changes the meaning in subtler ways by turning the phrase "overestimating potential benefits" into *potentially overestimating benefits,* which isn't the same thing.

Chapter 2
Reading
Comprehension

OVERVIEW OF THE READING COMP SECTION

If you are like many students, the Reading Comprehension section of the GMAT Verbal section is not something you would do for fun on a Saturday afternoon. There is no way around the simple fact that most of the reading comp passages on the GMAT are mundane in content and tedious in structure. Moreover, the questions often seem to ask you to delve into the mind of the author and make assumptions about their beliefs.

But is this really true?

The bad news is that, yes, the passages tend to be tedious and boring. The good news, though, is that the questions do not ask you to make assumptions about what an author believes. In fact, the Reading Comprehension section is designed so that every question can be answered based on information from the passages.

The best news is that this chapter touches on all of these issues and more, and introduces you to the practices taught in our test prep classrooms. One time-tested principle remains as true for the Reading Comprehension section as it does for all other sections on the GMAT: *You must practice in order to achieve your optimal score.* Remember, you can improve on the Reading Comprehension section, and for the rest of this chapter, you will learn how.

The Structure

You will encounter four Reading Comprehension passages on the verbal portion of the GMAT. In all likelihood, you will see three short passages and one long passage. The passages range anywhere from 30 to 70 lines of text, with about six to eight words per line. Shorter passages are typically accompanied by three questions, while longer passages have four questions. It's also possible that you will get two short passages and two long, which means there will be a total of either 13 or 14 questions on the reading comp section (out of the grand total of 41 questions in the Verbal section).

Computer-Adaptive Reading Comp

The GMAT test writers create passages that range from short and fairly simple to long and complicated, filled with unfamiliar terminology and difficult sentence structure. As with all computer-adaptive exams, passage difficulty is dependent on the computer's perception of your ability as you progress through the test. However, *question* difficulty will not change once you have been given a passage, regardless of how you perform on the questions. For example, if you are doing well and the computer gives you a difficult passage, you will continue to be presented with questions that are appropriate for the passage's difficulty level, and your score will not change until you have completed all questions associated with that passage.

What Your Screen Will Look Like

Passages appear on the left-hand side of the screen. When a passage is too long to fit on one panel, you will be prompted to scroll down in order to read all of it. The question appears on the right side of the screen, next to the passage. Your screen will look a lot like this:

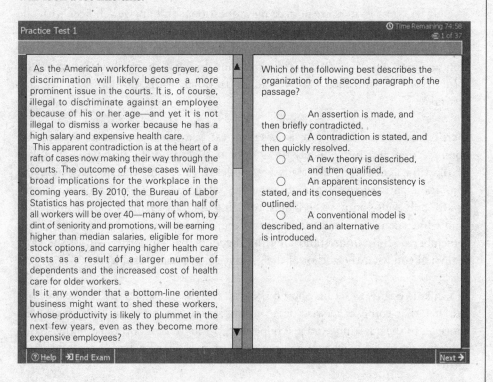

Types of Passages

Passages on the Reading Comprehension section cover a variety of topics from four primary areas:

- **Social sciences:** Social or historical issues, such as the civil rights movement or World War I

- **Physical sciences:** Natural science topics, such as photosynthesis or black holes

- **Biological sciences:** Topics related to living organisms and how they interact with their environment

- **Business:** Business-related topics; for example, management strategies or the loosening of international trade restrictions

It is worth noting again that the passages can be tedious. The test writers know this and purposely create passages that the average test taker will have to read and re-read multiple times to fully comprehend. Basically, the test writers want to trick you into doing what they want you to do. Don't do what the writers want you to do!

DON'T BE AVERAGE

Imagine you are a test writer for the GMAT. You are tasked with creating questions that will be used to evaluate one student against another, and you're responsible for the Reading Comprehension section. How would you go about it?

The GMAT test writers create passages, questions, and answer choices with the average test taker in mind. They know how the typical test taker reads passages and responds to questions the majority of the time, and they use this information against you. The best strategy is to not do what the test writers want you to do. Don't be who they want you to be. In other words, do not be the average test taker.

Here's a common scenario for an average test taker. She encounters the reading comp section and immediately dives right into reading the first passage. Aware of the time remaining, she reads very quickly. After all, the questions are the important part, right? She might read the whole passage or, if a bit more self-aware, only half the passage before realizing she has retained hardly any of it. And while she may have a vague idea of the passage's main subject, she does not remember or fully understand anything beyond that—in other words, she can't really tell you what the author of the passage said about the subject.

Now panic begins to set in. Should she read the passage again and waste precious minutes that could otherwise be spent answering the questions? Or should she move on to the questions and just hope that, through some sort of computer-based osmosis, she picked up enough important details to help her choose the right answers?

Either way, in this type of scenario, the average test taker has played right into the hands of the test writers. She has become slightly panicked and is wasting time, and is thus more susceptible to making the mistakes that the test writers want her (and you) to make—which, of course, ultimately lead to wrong answers.

HOW TO BE DIFFERENT

Active Reading

Average vs. Active
Average test takers read for speed, but active readers read for understanding and efficiency.

One way to differentiate yourself from the average test taker and avoid the same mistakes is by practicing **active reading**. The average test taker reads for speed, does not pick up relevant information about the passage's content or author, and, as a result, ends up wasting more time re-reading the passage than would have been spent *actively* reading the first time around.

So what is active reading? How does one go about reading "actively"? Are there any effective practices to help you learn this skill? There sure are, and this section outlines them for you. Simply reading about this technique, however, is only half the battle. You must practice active reading as well—and we've helped you out with that by providing some practice material at the end of the chapter.

How to Be an Active Reader

An active reader is able to follow an author's argument or thesis throughout an entire passage. Active readers are on a mission to seek out and identify an author's main point, as well as the facts and evidence used to support that point. To become an active reader, you should do the following things (at the very least):

- **Ask questions while reading.** While you are reading, try to get as much information as you can from the passage. What is the subject or main idea? What does the author think about the subject or main idea? Is the author merely providing facts or trying to convince you that his or her viewpoint is correct? What is the author's tone? By asking these kinds of questions, you will be able to follow the passage and remain engaged with the author.

- **Identify the structure of the passage.** Reading comprehension passages on the GMAT largely follow the same structure. Being aware of this structure will help you to identify the subject or main idea of the passage, as well as the author's claims about that subject or idea. Typically, passages are general at first and then move to the more specific, and then finally move back to general. Individual paragraphs may also follow this structure, with the opening sentence serving as the (general) topic sentence and the sentences that follow as the specific details and information. The last sentence is often a more general statement that sets up the next paragraph.

- **Look for topic sentences.** An active reader acknowledges topic sentences. The topic sentence is usually the first sentence of a paragraph, and you'll need to examine the remainder of the paragraph to find information that further explains or supports the topic sentence. Because each paragraph flows into the next, look to the last sentence of the paragraph for clues about the main idea of the paragraph that follows.

By reading actively, you will be able to create a roadmap for a passage to which you can refer back when you get to the questions. Mapping the passage is a key component in making sure you are not being the average test taker, thereby helping you achieve your maximum score.

Mapping the Passage

If you were actively reading the last section, then you may have guessed that the next section (this one) will touch on mapping out passages. If you didn't pick up on this, go back and read the last paragraph again. Active reading often helps you predict where the author is going next.

Want More?

If you want more practice, grab *Cracking the GMAT* for additional questions and insight into the test.

Now let's discuss mapping out passages. Think back to the common scenario of the average test taker that we described earlier. Let's say the same average test taker reads the previous section on active reading but decides to skip this section on mapping passages. What do you think would happen?

Well, if she reads the passages actively, she will likely have a better understanding of a passage's content and main points. But when she reads the first question, she will likely spend the next few seconds trying to remember where in the passage the relevant information is located. Now time is ticking by and panic sets in. She does not remember where in the passage she read that relevant information, forcing her to return to the passage and re-read.

But is re-reading the passage really necessary? Most likely, no. And has she wasted valuable time searching for a piece of information that she would have already had by mapping out the passage? Yes.

Map It Out

When you map out a passage, you'll find the answers to the questions more quickly.

Mapping the passage is the best way to keep yourself organized as you tackle the passages. When you map out a passage, you can quickly refer to pieces of information and remember where they are located in the text. In short, you will be able to find the answers you need more quickly.

Of course, the only way to map a passage is to do something that the average test taker almost never does on the Reading Comprehension section: write things down.

Pick Up That Pencil…No, Seriously

Just because the Reading Comprehension section is based on reading does not mean you are excused from writing important things down. Mapping the passage is a straightforward and effective strategy, but it means you have to do some writing.

The best way to map a passage is to look for *key sentences*. Read the passage one paragraph at a time. At the end of each paragraph, stop and think about which sentence in that paragraph seems most like an opinion, recommendation, conclusion, or reason. Then, on your noteboard, write down a short summary of the sentence. There's no need to copy down the whole sentence; just write enough to give you a clear idea of what the sentence is about and what it means in relation to the paragraph as a whole.

Mapping a passage in this way will allow you to see the big picture and, in turn, have a better understanding of the passage's main ideas and points. You will also be able to quickly reference key details and information.

Practice, Practice, Practice

The following passage was written shortly after the European Central Bank, or ECB, was established in 1998. Read the passage, and then practice your active reading and mapping skills by writing summaries in the spaces provided. Compare your summaries to the ones on page 67 to see how you did.

It comes as no surprise that there is little consensus among economists who study the prospects for the new European Central Bank (ECB). Some are overwhelmingly enthusiastic about the ECB's potential to eliminate exchange-rate currency fluctuations among its eleven member economies, while others are convinced that cultural differences and inevitable squabbles over monetary policy doom the central bank to failure.

The pessimists have a valid point. The ECB's primary goal, as specified by the Maastricht treaty, is to bring about price stability within its area of sovereignty. This stability, however, is predicated on reducing the current incongruity of prices throughout the region. Currently, though, there are too many cultural and financial variables that prevent prices from coming into alignment anytime soon.

For a start, the prices of many products sold in Europe already vary from country to country by large margins. The average cost of a pair of blue jeans is 34 percent higher in Germany than it is in Italy. Some reasons for this can be remedied through legislation. If Germany were to repeal its law prohibiting supermarkets from stocking aspirin on their shelves, for example, aspirin prices might come in line with the rest of the European Union. But most price differentials derive from seemingly immutable standards of living. Personal incomes in Spain and Portugal are well below the European average, as they have been for decades. Thus, prices stay lower to accommodate weaker buying power. And since Scandinavian countries show no sign of adopting the high demand for coffee products that exists in France and Italy, coffee prices will remain much higher in southern Europe than in the north.

Until now, Europe's different currencies have done well to divert consumers' attention from these price differentials. But now that Europe has adopted its one currency, the euro, Europeans are more likely to seek out the best price regardless of geography. This could mean depressed localized economies of scale. Many countries will not recover from this situation in the short term.

Fortunately for the ECB's architects, there are two extraordinary financial models to study and replicate: the German Bundesbank and America's Federal Reserve Board. Each country within the European Union, regardless of its population or the size of its gross domestic product, will be represented equally in the ECB's governing council, which will dictate the policies that the various national central banks will implement. As long as the lines of communication remain open and country representatives keep an open mind toward what may become a radical overhaul within European commerce, the euro and the ECB have a fighting chance to survive.

Paragraph 1:

_____

_____

Paragraph 2:

_____

_____

Paragraph 3:

_____

_____

Paragraph 4:

_____

_____

Paragraph 5:

_____

_____

Overall Main Idea:

_____

_____

Now compare your summaries to those provided below.

Paragraph 1: Introduction: Some economists believe the ECB will thrive, while others believe that it will struggle due to differences among countries.

Paragraph 2: The author agrees with the pessimists, as there are too many variables that separate cultures to find financial common ground and make the ECB work.

Paragraph 3: Cites examples of how countries are different to support paragraph 2

Paragraph 4: Introduces new currency, the euro, and mentions more issues with the currency

Paragraph 5: There is a chance the ECB can thrive (author gives two examples of similar banks), but it will be difficult.

Overall Main Idea: The ECB and the euro have many difficult challenges to overcome, but success is possible.

Answering the Questions

As outlined in the previous section, test writers like to create situations in which the average student is at a disadvantage. Again, your job is to try your best *not* to be average. You already know how ill prepared the average test taker is to answer questions in the first place due to their deficiency in developing a true understanding of a passage.

So how does the average test taker approach answering the questions? Well, he or she will most likely attempt to find the correct answer in the passage and then choose it, which sounds reasonable. However, a much more effective strategy is to eliminate the bad answer choices through Process of Elimination (POE). And in order to identify a bad answer choice, you should know the types of wrong answer choices commonly seen on the GMAT.

Answer Choice Capers

The test writers employ a few different types of answer choices that trick and tempt students to pick them. The writers are skilled in creating wrong answers that appear correct. The most effective way to combat these answer choices is to understand why test writers use them and how they create them. Once you can identify common ways that incorrect answer choices are made, you will become more skeptical of answer choices and be able to spot—and then eliminate—those that are incorrect.

Wrong Answer Choices

Imagine again that you are a test writer. You have created a reading comp passage and question, and now you must create answer choices that contain some traps. Because the correct answer must come from information in the passage, you, the test writer, need to find a way to make wrong answers appear correct—or else the Reading Comprehension section would be way too easy, right?

As the test writer, you must consider the average test taker. Test writers believe that the average test taker is susceptible to certain tools at their disposal, and the writers use these tools to create their answer choices.

A number of strategies are used in constructing wrong answer choices:

- Memory traps and recycled language

- Extreme language

- No such comparison

- Reversals

- Emotional appeals

- Outside knowledge

Let's look at each of these in a little more detail.

Memory Traps and Recycled Language

A **memory trap** is a common technique used to create wrong answer choices. Memory trap answers contain words or phrases that evoke a strong memory from the passage.

When the average test taker reads a memory trap answer, he or she will be immediately reminded of something in the passage and be prompted to choose that answer.

The truth is that most correct answers on the GMAT are paraphrases of information contained within the passage. It is rare for a correct answer to be a direct quote or phrase from the passage itself. However, memory trap answer choices are so appealing because they look familiar; and since the average test taker does not, as we determined, have a clear understanding of the passage, he or she will likely choose the memory trap answer for that exact reason.

Recycled language is a type of memory trap that pulls words or quotes directly from the passage. Be suspicious of any answer choice that contains words or phrases just as they appear in the passage.

When you encounter an answer choice that you think might be a memory trap, do some more investigation to find a concrete reason to eliminate it. Very often you will find that the passage mentions the subject or main idea of a recycled language answer, but in a different context than the question poses. Consult your passage map and search the passage for the recycled language and, when you locate it, determine the context in which the passage mentions it. If the answer choice uses words or phrases out of this context, eliminate it.

Extreme Language

Another common way that test writers create wrong answer choices is by using strong language that is too powerful or overt, including words such as must, *always, never, only,* and *best,* among others. Strong verbs like *prove* or *fail* are also frequently used.

Answer choices with **extreme language** often state that the purpose of the passage is to do something specific, like defend or support an idea. The average test taker feels comfortable choosing this type of answer choice because it seemingly conveys the main idea of the passage. But if you read actively and map out passages, extreme language becomes much more noticeable. Correct answer choices typically use language that is passive or "soft" so that they can be more easily defended if a student challenges the scoring of the test.

The following table lists common "extreme" words. If you see an answer choice that contains one or more of these words, be skeptical.

Refer to the Passage

When you read an answer choice, refer to the passage and your notes to see whether or not that choice can actually be supported. If it can't, eliminate it.

Common Extreme Words			
never	not	defend	contradict
always	no	attack	failure
only	must	denounce	
none	prove	counter	

No Such Comparison

As their name implies, **no-such-comparison** answer choices draw a comparison between two items that are discussed in the passage but not actually compared. Words that commonly appear in this type of answer choice include better, more, reconcile, less, decide, or more than. The presence of any of these words in an answer choice is cause for skepticism. Always refer back to the passage and your notes.

Reversals

Reversal answer choices are designed to confuse test takers. These choices reverse the main idea or what the passage says about the focus of a question. While there is no list of common words or phrases specific to this type of answer choice, you can avoid reversal answers by reading actively and mapping out passages. Always double check the ideas conveyed in an answer choice against the passage itself.

Emotional Appeals

Although this type of answer choice rarely appears on the GMAT, it's still worth mentioning. **Emotional appeals**, which are often found in conjunction with memory traps, try to appeal to a test taker's beliefs. The average test taker might select this type of answer choice simply because they agree with it. Beware of any answer choice that seems a little too opinionated, and check it against the information presented in the passage.

Outside Knowledge

Important!

Any answer choice that requires or involves outside knowledge is automatically incorrect.

Much like emotional appeals, outside knowledge answer choices are seen infrequently on the GMAT and usually appear in conjunction with memory traps. These answer choices can be very tempting for the average test taker, who may have knowledge that is not mentioned in the passage but is reflected in an answer choice. Remember, correct answers on the reading comp section always come directly from the passages. So if you see a piece of information in an answer choice that isn't relevant to the passage, look back to the passage and find out. If it is not addressed in the passage, eliminate it—even if it's true. Answer choices that require outside knowledge are incorrect.

Reading the Questions

The final step in learning how to *not* be the average test taker is to become familiar with the types of questions you'll likely encounter on the Reading Comprehension section. The average test taker spends a considerable amount of time reading and re-reading a question in order to fully understand what it's asking. But this process costs valuable time that is better used in other ways—time that can be saved if you're aware of a few common question types, as well as what you need to do after you read a question: Figure out the question's subject and task.

Subject and Task

Once you read a question, your first job is to find its subject and task. Many test takers struggle with this because it requires actively reading the question. If you read the question actively, you can quickly identify the subject and task and then begin the process of eliminating wrong answers through POE.

The following is a sample question. See whether you can identify the subject and task before reading on.

> The author's attitude toward the success of the
> ECB can best be described as

The subject of this question is the *author's attitude toward the success of the ECB*, and the task is to find what it is best...*described as* in the passage. To answer this question, look at your notes and refer back to the passage to determine the author's attitude. Then eliminate the answer choices that do not match the passage.

Common Question Types

In addition to finding subject and task, knowing types of common questions is also very useful when it comes to tackling the reading comp section. Generally speaking, there are three question types found in the Reading Comprehension section: *general, specific,* and *complex.* Each of these categories is further divided into four subcategories.

General Questions

The four types of general questions are **main idea, primary purpose, tone,** and **structure.**

Main idea questions ask you to consider the main claims an author makes in a passage, and generally ask what the passage is about. The goal of a main idea question is to get you to summarize what the author wants you to remember about the passage. The phrase "main idea" or any reference to an overall claim usually appears in the question stem. The answer choices for main idea questions typically contain memory traps, recycled language, extreme language, or reversals.

The following question for a passage on women's history is an example of a main idea question:

> The author of the passage would be most likely
> to make which of the following recommenda-
> tions to scholars of women's history?

The subject of the question is *scholars of women's history,* and the task is to find *which of the following recommendations* the author would make to the scholars. This is a main idea question because it asks you to refer back to the passage to find the author's main point.

Primary purpose questions may seem very close to main idea questions, but they differ in one important way. While main idea questions ask what the passage is about, primary purpose questions tend to ask why the author wrote the passage. Moreover, primary purpose questions sometimes even contain the phrase "primary purpose" in the question stem. Wrong answer choices that commonly accompany this type of question are memory traps and recycled language.

**Reading Comp
Question Categories**
There are three main types of questions in the reading comp section: general, specific, and complex. These types are further divided into four subcategories.

The following is an example of a primary purpose question:

> The passage is primarily concerned with

As you can see, this question seems very similar to a main idea question. But when you know the difference between these two question types, you'll notice that the answer choices have more to do with why the author wrote the passage rather than the passage's main idea.

Tone questions ask you to evaluate the opinion of the author and how strong his or her position is. The author's opinion is often stated somewhere in the passage, and is usually synonymous with the passage's main idea. If you have taken all the necessary steps to fully understand the passage, deciphering the tone is a manageable task. Tone questions are readily identifiable, since they frequently contain the words "tone" or "attitude" in the question stem. However, tone questions can also be made a bit more challenging by the presence of extreme language in the answer choices. Consult your notes and the information in the passage, and then use POE.

Pro Tip

It is not uncommon to encounter a tone question with five answer choices that all begin with a strong verb.

A tone question might look something like the following:

> The author's attitude toward the success of the ECB can best be described as

This question refers to author's *attitude*, which is a clear indicator that it's a tone question. As you may have noticed, it's also a fairly general question.

Structure questions ask about the flow and organization of a passage. To answer this type of question, look through your notes and the passage to determine its structure. Usually the author presents an opinion followed by some counterpoints, and then establishes evidence that supports his or her opinion. The task of a structure question is to identify the order in which the author presents the argument. Reversals and extreme language often show up in the answer choices for this type of question in order to confuse you, as the difference between the correct answer and the incorrect ones is often very small.

The following is an example of a structure question:

> Which of the following best describes the organization of the passage?

Here the subject of the question is the *organization* of the passage, and the task is to find which of the answer choices *best describes* the organization. To find the correct answer, you must first review how the author constructs the passage. When you map out the passage beforehand, this task is fairly straightforward.

Specific Questions

The four types of specific questions found in the Reading Comprehension section are **retrieval, inference, purpose,** and **vocabulary in context.**

Retrieval questions, which ask you to find a specific fact or detail in the passage, can be identified by the phrase *according to the passage* or a similar phrase that points you back to the text. The correct answer to a retrieval question is usually simply a paraphrase of the passage. Incorrect answer choices that often show up in this type of question are memory traps and recycled language, but reversals might also be used.

Here is an example of a retrieval question:

> According to the passage, which of the following shapes the oral narratives of women storytellers?

The phrase *according to the passage* is a dead giveaway that this is a retrieval question. The subject of the question is *oral narratives of women storytellers*, and the task is to find the answer choice that *shapes* those narratives.

Inference questions are common in the Reading Comprehension section and are most troublesome to unaware test takers. These questions usually say something along the lines of "What can be inferred from the passage?" Inference questions always ask about something very specific in the passage and are thus very similar to retrieval questions. However, inference questions can be distinguished by the presence of words like *infer, imply,* or *suggest*. These key words might cause some test takers to assume the answer does not lie within the passage but, as mentioned earlier, this is never the case for questions on the GMAT. Outside knowledge is not required; the correct answer will always be found in the passage.

Therefore, treat these questions like retrieval questions, and look through the passage as well as your notes for reasons to eliminate answer choices. In inference questions, watch out for memory traps, recycled language, no-such-comparisons, and outside knowledge in the answer choices.

Take a look at the following example of an inference question:

> It can be inferred from the passage that which of the following is a true statement about sea snakes?

You can tell this is an inference question because the word *inferred* is in the question stem. The subject here is *sea snakes*, and the task is to find the answer choice that is a *true statement* based on the passage. In other words, the answer is somewhere in the text. Refer to your notes and the passage to find what the author says about the subject, and then eliminate the answer choices that don't match.

Remember!
Outside knowledge is never required on the GMAT, so don't let words like *infer* or *imply* confuse you.

Purpose questions are similar to primary purpose questions in the sense that they both ask *why* the author includes something in the passage. However, while primary purpose questions focus on the bigger picture, purpose questions ask about something very specific, such as a fact, detail, sentence, or entire paragraph. Purpose questions typically contain phrases like *in order to* and *serves which of the following functions,* for example. Incorrect answer choices that frequently accompany this type of question are memory traps, recycled language, extreme language, and no such comparison.

An example of a purpose question is the following:

> In the context of the passage as a whole, the
> second paragraph serves primarily to

Don't let the word *primarily* confuse you; this is not a primary purpose question. The subject of the question is *second paragraph*, and the task of the question is to figure out the role it plays in *the context of the passage as a whole*. Since the question is asking about a specific piece of the passage, it is a purpose question.

Vocabulary-in-context questions reference a word or phrase from the passage that the author uses to prove a point. The task of such questions is to determine the point or meaning of the word or phrase. Extreme language commonly shows up in the answer choices, and don't be surprised to find some memory traps in there as well.

Keep an Eye Out

Extreme language and memory traps often show up in answer choices for vocabulary-in-context questions.

The following is an example of a vocabulary-in-context question:

> In the context of the passage, the word "ex-
> cessive" (line 23) most closely corresponds to
> which of the following phrases?

Note that in the vocabulary-in-context questions you'll see in this book, the word or phrase in question will be quoted and accompanied by a line reference to help you find it in the passage more easily. On the actual exam, though, the word or phrase will probably be highlighted onscreen, and the question will refer to the "highlighted word."

The subject of vocabulary-in-context questions is always the highlighted word or phrase in the passage, and the task is to figure out which of the answer choices is most closely synonymous with that highlighted word or phrase.

Complex Questions
Complex questions are also divided into four types: **evaluation**, **weaken/strengthen**, **analogy**, and **application**.

Evaluation questions require you to compare or analyze information in the passage. These questions are rare, so there aren't common phrases you can look for to identify them. An evaluation question might, for example, ask you to choose the statement that an author would be most likely to agree with. Wrong answer choices are often no-such-comparisons or contain recycled language.

Check out the following example:

> Which of the following most accurately summarizes the relationship between Arizona v. California in lines 38-42, and the criteria citing the Winters doctrine in lines 10-20?

Like vocabulary-in-context questions, evaluation questions on the actual GMAT most likely contain highlighted phrases or sentences onscreen instead of quotes and line references. The point remains, however, that this type of question asks you to evaluate the relationship between two things mentioned in the passage. Here, the subject of the question is *Arizona v. California* and the *Winters doctrine*, and the task is to *summarize the relationship*.

More common than evaluation questions, **weaken/strengthen questions** ask you to weaken or strengthen an author's claim. Often, this requires you to consider possible scenarios that could affect the outcome of the claim. Weaken/strengthen questions usually include the words *weaken* or *strengthen*, and the incorrect answer choices are usually reversals or outside knowledge answers.

A weaken/strengthen question might be something like the following:

> Which of the following, if true, would most clearly weaken the chances of ECB's survival?

This is a weaken question, as indicated by the word *weaken*. If you substituted it with *strengthen*, you'd have a strengthen question. The subject of this question is the *chances of ECB survival*, and the task is to determine which of the choices would weaken it.

In **analogy questions**, the answer choices are used to draw comparisons with information discussed in the passage. The correct answer is the one that completes a reasonable analogy. In general, analogy questions can be identified by the key phrase *most similar*. Incorrect answer choices are typically no-such-comparisons or contain extreme language.

Sometimes a question will ask you to apply information from the passage to a new scenario. This type of question is an **application question**. Look for words like *scenarios, situations,* or *assertions* in the question stem to figure out if it's an application question. Reversals, emotional appeals, extreme language, and no-such-comparisons often show up in the answer choices for this type of question.

Take a look at the following example of an application question. (Again, application questions on the computer-adaptive GMAT use the highlight feature rather than quotes and line references.)

> Which of the following best exemplifies "an 'Aha!' experience" (line 30) as it is presented in the passage?

Each answer choice conveys a distinct scenario that you must relate to the high-lighted word, phrase, or sentence in the question, which, of course, comes directly from the passage.

THE ART OF INFORMATION GATHERING

Now that we have established an understanding of the details that go into making incorrect answers, deciphering answer choices, and determining the subject and task of a question, let's take a minute to discuss in more detail useful ways to gather information from reading comprehension passages. Everyone reads something at some point in his or her day, even if it's just a stop sign at the cross-walk. Very few of us, though, are required to read actively as part of our daily lives. In fact, reading for adults usually falls into two categories: (1) reading for work, which usually involves skimming websites, newspapers, trade publications, specialized magazines, and internal correspondence (e-mails, memos, and the like), and (2) reading for pleasure, when you read something that is interesting to you at your ideal pace. Neither of these practices is adequate training for the Reading Comprehension section of the GMAT.

Minimize Re-Reading

The key to becoming a better reader is to train yourself to understand what you've read the first time you read it.

Improving your skill on reading comp questions is really about active reading, which enables you to read with a purpose (as outlined at the beginning of this chapter). The more purpose with which you read a passage, the less likely it is that you may have to reread the passage in its entirety before answering the questions. Many test takers spend too much time reading paragraphs again and again, mainly because it's hard to concentrate on the subject matter when you're under such time pressure. No one expects you to eliminate re-reading altogether, but if you can train yourself to understand what you've read the first time you read it, you'll be amazed at how much easier the reading comp questions will become.

Reading Paragraph by Paragraph

Have you noticed that reading is a lot easier when the text is broken up into a lot of paragraphs? That's why the average paragraph in a newspaper story is usually no longer than seven or eight lines of text. (That's also why your AWA essay should have many paragraphs, so that the readers have an easier time reading them—but more on that later.) Rather than regarding the reading comp passage as a large, imposing hulk of material to read, look at it as the sum of several smaller parts. If you assimilate little bits of information at a time, you will have read (and under-stood) the whole thing before you know it.

The Three C's

A useful way to gain a better understanding of any written paragraph is by using the three C's. Pick a paragraph anywhere in this book, read it once, then close the book and ask yourself, "What did I just read?" The summary you come up with should be clear, concise, and conversational:

- **Clear:** Any person older than ten should be able to understand it thoroughly. That means no ultra-big words. If you see the words "infatuated with" on the page, think "crazy about" in your head.

- **Concise:** Keep the thoughts as brief as possible and avoid redundancy. Once you've got the basic idea, move on.

- **Conversational:** Rethink what you read as if you're explaining it to a close friend, your spouse, your kids, or anyone else with whom you speak informally and casually.

Let's try an example. Suppose you were visiting an art museum with your 10-year-old niece and you read this on the wall next to a particular painting:

> In 1949, Erno Blenckmann established a highly reductive compositional format: the vertical alignment of expansive, soft-edged, rectangular forms suspended within a monochromatic field.

At this point, the kid is scratching her head quizzically (and frankly, you might be too). If you were to translate this sentence into kid-speak, it might sound something like this:

> Blenckmann painted some fuzzy boxy shapes stacked on top of each other.

See? You've turned 23 words of dense babble into something anyone could grasp at first sight. Of course, using the three C's is often only as good as your vocabulary, so make sure to study up! If you can develop a talent for this, you'll be able to remember the content of reading comp passages a lot more readily.

Remember These C's
When summarizing what you've read, keep it clear, concise, and conversational.

START PRACTICING NOW

Just as your first driving lesson shouldn't take place among the Indy cars at Le Mans, your first attempts to read actively shouldn't be on reading comprehension passages. Start out with your favorite magazine or newspaper because odds are that (1) you'll find the subject matter at least remotely interesting and (2) the text will be divided into small, easy-to-digest paragraphs.

Let's look at the first few paragraphs from a sample article in the newspaper and try to translate them using the three C's:

Turkish Foreign Policy Still Vibrant Despite Domestic Strife

by Gordon Hobbie

ISTANBUL, Turkey—Though Turkey has lurched forward without a functioning government for more than six weeks since its prime minister, Mesut Yilmaz, lost a confidence vote in Parliament, its foreign policy has remained assertive. Turkish leaders have learned to exploit its Eurasian position and burgeoning economy to achieve its policy goals.

Translation: Turkey's government is a mess right now, but it still has some money and some international clout.

See? When you explain something to a 10-year-old kid, you can't use higher-level vocabulary words like *assertive* and *burgeoning*. Boiling passages down to simple English makes it easier to absorb right away.

Here's the next paragraph:

Despite stern warnings of economic sanctions and military intervention, Turkey has benefited from a growing power vacuum in the Middle East, which for decades has been dominated by Russia, Iran, Iraq, and former satellites of the now-defunct Soviet Union. In recent months, a series of foreign policy successes has emboldened the Turks to flex their muscles and build their influence in this chaotic region.

Translation: Other countries are weaker, so the Turks are taking the opportunity to act tough, and they've had some success lately.

Given the content of the last sentence, and your knowledge of active reading from earlier in this chapter, can you predict what the next paragraph will discuss? It will probably give details of the "successes" to which the article refers.

Turkey's most recent foreign policy success came on the tense island of Cyprus, where the Greek-backed government had planned to test antiaircraft missiles recently acquired from Russia. When Turkey threatened to bomb the Greek side of the island, the Cypriots acceded to Istanbul's demands.

<u>Translation (as predicted):</u> For example, Turkey just bullied the Greeks on Cyprus into not shooting off their new Russian rockets.

Though NATO was instrumental in helping the Turks resolve the Cypriot standoff, Turkey has also won some important battles strictly on its own. Last October, Syria agreed to release the Kurdish rebel leader Abdullah Ocalan after Turkey amassed troops along the Syrian border in a tacit threat of invasion.

<u>Translation:</u> Sometimes they need help to get what they want, but sometimes they do it all by themselves—like when they bossed Syria around and got that guy Ocalan released.

You get the idea. Now, to get a basic grasp of the material from the article thus far, combine the information you have gathered into one full description:

The Turks haven't got a prime minister, but they're looking a lot tougher to their neighbors because they've bossed some people around and absorbed some of the power that other traditional powers in the area have lost.

Keep It Concise

When you first try this exercise, don't be surprised if your summaries become longer than the text itself. This happens a lot because most students are not comfortable leaving out any details. That's fine at first, but as you practice, you should concentrate on making your synopses more concise.

Whatever you do, resist the temptation to cheat by looking back at the page. That's no help at all. Make yourself remember what you read without refreshing your memory. If you struggle at first, don't take any sneak peeks. Start again from scratch. It will get easier as you practice.

If You Can Explain It, You Know It

If you can train yourself to understand the stuff you read as you read it (and you can take notes at first, if you have to), you'll be in great shape to improve your overall verbal score. And the best part about this whole exercise is that you haven't yet forced yourself to do the hardcore reading for content yet.

Partner Up

If you lack the discipline to keep from looking back at the text (and you're not alone if you do), try working with a friend.

There are two reasons for this:

- Because reading for content is difficult, why not make it as easy as you can on yourself?

- Because the questions pertain only to a portion of the passage, the more you understand the passage, the easier it will be to find the content in the passage that answers a question later on.

Drill 1: Translating

Here are some paragraphs containing text you might see on the GMAT. The first two have been "translated" for you; use the blank lines provided to write your own translations for the other ten. Try to boil them down to their most basic meaning using the three C's.

Practice 1:

> Reasons for the big movie studios' disappointing holiday film season extend far beyond the fact that Christmas fell on a Friday, which cut short the most profitable week of the season. Throughout the six weeks between Thanksgiving and New Year's Day, blockbusters were few, and those rare films that received both critical acclaim and modest financial success were released by smaller art houses.

Translation:

> There are many reasons why the big studios didn't make a lot of money between Thanksgiving and New Year's, and most of their big movies lost out to smaller films.

Practice 2:

> Sir Walter Scott's memoirs revealed his fierce Scottish patriotism during the last seven years of his life. The breadth of his political influence suggests that he had become an uncrowned monarch upon whom most Scots relied for inspiration and leadership.

Translation:

> Walter Scott's book about himself shows that many people in Scotland listened to him and looked up to him as if he were king (even though he wasn't).

Although there are no correct answers for these exercises, turn to page 98 for approximations of the length of your translations and the type of language you should use.

1. Among academic historians, a rift of sorts has arisen between social historians, who pinpoint their studies on the suffering of victims of prejudice, and traditional historians, who prefer to emphasize wars, diplomacy, and the great personalities involved.

Translation:

_____

_____

2. Botanists have recently undertaken to recreate the natural diversity among species of trees in Hong Kong's forests. Massive deforestation before World War II denuded thousands of acres of land, and the consequent soil erosion that the southern coastline has endured is endangering several indigenous animals and plants.

Translation:

_____

_____

3. Two prominent Japanese investment banks, Nikko and Nomura, are endeavoring to pattern themselves after their American counterparts. Rather than charge high fixed commissions, these two financial powers have shifted some of their emphasis to building wealth for individual investors.

Translation:

_____

_____

4. Tchaikovsky received financial support for nearly fourteen years from his patron, Nadezhda von Meck, the widow of a wealthy German railroad magnate. It has been rumored that Tchaikovsky resisted meeting her because he was too paralyzed with self-doubt to convey his love for her.

Translation:

_____

_____

5. The clearest advantage that the new Ferroelectric Random-Access Memory (FeRAM) chip has over its predecessor, the Dynamic RAM chip, is FeRAM's ability to retain and reproduce information with far greater security and at much greater speed. It will be at least a decade, though, before FeRAM is inexpensive enough for mass production.

Translation:

_____

_____

6. Given the recent rise of unemployment and a rapid drop in the prices of Korean stocks, a rapidly increasing number of Korean parents have found themselves unable to send their children to the same elite American and European private schools that they themselves attended many years ago.

Translation:

_____

_____

7. A new group of investment advisors has started a new website designed to disabuse average citizens of the complexity of personal investing. In order to encourage repeat visits to the website, the group will begin a real-money portfolio and encourage investors to follow it day by day.

Translation:

_____

_____

8. Throughout the Midwest, the number of visitors that come to state fairs has tripled within the last decade. These fairs offer tens of thousands of attendees the opportunity to sample local agricultural products, enter various contests, and attend political rallies conducted by candidates for local office.

Translation:

_____

_____

9. The International Monetary Fund (IMF) has declared that before it will green-light any further funding, the country's new leaders will have to commit themselves to creating a functional market economy and not succumb to populist resistance to change. The new government is convinced that it can live up to the IMF's demands and repay all loans within five years.

Translation:

_____

_____

10. Due to a peculiar phenomenon known as orbital decay, satellites gradually accumulate vast quantities of atmospheric particles that cling to the external navigation mechanisms. Burdened with this debris, the satellites lose an average of 10 percent of their altitude within 12 months after launch.

Translation:

_____

_____

ANTICIPATING WHAT'S NEXT

Of course, it shouldn't be ALL work. If you are reading actively, then you should be able to accurately predict what the passage will discuss next.

If you've ever consulted someone who has already taken the GMAT about reading comp passages, he or she might have advised you to circle words like *but, however, therefore,* and so on. That was a good idea on the paper-and-pencil test, but it's no longer an option (unless you have one of those cool telestrators that announcers use at televised football games). However, those words are still good ones to notice; they help show you if a supporting point (or a contrary point) is being made.

Take the second sentence of that last paragraph, for example:

That was a good idea on the paper-and-pencil test, **but** it's no longer an option.

The first part was a good point, and the *but* changed the direction and made a contrary point. Then came the word *However*; just by reading that one word, you knew that the remainder of that sentence would revert back to good reasons for circling the words.

Translation words such as these can keep the passage flowing in the same direction, or they can change the direction by signaling a contrasting thought. Either way, recognizing them can help speed the reading process a lot.

Words that suggest a *supporting or continuing point* come in several categories:

- Additional points (*furthermore, in addition, also, too*)

- Additional examples (*similarly, likewise, for example*)

- Structure (*secondly, thirdly*)

- Conclusions (*thus, therefore, in conclusion*)

Many passages on the GMAT explore both sides of an issue, and often the first paragraphs express one position and are followed by the other side's viewpoint. For example, if a sentence begins with *Although*, you can expect two contradictory thoughts to appear in it.

> *Although* cigarettes make you look really cool
> [first point], it has also been hypothesized that
> they can give you cancer and kill you [second,
> contradictory point].

Each of these words lets you know that a *contrary point* is on the horizon:

although, though, even though	however
but	nevertheless
despite, in spite of	unless
except	while

How Anticipation Works

Check out how anticipation works on this paragraph by concentrating on the bolder text and glossing over the gray text (just for now).

Scientists have posited for centuries that there is intelligent life living somewhere in the universe. In fact, most experts speculate that, somewhere in the outer regions of the universe, there are other carbon-based life forms that draw oxygen and expel carbon dioxide in order to survive. **However,** these musings are utterly without merit. There is now concrete, irrefutable proof that outer space is a bitterly cold, lifeless void.

From the first sentence and the word *However*, you can probably guess how this paragraph will play out without reading the rest of the text. Now read the whole paragraph:

Scientists have posited for centuries that there is intelligent life living somewhere in the universe. In fact, most experts speculate that, somewhere in the outer regions of the universe, there are other carbon-based life forms that draw oxygen and expel carbon dioxide in order to survive. However, these musings are utterly without merit. There is now concrete, irrefutable proof that outer space is a bitterly cold, lifeless void.

Did you anticipate correctly? You'll find that many GMAT passages work this way, and it's a great way to assimilate information as quickly as possible. Look at another example:

The Iridium satellite-telephone network **had been so named** because the network was reported to contain 77 satellites (and there are 77 electrons in an iridium atom). Subsequent research has concluded, **though,** that there are only 66 satellites in the network. Thus, it should be renamed as the Dysprosium network.

There's your opening thought; what do you think the rest of the sentence will say, and how do you know?

The Iridium satellite-telephone network had been so named because the network was reported to contain 77 satellites (and there are 77 electrons in an iridium atom). Subsequent research has concluded, though, that there are only 66 satellites in the network. Thus, it should be renamed as the Dysprosium network.

The key words *had been so named* tell you that something new has happened, and that the network probably has a new name by now. We call these indicators "translation words" because the first part of the sentence helps you predict what the second half will say.

Drill 2: Translation Words

As we'll discuss later on, using proper sentence structure is crucial to good writing. Anticipating structure is also helpful for better reading. If you see a sentence in the introduction that says *Toaster pastries will bring about the end of Western civilization for the following four reasons,* you can comfortably assume that those four reasons are forthcoming.

There are several common ways that the test writers express contrasting thoughts within its reading comprehension passages. In each of the following examples, indicate what you think the next sentence will be and circle the translation words. Turn to page 98 for the answers.

1. Most large corporations in the United States were once run by individual stockholders who owned most of the company shares and dominated the board of directors.

2. Normally, possums are timid, nocturnal creatures who rarely venture from their nests.

3. At first glance, Shays' rebellion of 1787 appeared to be the ineffectual revolt of a few destitute farmers.

4. Traditionally, stocks have been valued mostly by their price-to-earnings ratio.

5. Until the end of the eighteenth century, the fledgling American government had been dominated by the Federalist party.

KEEP PRACTICING!

The remainder of this chapter consists of practice passages and questions. The answers and explanations are found at the end of the chapter beginning on page 99.

Use the strategies you learned at the beginning of the chapter and practice your pacing. You don't ever want to rush through a reading comp section. With that said, you should work through the passages and questions at a reasonable pace.

Keep track of your progress and assess your ability as you go. Before you know it, you'll be thinking just like the test writers.

Comprehensive Drill: Reading Comprehension

Questions 1–4 refer to the following:

Within most animal species, the males must do their best to attract females by showing off—by attempting either to demonstrate sexual prowess or to intimidate rivals. A new study, however, suggests that males are actually submitting to a more genetic imperative. By displaying their most prized attributes or talents, hopeful males do the best they can to show off superior genetic qualities that lesser males cannot mimic.

Biologists at the University of Missouri conducted this new study by analyzing the mating calls of the gray tree frog. Females have been shown to gravitate toward males whose calls last longest, and it has long been theorized that a male's lengthy mating call is linked to superior fitness and energy.

Tree frogs were chosen for the experiment for two very important reasons. Since frogs fertilize their eggs externally, it is easy to trace the genealogy of each tadpole. Secondly, male frogs are utterly uninvolved with raising their offspring. This allows the scientists to address the "nature vs. nurture" conundrum directly by removing any chance that the tadpoles are "learning" anything from their fathers. Whatever strength or weakness the offspring displays, that characteristic must have been passed down through the father's genes.

To start the experiment, eggs were harvested from several females and then split into two groups. The first cluster was fertilized with the sperm of a long-calling male, the second with that of a male whose call was demonstrably shorter. The scientists compared the progress of all tadpoles with different fathers but the same mother. Mating calls are strictly a male trait, so the biologists later planned to compare the mating calls of certain males with those of their male offspring.

The results were astounding. The physical characteristics of all the male tadpoles were virtually identical at first, but within weeks the children of long-calling males grew into faster and stronger tadpoles who eventually would metamorphose into frogs much sooner than the offspring of short-calling males. Such a finding lends credence to the theory that calling is an honest and reliable indicator of genetic quality.

1. Which of the following is the primary focus of the passage?
   ○ Supporting a new theory by providing a new explanation for an accepted mode of behavior
   ○ Evaluating the results of two separate experiments and contrasting the relative merits of each one
   ○ Pursuing evidence in the "nature vs. nurture" debate
   ○ Dismissing a current phenomenon as inconsistent with common trends
   ○ Embracing a new system of analysis that is likely to overturn much of today's accepted knowledge

2. Which of the following statements about the gray tree frog is supported by the information in the passage?
   ○ Females teach their offspring to fend for themselves in the wild.
   ○ Males are more energetic and physically fit than are females.
   ○ Mating calls are restricted to the males of the species.
   ○ Offspring acquire more of their genetic information from their mothers than from their fathers.
   ○ The mating call of the female is hardly distinguishable from that of the male.

3. The passage suggests which of the following about the male tree frog?

○ It is now no longer prudent to assume that the length of a frog's mating call is linked to its sexual prowess.

○ Some females are attracted to long-calling males because of the quality of "parenting" that these males can provide.

○ A male that exhibits a demonstrably shorter mating call is probably also betraying its physical inadequacy.

○ A study comparing tadpoles with the same father but different mothers would yield similar results.

○ A frog that is unable to sound a mating call will never reproduce.

4. Which of the following, if true, would most undermine the scientists' conclusions regarding the gray tree frog?

○ Not all sperm that was harvested from the males was viable for fertilization.

○ Newts learn how to attract females by mimicking their fathers.

○ Offspring of long- and short-calling males are eaten by predators with equal frequency.

○ The long-calling male whose sperm was used in the experiment was younger than the short-calling male.

○ Mates of short-calling males usually produce twice as many offspring as mates with long-calling males.

Questions 5–8 refer to the following:

Most Americans are fascinated with their own history, particularly that of the colonial era. Whenever a crisis affects the current government, pundits and plebeians alike invoke the writings and teachings of the eighteenth century in order to support or denounce modern viewpoints. Many citizens wax nostalgic for the glorious times of their nascent union, when some of the most shrewd and free-thinking minds came together to construct "a more perfect Union." A new book by Nathan Parker, however, suggests that colonial New England was never the egalitarian Eden that modern Americans make it out to be.

Popular imagination holds that the Puritans were a virtuous group determined to create a new government through direct democracy. Communities convened town-hall meetings, at which policies were debated and decisions were made by the will of the people. Many renowned international thinkers, such as France's Alexis de Tocqueville and Hector St. John de Crèvecoeur, praised this new American commitment to the voice of the common man.

According to Parker, admiration for New England's first settlers is profoundly misplaced. In a typical show of their historical revisionism, Americans have mythologized these town meetings to the point of embarrassment. Parker asserts that town-hall meetings were open only to a select few male property owners who wielded a strong financial influence on the community. Thus, the laws that were put into effect as a result of these meetings hardly reflected the "consent of the governed." Therefore, there is vast evidence of voter apathy among the colonists. Citing the disparity between the roll calls of several meetings and the voter registries of the towns in which they took place, Parker demonstrates that attendance at town-hall meetings rarely exceeded 30 percent of all registered voters.

In making these points, Parker hopes to lay to rest the notion that simple, family-oriented colonial New England was far preferable to the modern America that many perceive to have outgrown pure democracy. His objective is to lay bare the true nature of eighteenth-century governance and thus assure Americans that progress can't kill an equality that never was.

5. The primary purpose of the passage as a whole is to
   ○ critique a system of logic
   ○ clarify an ambiguity
   ○ contrast two diverse notions
   ○ discredit a commonly held perception
   ○ question a dubious explanation

6. Which of the following best describes the purpose of the second paragraph?
   ○ It extols the virtues of the first American settlers who were not daunted by the prospect of creating an egalitarian society.
   ○ It introduces de Tocqueville and de Crèvecoeur, by whom Parker was first inspired to write.
   ○ It lists several perceptions about the early American colonies that Parker believes to be more myth than fact.
   ○ It serves to emphasize the massive impact that French thinking had on New England's first settlers.
   ○ It provides evidence that the Puritans were not nearly as virtuous as they asserted themselves to be.

7. According to the passage, the colonial period is often invoked in contemporary discourse in order to

○ advocate the importance of pure democracy to a fledgling capitalist nation

○ illustrate how American society has always depended upon the family unit that was so highly esteemed in the eighteenth century

○ establish a historical context for the celebrated writings of de Tocqueville and de Crèvecoeur

○ praise the perseverance of the Puritans, who never receive the recognition they so richly deserve

○ indicate that the country's rampant growth since its creation has caused it to stray from its original path toward absolute democracy

8. According to the passage, Parker asserts which of the following about early colonial town meetings?

○ Those who owned property in the area served as representatives for everyone in the community.

○ Attendance at these meetings was restricted to wealthy landowners.

○ All registered voters were permitted to attend, but fewer than one-third of them actually did.

○ They became the inspiration for what is known today as direct democracy.

○ They were looked upon as models by the framers of the Constitution.

Anyone who thinks that rabbits make cute and cuddly pets has never owned one and has most definitely never worked as a farmer or gardener. To people whose livelihood depends on agribusiness, rabbits are nothing more than ravenous vermin that inflict millions of dollars in damage to crops meant for both animal and human consumption. Until now, no one had undertaken to quantify the annual cost to a farmer's output for which a single rabbit is accountable. Great Britain's Ministry of Agriculture, however, has shown itself to be up to the challenge. Gordon McKillop, a biologist at the Central Science Laboratory in York, England, just finished a study that monitored the appetites of rabbits let loose to graze on several crops. As a result, farmers can gauge rabbit damage more effectively, allowing them to anticipate the crops they will lose and make necessary compensation.

During his three-year study, McKillop released a set number of rabbits into several enclosed regions, each containing one type of vegetation on which the rabbits subsisted. To keep numbers constant, each enclosure was surrounded by a fence that was entrenched ten feet into the ground, and all rabbits released in a certain area were of the same sex.

The rabbits did the least damage in the pens containing grass, which many farmers cultivate as grazing land for their livestock. The average rabbit ate almost 300 pounds of grass in one year, which reduced the yield of one hectare (about two and a half acres) by half a percent. This translates to more than $3 worth of damage per rabbit per year—a seemingly nominal sum until one considers that most grasslands are home to as many as forty rabbits per acre. The rabbits' taste for barley was about the same as that for grass in terms of percentage, but the cost was calculated to be almost $7 per rabbit. By far, the most endangered crop was wheat, which rabbits munch at a rate that depleted normal yields by more than 1 percent of the maximum. Because wheat is also the most expensive on the open market, McKillop's group calculated that one rabbit can eat almost $1 worth of the crop in one month. This can mean financial ruin for wheat farmers in areas with abnormally high rabbit populations.

Farmers may now be able to attach a dollar value to the crops that rabbits feed on, but they still lack the most important piece of information that Dr. McKillop's study did not reveal: how to stop them. Shooting and trapping rabbits is too time-consuming and inefficient to keep up with the approximate

2 percent increase in rabbit populations every year, and most rabbits have developed resistance to viral diseases such as myxomatosis and viral hemorrhagic fever that have been introduced to curb reproduction. Even the age-old remedy of releasing foxes on the property has been blocked by chicken farmers, whose commodity, according to the Ministry, contributes almost 14 percent of Britain's gross domestic product.

9. Which of the following statements best summarizes the purpose of McKillop's experiment?
   ○ He contrasted several methods for establishing more credible methods for controlling rabbit populations.
   ○ He set out to express the damage inflicted by rabbits on farmers' crops in a more tangible, monetary sense.
   ○ He endeavored to prove that rabbits are more destructive than most people perceive them to be.
   ○ He hoped to determine the crop for which rabbits showed the most ardent appetite.
   ○ He wanted to portray the rabbit in a less flattering manner.

10. The passage supplies information about each of the following EXCEPT
   ○ the population density of rabbits
   ○ the best way to prevent rabbits from decimating a certain crop
   ○ the duration of McKillop's study
   ○ the rate at which rabbits normally reproduce
   ○ the amount of grass usually grown annually upon a hectare of land

11. Each of the following can be inferred from the passage EXCEPT

○ in the agricultural marketplace, barley is at least twice as expensive as grass

○ at one point, myxomatosis and viral hemorrhagic fever were more effective than they are now

○ the power wielded by a certain type of farmer is at least partly influenced by financial impact of that farmer's product

○ the cost incurred by farmers to rid themselves of large rabbit populations far exceeds the monetary damage done to the farmers' crops

○ rabbits are unable to tunnel through the ground at a depth that is greater than ten feet

12. Which of the following, if true, would most seriously weaken the merit of McKillop's study?

○ Several rabbits develop a new strain of myxomatosis that renders each completely sterile.

○ Due to a decrease in supply, the price of barley suddenly doubles.

○ It is determined that younger, more energetic rabbits consume almost double the food that an older rabbit does.

○ A rare drought inhibits plant growth in the enclosures for several months.

○ Soon after the experiment begins, a predatory animal finds its way into some of the rabbit enclosures.

13. In the last paragraph, the author is primarily concerned with

○ exposing a problem to which McKillop's study has failed to supply a solution

○ suggesting that rabbit farmers and chicken farmers are often at odds when it comes to agricultural legislation

○ citing evidence that McKillop's study is woefully incomplete

○ comparing the various methods that farmers have used in order to keep rabbit populations under control

○ establishing that foxes have an equal appetite for rabbits as they do for chickens

Questions 14–17 refer to the following:

Multiple sclerosis, a disease that prevents electrical impulses from traveling along nerve fibers, is widely believed to be caused by the body's immune system. Medical researchers have long held that T cells attack and destroy myelin sheaths, the fatty coatings that protect most of the central nervous system, rendering the nerves inoperable. A new study, however, puts forth the theory that the immune system is not the primary culprit in the destruction of myelin sheaths. Instead, certain cells may be undergoing apoptosis, or "committing suicide."

Because the severity of multiple sclerosis rises and falls at irregular intervals within each patient, the disease is difficult to study. Relapses are impossible to predict and are seldom life-threatening. Drs. John Prineas and Michael Barnett, therefore, decided to limit their investigation to those patients who died during or soon after a relapse, assuming that evidence of the mortal trauma would lie within the victim's nerve fibers.

Upon studying the brains of several such patients, the doctors discovered that although many myelin sheaths had been compromised, there was no sign of T-cell activity. Instead, they found that microglia—cells that clean up dead or dying tissue—had surrounded the oligodendrocytes—the cells that create myelin. This proved to be a conundrum because microglia do not normally attack healthy cells.

Prineas and Barnett have thus concluded that the oligodendrocytes had killed themselves. Cells often do so if they "realize" they are infected with a virus or have a similarly pernicious effect on the body. It is reasonable to argue, therefore, that the sheaths had worn away because their creator cells had diagnosed a problem and shut down, causing the myelin sheaths to disintegrate. The cause of that problem was inconclusive and remains a subject of fierce debate.

14. Which of the following can be inferred from the passage about the human body's immune system?

   ○ T cells are part of the body's immune system.
   ○ Oligodendrocytes function to clean up dead or dying tissue.
   ○ Only people suffering from multiple sclerosis will have cells that commit apoptosis.
   ○ Microglia often times attack oligodendrocytes.
   ○ There is much debate still about whether or not microglia attack otherwise healthy cells.

15. The findings of Drs. Prineas and Barnett serve to

   ○ contrast two controversial hypotheses
   ○ undermine the work of colleagues
   ○ debunk a causal relationship
   ○ lend credence to a popular belief
   ○ settle a long-standing debate

16. According to the passage, the cells that are charged with protecting the central nervous system are

   ○ fatty coatings
   ○ microglia
   ○ myelin sheaths
   ○ oligodendrocytes
   ○ T cells

17. Which of the following, if true, would most severely weaken the doctors' hypothesis?

   ○ People born with lower levels of myelin in their central nervous systems have a greater risk of contracting multiple sclerosis.
   ○ In certain cases, microglia have been known to attack healthy cells.
   ○ The population of microglia in the human body doubles within the first half hour after the body dies.
   ○ New technologies have helped doctors predict the arrival of a relapse with increasing accuracy.
   ○ Relapses are far less life-threatening now than they were 15 years ago.

Questions 18–20 refer to the following:

In 1997, Missouri's General Assembly passed a law barring local governments from providing telecommunications services or facilities without state authority. Since then, ten more states have enacted legislation that restricts local governments from selling television, Internet, and phone services that compete with those offered by private-sector telecommunications companies. In their attempts to overturn these legislative acts, the municipalities argued that the 1996 Telecommunications Act encouraged competition in the industry and that permitting local governments to enter the telecommunications business created healthy competition that was in the public's best interest. Such competition would be the only way to keep prices down, restrict monopolistic practices, and help these mass-media outlets reach the most rural areas. Large private corporations countered that local governments would do better to maintain an equitable regulatory environment rather than enter the fray themselves and commit public funds to compete with private companies.

The dispute came to a head when a lawsuit brought by several regional telephone companies reached the Supreme Court. In an 8-to-1 decision, the Court ruled that states had the right to block municipalities from entering the telephone business. Although the ruling does not affect the offerings that were in place before the case was decided, it will inspire other states to approve similar laws and severely curb the proliferation of government-based communications services. Private-sector companies were understandably elated by the ruling, but municipalities fear that the telecommunications marketplace is destined to become far less competitive, to the detriment of the average consumer.

18. The primary purpose of the passage is to
○ explore the relative merit of public- and private-sector interests
○ illustrate the need for greater regulatory supervision of the telecommunications industry
○ outline both sides of a disagreement that has been legally resolved
○ describe a new technique in the practice of corporate law
○ criticize the intrusion of the Supreme Court on the capitalist system

19. The passage provides information about each of the following EXCEPT
○ the nature of products the municipalities were attempting to provide
○ speculation regarding the ramifications of the Court decision
○ the tangible benefits of competition in the telecommunications marketplace
○ the reasoning behind the Supreme Court's ruling
○ whether the Court's decision would affect municipalities with pre-existing services

20. The author of the passage mentions the Telecommunications Act in order to
○ refute the assertion that the actions of the Missouri General Assembly were unconstitutional
○ illustrate how municipalities were not guilty of alleged nefarious activity
○ supply an example of a federal law that has since been overturned
○ defend the use of public funds to sue a private company
○ indicate a legislative basis for the municipalities' challenge to the initial, state-level edicts

If you are no longer able to reproduce, are you evolutionarily dead? Such is the common wisdom among anthropological biologists, due to the startling correlation among many species between infertility and mortality in females. Curiously, however, humans belie this trend, as women, most of whom experience menopause by the time they are 50, continue to outlive men, who remain fertile well into their 70s, by an average of six years. Furthermore, the relationship between health and reproduction seems to be based more on the next generation; the mortality rate among human women tends not to rise until after their children are no longer able to reproduce. These data suggest that an organism's "usefulness" can persist long after it is unable to replace itself in the evolutionary chain. The explanation to this phenomenon may lie in the human-specific practice of caring for grandchildren.

Herbert Spencer may be credited for coining the phrase, "Nature is a question of the survival of the fittest," but the interpretation of the term "fit" is open to discussion. Among humans, "fitness" may pertain less to direct propagation of the species than to helping usher second-generation progeny into the world. This helps to explain the preferred utility, from an evolutionary standpoint, of the human female, long believed to possess a greater capacity and willingness to nurture than her male counterpart.

This hypothesis was the subject of a new study by Mirkka Lahdenpera at the University of Turku in Finland. From her work, Dr. Lahdenpera was able to discount the notions that a woman's post-reproductive survival is connected to the number of children she has had or to the socioeconomic stratum in which either she or her children were raised. Rather, the prolonged life span of older women is an evolved phenomenon that supersedes genetics or living conditions. Almost every trend led to the fascinating discovery that women with living mothers tend to have more children, and rear a greater percentage of them to adulthood, than those whose mothers are deceased. Nearness was also a crucial element, as women who live within 15 miles of their mothers tend to reproduce at a much earlier age and with greater frequency. All this suggests that greater quantities of children—and thus, the more successful propagation of the human species—are not due only to a grandmother's existence, but also her presence, as she is able to provide assistance or advice to the mother.

21. Which of the following statements, if true, could be used as an example to support the information provided in the first paragraph?
- ⭕ Domestic cats seldom come in contact with their second-generation offspring.
- ⭕ Medical advancements have helped females of all species retain the ability to have children for far longer than their ancestors did.
- ⭕ A female elephant who has reproduced lives an average of two years longer than her mother did.
- ⭕ Female lions whose offspring is predominantly female live longer than those who produce male cubs.
- ⭕ The average female chimpanzee dies within five years after its ability to reproduce is extinguished.

22. Which of the following statements regarding "the survival of the fittest" is best supported by the passage?
- ⭕ It is a fundamentally flawed view of species propagation that needs to be challenged.
- ⭕ The definition of a commonly understood term in the phrase merits re-examination.
- ⭕ Female existence should not be distilled to mere evolutionary "utility."
- ⭕ Superior intellect should make survival less reliant on fitness.
- ⭕ Biologists undervalue the hunt-and-gather instinct of the males of a species.

23. According to the passage, which of the following does Dr. Lahdenpera believe to affect the quantity of offspring produced by a female?

○ Socioeconomic status that the female was raised in
○ The genetics that the female inherited from her mother
○ The proximity of the female to her mother
○ Quality of education the female has received before motherhood
○ The hereditary traits of the male

24. Lahdenpera's study suggests that a woman might live longer if she were to

○ have a daughter very late in her reproductive life
○ have more than the average number of children
○ procreate to ensure that she will have children to care for her
○ be financially stable
○ live close to her mother

DRILL ANSWERS AND EXPLANATIONS

Drill 1: Translating

There's no "correct" answer to these questions, of course, but these are approximations of the length of your translations and the type of language you should use.

1. Two groups who study history view it in different ways: One group likes to study the more famous people that shaped world events, while others prefer to study the little people who get lost in the shuffle.

2. Hong Kong lost a lot of trees during World War II, and a lot of other environmental damage has resulted. So, scientists are trying to replant all the trees and bring things back to normal.

3. Two Japanese banks are trying to copy the way that American banks do business by helping individual people, as well as big businesses, spend their money.

4. Tchaikovsky got a lot of money from this rich German lady, but he loved and respected her so much that he was too chicken to ever meet her in person.

5. The FeRAM chip is better than the Dynamic RAM chip because it's safer and faster, but it's also much too expensive for ordinary people to afford it.

6. Lots of Koreans can't send their kids to the same snooty private schools that they went to because the stock market is tanking and lots of adults are looking for work.

7. The goal of a new website is to help people understand that investing isn't that hard, and they'll show this by buying a bunch of stocks showing how they grow.

8. State fairs are full of people trying to sell stuff, win stuff, or talk about stuff, and three times as many people attend state fairs now as they did ten years ago.

9. The IMF won't shell out any more dough to this new country until the country's government shapes up and becomes capitalist. The country will repay everything in five years.

10. After a year in space, satellites get crusted up with a bunch of gunk that causes them to sink a little off course. This is called orbital decay.

Drill 2: Translation Words

1. It is no longer possible for an individual to wield such power today, because most corporate stock is owned by large institutions. Translation words: *were once run*.

2. If provoked, however, they'll rise up and attack. Translation word: *Normally*.

3. But further research shows that the rebellion revealed how close the new country was to absolute chaos. Translation words: *At first glance*.

4. In today's market, stocks are more valued for their potential for growth. Translation word: *Traditionally*.

5. After the ascension of Thomas Jefferson to the White House in 1801, the Republicans ran the show. Translation words: *Until the end of the eighteenth century*.

Comprehensive Drill: Reading Comprehension

1. **A** The main idea of the passage, as established in paragraph one, is that tree frogs exhibit their long calls to display their genetic superiority. This is demonstrated by detailing an experiment that explains this behavior. Choice (A) matches up well with this idea, so keep (A). Choice (B) refers to two experiments rather than the one detailed in the passage, and so should be eliminated. Choice (C) uses the recycled language of "nature vs. nurture"—a memory trap wrong answer. Eliminate it. Choice (D) should be eliminated, as it is a reversal of the passage's main idea. The trends discussed are emphasized, not dismissed. Finally, (E)'s use of the language "overturn much of today's accepted knowledge" is too extreme. Eliminate it. Therefore, (A) is correct.

2. **C** This inference question asks which of the following answers can be supported by the information in the passage. The correct answer will be directly supported by the passage. Choice (A) cannot be correct, as the passage states that males do not help their offspring but says nothing about females. Eliminate (A). The passage does not compare energy or physical fitness between males and females, so eliminate (B). Likewise, the passage makes no comparison between the amount of genetic information passed on by males or females. Eliminate (D). Finally, (E) reverses the information in the passage, which states that male mating calls are very distinctive, so eliminate it. Only (C) is supported by the information in the passage.

3. **C** The main idea of this passage is that the length and power of a male tree frog's mating call is correlated with its physical and genetic fitness. The correct answer to this inference question will be supported by this idea. Choice (A) is too extreme: A new theory does not necessarily mean that the old theory should be discarded. Choice (B) contradicts the third paragraph, which states that male frogs do not "parent" their spawn. Choice (C) can be directly inferred from the correlation established in the passage between length of call and physical fitness. Keep it. The passage does not offer information that supports the experiment proposed in (D), nor does it support the extreme statement in (E). Choice (C) is the correct answer.

4. **D** The experimenters' conclusion is that length of call is a reliable metric for determining physical and genetic fitness in frogs. The correct answer will weaken this conclusion. Choice (A) discusses sperm viability, not frog fitness, and so is out of scope. Choice (B) brings up another amphibian, a newt, which is too distant from the gray tree frog to be a viable comparison. Predation rates, as discussed in (C), are not a reliable indicator of whether long-calling frogs are physically superior or not. Choice (D) weakens the argument by introducing another explanation, age, which could have affected the results. Keep it. Choice (E) discusses quantity, not fitness, of offspring. It is out of scope, so eliminate it. Choice (D) is the credited response.

5. **D** The primary purpose of this passage is to critique the American tendency to romanticize the colonial era, which was not, in fact, a democratic utopia. The correct answer will highlight this critique. Choice (A) takes issue with the wrong subject, as the author critiques a perception, not a system of logic. Choices (B) and (C) don't match the author's technique because the author neither clarifies an ambiguity nor contrasts two options. Be careful of false comparisons. Choice (D), the credited response, correctly notes that the author's primary purpose is to critique a perception. Finally, (E) is incorrect because the author's critique concerns a perception, not an explanation.

6. **C** The author of the passage uses the second paragraph to indicate the inaccurate popular perception held by most Americans about colonial New England. Choice (A) highlights the nature of these perceptions, but the author does not extol the virtue of these colonists. The two writers are introduced, but there's no indication that Parker (or the first settlers) were inspired by them, so eliminate (B) and (D). Choice (E) is too extreme because the author does not attack the Puritans so directly. Choice (C) is the credited response.

7. **E** In the second sentence, the author claims that modern citizens often invoke the Puritans to criticize or support contemporary policy, since the Puritans were regarded as more purely democratic than modern polities. Neither capitalism nor the family unit are mentioned as being the target of admiration, so eliminate (A) and (B). The two authors are brought up by Parker himself, not by the contemporary discourse, so (C) is incorrect. Choice (D) reverses one of the passage's main points, namely, that the Puritans do receive a great deal of adulation. Only (E) matches the author's description of how Puritans are viewed by modern citizens, and is therefore the credited response.

8. **B** In the third paragraph, Parker states that the town-hall meetings of early colonists were open only to wealthy, land-owning male colonists. This dovetails well with (B). Choice (A) should be eliminated, as it is too much of a logical jump to presume that the landowners served as representatives. Choice (C) refers to a correct statistic (30 percent, which is noted in the third paragraph), but the first part of this choice is wrong—not all registered voters were permitted to attend. Choices (D) and (E) reverse Parker's sentiments about the Puritan colonists and, therefore, should be eliminated.

9. **B** The first paragraph of the passage states that McKillop conducted a study that allowed farmers to "gauge rabbit damage more effectively, allowing them to anticipate the crops they will lose and make necessary compensation." Choice (A) is a memory trap that uses the passage's mention of "controlling rabbit populations" to trick the test taker, so eliminate (A). Choice (B) is a good paraphrase of the passage, so keep it. Choice (C) is an appeal to outside knowledge, but McKillop does not endeavor to prove how destructive rabbits are in comparison to how much damage people think they do. Therefore, eliminate (C). Choice (D) is a memory trap: Although McKillop's study was about the rabbit's appetite, determining the appetite was not the purpose of the experiment, so eliminate (D). Choice (E) is a no-such-comparison answer, as the purpose of the experiment was not to portray the rabbit in any manner. The correct answer, therefore, is (B).

10.   **B**   This is an EXCEPT question, so look at the answer choices and compare them to the information in the passage to find the one that was not mentioned. Choice (A) is mentioned in the third paragraph, which states that "most grasslands are home to as many as forty rabbits per acre," so eliminate (A). Choice (B) is not mentioned at all in the passage. In fact, the passage states that the one thing the study did not do is reveal "how to stop [the rabbits from eating the crops]," so keep (B). It's stated in the second paragraph that the study took three years, so eliminate (C). Choice (D) is mentioned in the fourth paragraph, so eliminate it. Choice (E) uses information found in the third paragraph, so eliminate this one as well. The correct answer is (B).

11.   **D**   This is an EXCEPT question, so look at the answer choices and compare them to the information in the passage to determine which choice cannot be inferred. Choice (A) can be inferred because the third paragraph says "the rabbits' taste for barley was about the same as that for grass," but the cost of barley ($7) is more than double that of grass ($3). The last paragraph states that rabbits "have developed resistance to viral diseases such as myxomatosis," so it must be true that the disease used to kill a lot more rabbits than it does now. Therefore, eliminate (B). Choice (C) can also be inferred because, according to the last sentence, chicken farmers have strong influence in government due to their significant contribution to Britain's gross domestic product. Choice (D) is not supported from the passage, so keep it. Choice (E) can be inferred from the second paragraph, which states that all fences were entrenched 10 feet into the ground in order to control populations. It must therefore be true that rabbits cannot tunnel below that, so eliminate (E). The correct answer is (D).

12.   **E**   To figure out what would weaken the merits of the study, first try to understand how McKillop's study was completed. The study relies heavily on population control, as evidenced by the parameters of the experiment detailed in the second paragraph. McKillop takes the amount of damage done and divides by the number of rabbits in each enclosure. Look to see if any of the answer choices reflect this idea. Choice (A) would not diminish the merit of the study because McKillop doesn't want the rabbits to reproduce, which is evidenced by the fact that they are all the same sex. Eliminate (A). If the price of barley doubled, McKillop would still be able to calculate the financial cost of the rabbits' eating habits, so (B) is incorrect. Since McKillop's data is based on the group in each enclosure, and it's impossible to predict if younger rabbits eat more, eliminate (C). Choice (D) would not decrease the merits of the study, as a drought over several months would not drastically impact a three-year study, so eliminate (D). Finally, (E) would greatly impact the study: If some of the rabbits were missing because a predatory animal ate them, the data is wrong and the rabbits actually would do a lot more damage. The correct answer, therefore, is (E).

13.   **A**   The last paragraph states that farmers "still lack the most important piece of information that Dr. McKillop's study did not reveal: how to stop [the rabbits]." Look for the answer choice that reflects that idea. Choice (A) is a good paraphrase of this, so keep it. Choice (B) is a memory trap that attempts to rely on a reference to legislation, so it can be eliminated. Choice (C) uses extreme language: The author does not say that the study is incomplete, only that it doesn't address an issue for farmers. Eliminate (C). In the last paragraph, the author does compare various methods

for controlling rabbit populations, but this is not the primary concern of the passage, so eliminate (D). Choice (E) is a memory trap with the mention of foxes, but the appetite of foxes is not the focus of the passage. The correct answer is (A).

14. **A** This is an inference question about what the passage says regarding the immune system, so determine which answer choice is supported by information in the passage. Choice (A) can be inferred because even though the passage never explicitly says that T cells are part of the immune system, the first paragraph states that multiple sclerosis is "widely believed to be caused by the body's immune system" and "medical researchers have long held that T cells attack and destroy myelin sheaths." This indicates that T cells are a part of the immune system, so keep (A). Choice (B) is a recycled language answer, as oligodendrocytes are mentioned in the same sentence as the phrase "clean up dead or dying tissue," but this phrase is not used to describe them. Eliminate (B). Choice (C) contains the word only, which is extreme language: The passage does not support the claim that only people with multiple sclerosis have cells that commit apoptosis. Eliminate (C). Choice (D) is incorrect and uses both a memory trap and extreme language. Although the passage suggests that microglia had attacked the oligodendrocytes, it does not mention the frequency of these attacks other than to say that microglia usually do not attack healthy cells. Finally, (E) uses a memory trap in its mention of a debate still being had by doctors; however, the debate is not about the properties of microglia. Eliminate (E), leaving (A) as the correct answer.

15. **C** This question is asking for the purpose of the doctors' findings. According to the passage, the doctors found that T cells did not cause the destruction of myelin sheaths, as was the widely held belief. Rather, the sheaths were "compromised" without the presence of T-cell activity. The doctors posited an alternate cause—the destruction of the oligodendrocytes. So look for an answer choice that reflects this idea. Choice (A) is a no-such-comparison answer because the findings did not contrast anything. Choice (B) contains extreme language in its use of the word "undermine" to attract the test taker. The findings serve as an alternate theory but do not necessarily undermine the doctors' colleagues. Choice (C) is a good match for the purpose of the findings, so keep it. Eliminate (D) because the findings are new, not part of a "popular belief." Choice (E) is also incorrect, since the findings did not settle a debate. Choice (C) is the correct answer.

16. **D** The passage defines oligodendrocytes as "the cells that create myelin" and myelin sheaths as "the fatty coatings that protect most of the central nervous system." Therefore, the cells that protect the central nervous system are those that create myelin for myelin sheaths. Those cells are oligodendrocytes. Choice (D) is the answer. Choices (A) and (C) may be tempting, because the myelin sheaths protect the nervous system and are referred to as fatty coatings, but the sheaths themselves are not cells. Choice (B) is incorrect because microglia cells "clean up dead or dying tissue." While the passage does not make clear the role of T cells, it also does not say anywhere that these cells protect the nervous system, so (E) can also be eliminated. Choice (D) is correct.

17.   **B**   The doctors' hypothesis is that oligodendrocytes kill themselves, so another explanation for oligodendrocyte death would weaken the hypothesis. Choice (A) neither addresses the oligodendrocytes nor weakens the hypothesis, as it appears that most doctors agree that myelin protects the nervous system. Choice (B), on the other hand, weakens the hypothesis by suggesting that the microglia, which "do not normally attack healthy cells," might be the reason why the oligodendrocytes are dying. So keep (B). Choice (C) does not refute the idea that oligodendrocytes are killing themselves and, moreover, the volume of microglia in the body does not weaken the hypothesis, so eliminate (C). While (D) may help track multiple sclerosis, it does not weaken the hypothesis. Choice (E) does not address the hypothesis directly and thus cannot weaken it. Choice (B) is the correct answer.

18.   **C**   This is a primary purpose question, so determine why the author wrote the passage. The main issue discussed in the passage is whether local governments can sell TV and other communications services. The passage presents both sides of the argument—that of municipalities and big corporations—leading up to the last paragraph, which indicates that the issue was decided by the Supreme Court. Therefore, this passage is an overview of a disagreement that has already been resolved. Look for an answer choice that reflects this idea. Choice (A) is a memory trap: Public and private interests are discussed throughout the passage, but the purpose is not to "explore the relative merit" of them. Eliminate (A). Choice (B) uses recycled language with the term "regulatory supervision," which was mentioned in the passage but is not its primary purpose. Choice (C) provides a good paraphrase, as the passage does in fact "outline both sides of a disagreement that has been legally resolved." Keep (C). The passage does not describe a new technique in corporate law practice, and it does not criticize anything, so eliminate (D) and (E). Choice (C) is the correct answer.

19.   **D**   This is an EXCEPT question that uses the phrase *each of the following*, so examine each answer choice and compare it to the passage to see if there is any information provided about it. If there is information about an answer choice, that choice is incorrect. (Remember, look for the EXCEPT.) The first paragraph indicates that municipalities wanted to sell "television, Internet, and phone services," so (A) is incorrect. Choice (B) is discussed in the last paragraph, which states that the Supreme Court's decision "will inspire other states to approve of similar laws." Therefore, eliminate (B). The benefits of competition, (C), are mentioned in the first paragraph, where it is stated that competition "would be the only way to keep prices down, restrict monopolistic practices, and help those mass-media outlets reach the most rural areas." Choice (C) is incorrect. The Supreme Court ruling is mentioned in the last paragraph, but no information is given about how or why that ruling was reached, so keep (D). Finally, (E) is addressed in the last paragraph, which says "the ruling does not affect the offerings that were in place before the case was decided." Choice (E) can be eliminated. The correct answer is (D).

20.   **E**   The subject of the question is the Telecommunications Act, which is first mentioned in the first paragraph of the passage: "In their attempts to overturn these legislative acts, the municipalities argued that the 1996 Telecommunications Act encouraged competition in the industry and that

permitting local governments to enter the telecommunications business created healthy competition that was in the public's best interest." The municipalities used the Telecommunications Act as a basis for their argument about they should be able to provide telecommunications services. Now look at the answer choices. Choice (A) uses a memory trap and extreme language. The passage mentions the Missouri General Assembly but does not seek to refute anything, so eliminate (A). Choice (B) is tempting, but actually uses extreme language. The author does not seek to illustrate any ideas, but seems to be simply providing information about a situation. Therefore, (B) cannot be the answer. Choice (C) is tricky but incorrect; the passage states that the Supreme Court eventually ruled in opposition to the municipalities mentioned in conjunction with the Telecommunications Act, but it does not say that the Telecommunications Act was overturned. Eliminate (C). Choice (D) uses extreme language ("defend") and recycled language ("use of public funds"), but does not describe the purpose of mentioning the Telecommunications Act in the passage—so eliminate (D). Choice (E) accurately sums up the purpose of including the Act in the passage and is the correct answer.

21. **E** The first paragraph indicates "the startling correlation, among many species, between infertility and mortality in females." Look for an answer choice that reflects this idea. Choice (A) is incomplete because it doesn't address whether this lack of contact is linked to mortality among the species. Choice (B) is incorrect because the phenomenon among women is not their extended fertility, but that they live longer than men even though they lose their fertility sooner. Choice (C) is incorrect and is a no-such-comparison answer choice because the passage does not compare life spans of mothers and grandmothers. Eliminate (D) because there is no mention of whether the gender of the offspring is a factor. Choice (E), however, is a good match for the first paragraph. The correct answer is (E).

22. **B** This is a retrieval question. The subject of the question is "survival of the fittest," so look in the passage for a discussion related to this topic. The second paragraph states that the term fit is "open to discussion...Among humans, 'fitness' may pertain less to direct propagation of the species than to helping usher second-generation progeny into the world." Therefore, the author believes that fit doesn't necessarily refer to only physicality, but could also refer to the ability to nurture. Look at each answer choice to find one that offers a different way to define fitness. Choice (A) is incorrect because it is too extreme: The author suggests that there may be another way to look at "survival of the fittest," not that it is a flawed view. Choice (B) is a good paraphrase of this idea—the author believes the phrase warrants re-examination because it may carry a different meaning than is commonly understood. Keep (B). Choice (C) uses recycled language ("utility") and emotional appeal, but it is not supported by the passage, so (C) is incorrect. Choice (D) makes a comparison that is not present in the passage, since the author does not seek to relate intellect to fitness, but rather the ability to nurture to fitness. Eliminate (D). Finally, (E) introduces males, which are not covered in the passage, so eliminate this choice. This leaves (B), which is correct.

23. **C** This is a retrieval question. The subject of the question is what Dr. Lahdenpera believes, and the topic is "the quantity of offspring produced by a female." The third paragraph of the passage states that "women with living mothers tend to have more children," and "nearness was also a crucial element, as women who live within 15 miles of their mothers tend to reproduce…with greater frequency." So the passage suggests that women with living mothers who live close to them see an effect on the quantity of offspring. Look for an answer choice that paraphrases one of these ideas. Choice (A) is a memory trap from earlier in the third paragraph, but the passage states that socio-economic stratum is not a factor, so eliminate this choice. Choice (B) is also a memory trap from the third paragraph but, as in (A), genetics is not described as a factor. Therefore, (B) can also be eliminated. Choice (C) is a good paraphrase of the passage, so keep it. The quality of education received by a woman before motherhood is not listed as a factor, so eliminate (D). Males are mentioned only once in the passage, and their hereditary traits are not discussed, so eliminate (E). The correct answer is (C).

24. **A** In the first paragraph, the passage states that the mortality rate among women tends not to rise until after their children are no longer able to reproduce. Therefore, if a woman has a daughter later in her life, the daughter will likely remain fertile until her mother is a much older woman. Find an answer choice that paraphrases this idea. Choice (A) is a good paraphrase, so hold on to it. Choice (B) is a memory trap: Although the passage mentions the number of children a woman has in relation to the longevity of life, it states that there is not a correlation. Choice (C) is incorrect because the passage does not indicate that there is evidence of increased life span in relation to adults caring for their elderly parents. Choice (D) is another memory trap because, much like (B), socioeconomic status is mentioned in relation to longevity, but a correlation is not found. Choice (E) is mentioned as a factor in the number of children a woman tends to have, but not as a factor in the longevity of the woman's life, so eliminate it. The correct answer is (A).

Chapter 3
Critical
Reasoning

THE NUTS AND BOLTS OF CRITICAL REASONING

Roughly one-third of the 41 verbal questions on your GMAT will be critical reasoning questions. Each question starts with a terse little nugget of information that's about three to four sentences long, followed by a question about the passage and five answer choices:

> Scientists estimate that the cost of an Aerosonde, an unmanned airplane designed to collect atmospheric data during a transatlantic flight, is approximately $20,000. An ordinary weather balloon, by contrast, can collect virtually the same information for about $200. Therefore, weather balloons are clearly the more cost-efficient method for gathering information.
>
> Which of the following, if true, calls the above conclusion into question?
>
> ◯ Aerosondes are less costly than piloted planes and also do not put human life at risk.
> ◯ Politicians who have lobbied for federal funds to construct the Aerosonde are astonished at its in-flight agility.
> ◯ Weather balloons are subject to violent weather changes that can blow them miles off course.
> ◯ Aerosondes can be used over and over again, but weather balloons, because of their frailty, can only be used once.
> ◯ In the time it takes to launch an Aerosonde, it is possible to launch more than 100 weather balloons at once.

Your first goal on every argument is to understand what the statement is saying as quickly as possible with minimal re-reading.

Translating Arguments

Most GMAT students admit that they spend even more time re-reading arguments than they do re-reading reading comp passages. This stands to reason because the wording of arguments can be a lot more subtle; once you've eliminated a few answer choices (and you probably have more than one left), you usually have to re-read to determine which of the remaining choices fall by the wayside and which one is left standing.

Still, getting the gist of an argument the first time can create a lot more time to ruminate on the answers. Follow the math: There are about 13 or 14 arguments on the GMAT. If you can save 30 seconds per question, that's more than seven minutes of extra time to spend playing the answer choices off each other.

In the following drill, translate the arguments into your own words to make them easier to understand. When you are finished, turn to page 153 to compare your translations to the ones we came up with. Remember, there are no absolutely correct answers here.

Translating Arguments Drill

1. It is unwise to dismiss rural homeowners as a key advertising demographic for luxury items. Because the cost of living is much greater in urban and suburban areas, the disposable income of the average rural homeowner is a greater percentage of his or her overall income.

Translation:

_____

_____

2. Due to the city's crumbling transport infrastructure, the comptroller has suggested that several renewal projects be privatized in order to ease the residents' tax burden. Objectors to this plan cite London's newly privatized commuter railroad, which has endured countless delays and breakdowns since the government sold it off.

Translation:

_____

_____

3. Ratings made by large investment banks on certain bellwether stocks are not the most reliable benchmark for investment. Many of these banks maintain large mutual funds, and it is possible for a bank to invest in a company and then assign a favorable rating to its stock in order for its own portfolio to increase.

Translation:

_____

_____

4. Buying advertising space during the Super Bowl is no longer cost-effective. None of the teams with the largest fan bases is likely to reach the game anytime soon, so it doesn't make fiscal sense to spend excessive amounts of the marketing budget on production of a one-day advertisement that fewer viewers are likely to see.

Translation:

_____

_____

5. Many institutions of higher learning enjoy increased enrollments during periods of strong economic growth. Graduate programs, however, suffer declines in applications because there is greater incentive to stay in the work-force and make the money that has become available.

Translation:

_____

_____

6. The dramatic increase in the use of antibiotics has put excessive strain on pharmaceutical companies. Several bacteria have developed resistance to the drugs that are currently being administered, and drug companies must expand research to create newer products that are more effective against superbugs.

Translation:

_____

_____

7. When people neglect to pay the income tax they rightfully owe, they end up costing themselves more money. Tax evasion results in insufficient government funds and forces lawmakers to raise income tax rates to make up the difference. Higher rates encourage tax evaders to maintain their illicit practices until they are eventually caught and fined rigorously.

Translation:

_____

_____

8. Many people assert that aggressive advertising on billboards and in magazines should be curbed because it encourages teenagers to experiment with alcohol and thus break applicable laws pertaining to underage drinking. But in France, where alcohol-related advertising is commonplace, rates of teenage crime and disease in which alcohol is involved are half those in the United States.

Translation:

_____

_____

9. Waylon Phipps, a collector known throughout New Orleans as the consummate connoisseur of antique writing desks, has publicly asserted that a cache of hidden furniture recently found in the basement of the Palace at Versailles is a blatant forgery. None of the tables bears the trademark of Louis XVI on its underside, nor do the top drawers feature the burled mahogany struts of which the king had been quite fond.

Translation:

_____

_____

First Things First

Now that we've covered translating arguments, get ready for the next big revelation: When you see an argument question, train yourself to read the question first.

Here's why: The test writers know that the average human likes to start reading at the top of the page; therefore, the question appears below the argument. If you read the argument first and then read the question, what do you usually end up having to do? Read the argument again, that's what. Save yourself a little time. Fifteen seconds might not seem like much for one question, but if you multiply that by 14 questions, you stand to save almost four minutes of reading time that would otherwise be wasted.

Second, the questions on the Critical Reasoning section fall into a few basic categories, and each question type involves slightly different techniques. If you read the question to each argument first, you can read the argument with your ultimate goal already stored in the back of your mind.

Don't Think So Much

Each argument is a self-contained bit of logic that doesn't require any outside information. As you consider the answer choices, you may be tempted to consider other thoughts of your own that, though valid, are immaterial to the argument. Don't do it.

> Everything you need to consider on an argument question is right there in front of you.

As we'll discuss later, the vast majority of wrong answers to argument questions are incorrect because they're irrelevant. Therefore, the best way to avoid picking irrelevant answer choices is to develop a sense of tunnel vision to help you ignore the stuff that doesn't matter. That's another difference between the GMAT and real life: On the GMAT, it's actually better to have a very narrow mind.

THE PARTS OF AN ARGUMENT

Most arguments are constructed using two basic building blocks: *premises* and *assumptions*. The author uses these ideas as supporting points for the argument's *conclusion*. Most arguments follow the conclusion-premise-assumption construct; we'll call it the CPA Model just to make you accountants feel at home.

The difference between the two types of supporting points is that premises are stated within the passage, and assumptions are not (they're assumed). Let's look at an example of how the test writers build arguments:

> I want to go to the movies. My car broke down last week. Therefore, I need to buy a new car.

This seems like an overly simple example, but the logic doesn't get much more complicated. (It's just the complicated word usage they use that muddies the water.) From the use of the word *Therefore*, you can tell that the last sentence is the conclusion:

> **Therefore**, I need to buy a new car.

The CPA Model

Most arguments on the GMAT follow a structure we call the CPA Model: conclusion, premise, assumption.

The author has concluded that he needs to buy a new car, based on two stated premises:

Premise 1: I want to go to the movies.

Premise 2: My car broke down last week.

These are the premises because they appear in black and white, right before your eyes. But arguments cannot stand on premises alone. There have to be other supporting points that are *assumed* to be true in order for the conclusion to work. What does the author assume?

Assumption 1: The only way to get to the movies is by car.

The author has concluded that he needs a new car because he wants to go to the movies. The author assumes, then, that his automobile is the only mode of available transportation. If it were possible that he could take a bus or a subway to the movies, he wouldn't have to get a new car.

Assumption 2: The car can't be repaired.

This is also a big assumption. If he could fix his car, then he would not need to buy a new one. In both cases, the assumptions have to be true in order for the conclusion to be valid. Keep this idea in mind because we'll talk more about it in the weaken/strengthen portion of the chapter.

That's the basic construction of most GMAT arguments: a conclusion that rests upon a few supporting points (either explicit or assumed). The confusion sets in because the text of most arguments is deliberately hard to grasp right away.

PROCESS OF ELIMINATION

POE is especially useful on the Critical Reasoning section because of this fact:

> Most of the wrong answers to argument questions are incorrect because they're irrelevant.

After you read an answer choice, you're more than likely to ask yourself, "Who cares?" That's because the information in the choice won't have a direct bearing on the passage.

Take a look at the following example:

> **[argument]** Because of an unusually cold winter, Nebraska's annual corn output will be one-third of what it was last year. As a result, the price of corn is sure to rise, and moviegoers can expect to pay an extra dollar for a large serving of popcorn.

> **[question]** Which of the following, if true, most seriously weakens the argument above?

The argument states that popcorn prices are going to rise, and you have to weaken it. Thus, you're looking for answer choices that suggest that popcorn prices *won't* rise. Now look at some answer choices:

- ◯ Meteorologists are predicting that next winter will be even colder than this past one.
- ◯ This year, theaters are expected to spend upwards of $50 for a bushel of popcorn.
- ◯ Several theaters that have offered their patrons the choice of regular or caramel-covered popcorn have enjoyed steadily rising popcorn sales in each of the past four years.
- ◯ The cold winter did not have as detrimental an effect on Nebraska's barley output.
- ◯ Studies show that movie ticket sales soar during periods of especially cold weather.

Which of these answer choices is relevant to the argument? Don't stare at them too long because it's a trick question—they're all irrelevant! And when we say irrelevant, we mean *irrelevant to the argument*. Each answer choice contains subject matter that pertains to cold weather and/or the price of popcorn, but none of them addresses the validity of the argument that the cold Nebraska winter will ultimately force you and me to shell out more dough for a bucket of popcorn.

- ◯ Meteorologists are predicting that next winter will be even colder than this past one.

Analysis: This might be true, and it might result in even higher prices in the future. But what about the present? We're concerned with the here and now, not the there and then.

Decision: Irrelevant.

- ◯ This year, theaters are expected to spend upwards of $50 for a bushel of popcorn.

Analysis: Great. So we know how much popcorn costs. Big deal! Is this any proof that the price can't go higher? In fact, this choice is especially evil because it wants us to think that popcorn is already expensive. ("Fifty bucks? Wow, that's a lot. That's even more than this book costs.") But we have no other prices for comparison. Last year, the per-bushel price could have been $5 or $500, so we don't know the price is rising or falling.

Decision: Irrelevant.

○ Several theaters that have offered their patrons the choice of regular or caramel-covered popcorn have enjoyed steadily rising popcorn sales in each of the past four years.

Analysis: This one wants to put a positive spin on the situation by stating that movie patrons are buying more popcorn. That doesn't mean the price won't rise, though.

Decision: Irrelevant.

○ The cold winter did not have as detrimental an effect on Nebraska's barley output.

Analysis: Okay. Is popcorn made out of barley kernels? If not, then we have no reason to consider this one any further.

Decision: Irrelevant.

○ Studies show that movie ticket sales soar during periods of especially cold weather.

Analysis: This one is especially nutty. It tries to appear relevant by linking two separate parts of the passage, but it omits a crucial point: What about popcorn? Do we know that any of these moviegoers buy popcorn at theaters?

Decision: Irrelevant.

The Relevant Choices

The argument says that prices will rise because supply will fall. Therefore, there are several very important assumptions in play here (and none of the previous five choices addressed them). Each of these, however, is much more likely to be a credited response:

○ Other corn-producing states enjoyed an unseasonably warm winter, and their corn production will be higher than usual.

Analysis: The choice pertains to the assumption that Nebraska is the only state in which corn is grown. If other states are also supplying corn that will make up for Nebraska's shortfall, then prices are unlikely to rise; thus the argument is weakened.

○ Most theaters have struck long-term deals with corn wholesalers to purchase popcorn kernels in bulk at a fixed price.

Analysis: The argument also assumes that supply and price are always directly related. In this instance, however, theater owners won't be affected by fluctuations in supply because their popcorn costs are fixed. Again, this weakens the argument.

○ The majority of Nebraska corn farmers anticipated the cold winter and stockpiled vast quantities of corn during the fall.

Analysis: The supply isn't so low after all because corn farmers can compensate for this year's drop. Weakened again.

○ In response to their more health-conscious clientele, many theaters are replacing the popcorn they normally sell with miniature rice cakes.

Analysis: This choice attacks the assumption that demand among theater owners for popcorn will remain the same. If theaters aren't buying as much popcorn anymore, then the decreased demand will match the decreased supply and prices won't rise. This, too, weakens the argument.

○ The last time the price of popcorn was raised by a dollar, protest riots broke out all over the country, causing many theaters to close for months for repairs.

Analysis: Okay, this one is sort of goofy. But it's relevant to the argument because the argument assumes that theater owners always want to turn a profit at their concession stands. If this answer choice were true, theater owners might think twice about raising the price and instead just ride out the tough times until popcorn was plentiful again. This weakens the argument.

When you read an argument, don't sit and think of all the possible assumptions that could pertain to it. You'll lose lots of valuable time and still not find the one related to the correct answer. It's better to scan the answer choices and learn to recognize which ones involve the argument's assumptions and which do not. All of this relates to relevance to some degree, but there is also a quality technique that we'll talk about in the section about assumption questions later in the chapter.

THE PLAN OF ATTACK

Remember the five-step plan in Chapter 1? Well, we're all really fond of step-by-step programs here at The Princeton Review, so here's the four-step plan for each argument you encounter on the Critical Reasoning section:

1. **Read the question first and identify what type of question it is.**

   There are fewer than ten types of critical reasoning questions, and each has its own considerations. Take a moment to read the question first and determine what exactly is asked—especially if the question has a lot of double negatives that are meant to confuse you. Then move on to the argument.

2. **Work the argument.**

   After reading the question, it's time to read the argument. You want to read for understanding, so try to paraphrase the information to make sure you understand. Also, identify the important parts of the argument. For most arguments, this means identifying the conclusion and the premises. Having a firm grasp of the main point (conclusion) of an argument and the evidence it uses (premises) to support that point is one of the keys to succeeding on argument questions.

3. **Predict what the correct answer should do.**

   Before you turn to the answer choices you want to have an idea of what you're looking for. Applying POE to the answer choices will be easier if you already have a sense of what the correct answer needs to do. This will change depending on the specific question type (weaken, strengthen, assumption, and so on), but as you learn about each one you'll learn what to look for.

4. **Use POE.**

   Remember, you're ultimately looking to eliminate four wrong answers. So focus on flaws in the answer choices. Decide which answers are irrelevant and have nothing to do with the logic of the argument. Use your prediction from Step 3 to help you, and focus on differences between the answers, particularly when you've narrowed it down to two or three.

THE QUESTION TYPES

Reading the question first is useful because you're only going to see about 14 arguments on your GMAT. These questions will all fall within the categories we're about to discuss.

Weaken and Strengthen Questions

Probably half of the arguments that you see on the GMAT will ask you to weaken or strengthen an argument. Depending on the difficulty of the question, the test writers will also try to phrase the weaken question in several ways, varying from the straightforward to the convoluted:

- Which of the following, if true, would most seriously **weaken the conclusion**?

- Which of the following, if true, **is the best basis for a criticism** of profit-sharing among construction unions?

- Supporters of the plan to force all politicians to shave their heads would likely **face the strongest opposition** if which of the following were voiced?

> When answering a weaken question, look for an answer choice that undermines the conclusion and is relevant to the premises. The answers to weaken questions usually refute an assumption.

Weaken and strengthen questions rely heavily on the CPA Model because they're closely related to an argument's assumptions. As you might imagine, strengthen questions are the reverse of weaken ones.

- Which of the following, if true, could **proponents** of the plan above most appropriately cite as evidence of the **soundness** of their plan?

- Which of the following, if true, taken together with the information above, best **supports** the conclusion that fire-eaters will pay more in insurance premiums?

> When answering a strengthen question, look for an answer choice that generally supports the conclusion and is relevant to the premises. The answers to strengthen questions usually reinforce an assumption.

Consult Your CPA

To answer the following questions (especially if you're down to two choices), it will usually be useful for you to consult the CPA Model.

Let's look at an argument and determine how assumptions factor into these types of questions.

A new interactive television company offering subscribers the ability to download movies off the Internet will have an easy time installing its new equipment in Hong Kong. Most of Hong Kong's residential buildings are easy to rewire and in close proximity to one of the company's central video servers. Thus, this new service is destined to succeed, despite the high cost to subscribe.

Which of the following, if true, casts the most doubt on the validity of this argument?

- ⬭ There are no plans to set up similar services in any other major Asian city in the next decade.
- ⬭ Surveys indicate that many of Hong Kong's residents would like the option of American movies that are subtitled rather than dubbed, and the new company cannot offer that yet.
- ⬭ The residents of Hong Kong who have the most wealth, and are thus most likely to subscribe to the service, live too far away from the city center to be connected.
- ⬭ The current cable-television provider in Hong Kong has lost money in each of the past four years.
- ⬭ Hong Kong's Bureau of Zoning has authorized the construction of more than 20 new movie theaters next year.

Each of these answer choices has something positive to say about the cable industry in Hong Kong. Your job is to determine which one is relevant to the premises that are given.

- ⬭ There are no plans to set up similar services in any other major Asian city in the next decade.

Analysis: Nice try, but we're looking at the problem in Hong Kong; the situation anywhere else is not necessarily comparable.

Decision: No.

○ Surveys indicate that many of Hong Kong's residents would like the option of American movies that are subtitled rather than dubbed, and the new company cannot offer that yet.

Analysis: This one serves to undermine the popularity of the service, but the key word is yet. It's possible that the new company will eventually find a way to give the people what they want.

Decision: So long.

○ The residents of Hong Kong who have the most wealth, and are thus most likely to subscribe to the service, live too far away from the city center to be connected.

Analysis: The argument says that the cost to subscribe is high, and the author assumes that everyone who lives close enough to get wired for the new service will want to buy it. The company won't succeed if the only people who can afford the service can't get it.

Decision: Yes!

○ The current cable-television provider in Hong Kong has lost money in each of the past four years.

Analysis: Again, we're making a comparison—this time between the current cable provider and the new interactive TV company. We can't assume that the two are comparable because their products are probably very different. And the management teams could run their businesses in different ways.

Decision: Move on.

○ Hong Kong's Bureau of Zoning has authorized the construction of more than 20 new movie theaters next year.

Analysis: The test writers would like us to think that these new movie theaters will threaten the home-viewing business. This may be true, but it's also possible that Hong Kongers would still prefer to stay home if the service were available to them.

Decision: Bye-bye. The answer is (C).

We've established that the assumption of this argument is that the people who live close enough to a central video server will be willing and able to afford the service. Therefore, there are several ways to strengthen the argument using this assumption.

- ◯ As the required technology becomes more commonplace, subscription prices are sure to come down.
- ◯ People would pay more to stay home and watch a movie whenever they want rather than be obligated to go out and adhere to a theater's projection schedule.
- ◯ Surveys indicate that movies are by far the most common form of entertainment among Hong Kong's residents.

Each of these answer choices strengthens the argument because each one is directly relevant to the assumptions that people will be able to afford the service and they will want to pay for it. It is important for you to distinguish relevant answer choices from irrelevant ones.

Make It Strong

When it comes to weaken/ strengthen questions, look for answer choices that use strong language. The correct answer will likely be strongly worded.

One last thing to know about using the Process of Elimination on weaken and strengthen questions is that strongly worded answers are good. It isn't *necessary* that a correct answer use strong language, but because we're trying to weaken or strengthen the answer as much as possible, we like strong answers more than moderate ones as long as they are relevant to the argument.

Flaw Questions

Questions that want you to find the mistake are closely related to weaken questions, but they're not the same. They usually look something like this:

- Which of the following indicates a **flaw** in the reasoning above?

- The above argument is most vulnerable to criticism on the grounds that…

In a weaken question, you have to determine which answer choice (which represents *new* information) would make the conclusion less plausible. In a flaw question, the mistake is already there, and you have to determine what it is.

> There is some truth to the speculation that the Olympic boxing judge from Country M has been favoring athletes from his home country. Of all the boxing matches he has assessed that involved a boxer from Country M, he has judged his country-men to be victorious 75 percent of the time.
>
> Which of the following statements suggests that the above argument is flawed?

This argument is just plain sneaky because it exploits our innate sense of numerical fairness. Because the judge has favored his countrymen more than half the time, he must be a crook, right?

But look at this potential answer choice:

◯ The other judges who presided over the
same Olympic fights as the judge from
Country M judged that Country M's boxers
should have won in more than 80 percent
of the fights.

Even though Country M's judge supported his boxers 75 percent of the time, it's possible that Country M is a nation of superboxers who deserved to win even more than they did. The argument is flawed because it wants to assume that unfair equals more than half, when unfair actually equals more than *they should*. For that reason, a correct answer might also appear like this:

◯ Though the judge from Country M favored his
countrymen more than half of the time, it is
possible that Country M's boxers deserved to
win even more than they actually did.

This should help you realize that no new information was added; the flaw in the logic was merely exposed.

Assumption Questions

In order for an argument to be valid, its assumptions must be true. Remember, there is always a gap between the premises and the conclusion, and the assumptions fill that gap. The assumption will always be something that is necessary for the logic of the argument to work, something that ties the conclusion to the premises.

The following are some examples of how assumption questions might be phrased.

- The argument above **assumes** that…

- Which of the following is an assumption on which the above argument depends?

- The conclusion drawn above depends on which of the following assumptions?

> On assumption questions, find the conclusion and determine which answer choice needs to be true in order for the conclusion to be valid.

When using the Process of Elimination on assumption questions, get rid of answer choices that weaken the conclusion, are irrelevant to the argument, or are too strong. Strongly worded answers are usually wrong on assumption questions.

Be Careful

Unlike weaken/strengthen questions, strongly worded answer choices for assumption questions are usually wrong.

The World Trade Organization (WTO) has stepped up its scrutiny of the offshore production facilities owned by the world's top producer of athletic footwear. A recent labor probe in Country P found that each of the company's production plants violated several labor laws, and the WTO forced the company to double the minimum wage of each of its workers within that country. Therefore, the company's costs of producing athletic footwear will rise.

The conclusion above is based on which of the following assumptions?

○ The company has never been forced to raise the minimum wage of its workers in the past.
○ Sales of the company's footwear in Country P will rise.
○ Footwear that is produced in Country P is superior to that produced in any other country.
○ The company will continue to produce its athletic footwear in Country P.
○ The company's public display of compassion for its workers will ultimately translate into a better image among consumers.

This is an assumption question, and the loose translation of the passage goes something like this: The WTO forced a company to pay its workers more money in Country P, so the company's production costs will go up.

Negation

One of the best ways to determine whether an answer choice is the sought-after assumption is to *negate* each one and see if the conclusion survives. Once you realize that an answer choice is crucial to the conclusion's survival, you know you've hit paydirt.

○ The company has never been forced to raise the minimum wage of its workers in the past.

Negation: The company has been forced to raise the minimum wage of its workers in the past.

Analysis: Whether or not this has happened in the past has no impact on what will happen in the future. And we still know nothing about costs.

Decision: Eliminate it.

○ Sales of the company's footwear in Country P will rise.

Negation: Sales of the company's footwear in Country P will not rise.

Analysis: The test writers would like us to believe that the workers in Country P will enjoy their new wealth by buying the shoes they're making (which will increase the company's *profits*), but what they do with their money has no impact on the company's *costs*.

Decision: Nope.

○ Footwear that is produced in Country P is superior to that produced in any other country.

Negation: Footwear that is produced in Country P is *not* superior to that produced in any other country.

Analysis: It sounds logical to us that the company would choose to make its product with the best workers possible, but we don't know that for sure. And how does this impact costs?

Decision: Eliminate it.

○ The company will continue to produce its athletic footwear in Country P.

Negation: The company will not continue to produce its athletic footwear in Country P.

Analysis: Yes! The author of the argument concludes that the company's production costs will go up because of the wage increase. It must be assumed, therefore, that the company will stay in Country P. If it decides to shift its production to another country, it's possible that the labor laws are different and the company will keep its production costs down.

Decision: We have a winner.

○ The company's public display of compassion for its workers will ultimately translate into a better image among consumers.

Negation: The company's public display of compassion for its workers will *not* ultimately translate into a better image among consumers.

Analysis: Watch out! The test writers are trying to toy with your emotions. Of course, we care about the oppressed workers, but a greater public image still does not address the company's production costs.

Decision: Gone. The best answer is (D).

Try It Out

Try to use this negation technique to figure out which answer choices are invaluable and which are irrelevant.

Evaluate-the-Argument Questions

This type of question is related to relevance. A conclusion is asserted, and the question will generally ask which choice helps to determine whether the conclusion is valid. Here are two examples of what evaluate-the-argument questions will be like:

- Which of the following determinations is most likely to yield significant information that would help to **evaluate** the researcher's hypothesis?

- Which of the following must be studied to **assess the validity** of the argument above?

On the AWA essay, you're asked to provide any other information that would help you to determine whether the argument makes logical sense. These questions work in much the same way. Wrong answers to evaluate the argument questions are usually just not relevant to the debate.

> A growing number of urban school districts have embraced the practice of "social promotion," whereby a student is automatically promoted to the next highest grade regardless of whether he or she has passed or failed English class. This policy is flawed because the only criterion that a student must fulfill in order to advance is to pass a state-wide standardized test.
>
> The answer to which of the following questions would be most useful in evaluating the validity of "social promotion"?
>
> ○ Do students have the option of taking a standardized test in a language other than English?
> ○ What is the rate of graduation from schools at which "social promotion" is commonly practiced?
> ○ How rigorous are the questions on these standardized tests that pertain to English skills?
> ○ How prevalent is "social promotion" among school districts in more suburban areas?
> ○ If a student fails a standardized test, is he or she given the chance to take it again before having to be kept back?

If you look at each of these choices separately, you'll see that all but (C) are irrelevant to the argument. If we knew more about the standardized test that the kids must pass, we would have a better idea of the English skills that the kids have. It might be that this test is a better judge of English skills than one's grades.

Identify-the-Reasoning Questions

Success with these questions derives from mapping out how an argument is structured and finding the answer choice that best describes the logic used. They're related to structure questions pertaining to reading comprehension passages.

> The Montridge Town Council has just voted to increase the local tax rate on all new commercial businesses within the town's border despite the possibility that some businesses might leave. The council believes that if it acts to keep the town as residential as possible, the town will attract wealthier people who will gravitate toward the town's charm and will not complain about an increase in property taxes.
>
> Which of the following best expresses the logical pattern underlying the Montridge Town Council's recent decision?
>
> ○ It rationalized that a drop in revenue from one source would ultimately be offset by an increase from another source.
> ○ It established its distaste for commercial activity within Montridge.
> ○ It questioned the assumption that all commercial businesses would react to the tax hike by leaving town.
> ○ It believes that in order to achieve goals, they must be prioritized.
> ○ It weighed several options and chose the one that it believed would result in the least collateral damage.

If you paraphrase the passage, you can see that the Montridge Town Council was willing to forgo corporate tax money in return for the residential tax money it would later collect from the rich folks who moved in. Therefore, (A) is the best answer.

WHEN THE CPA MODEL DOESN'T APPLY

From here on, don't worry about the CPA Model. The question types all have something quite different at stake.

Inference Questions

When you infer something, you determine that something is definitely true even though you weren't directly told so. If someone told you that she lived in a U.S. state directly south of Washington and directly north of California, you could correctly infer that she lived in Oregon. She didn't tell you directly; she *implied* it, and you *inferred* it. The questions will look something like the following:

- If each of the statements above is true, which of the following **must also be true?**

- Which of the following is **most directly supported** by the argument above?

- Which of the following can be **correctly inferred** from the statements above?

Inference questions don't deal much with the CPA Model. If anything, the passage is a series of premises and the correct answer choice is the only conclusion that can be properly drawn.

> When you see an inference question, you have to ask yourself only one question: "Which of the answer choices absolutely, positively, must be true based on what I've read?"

If you can't find direct proof that the answer choice is true, then it's out. Period. For that reason, stay away from answer choices that are too strong in their assertions. The right answer is usually a small detail that seems too obvious to merit mention.

Beware of Your Heartstrings!

We are all human, and we all have feelings. Because of this, the test writers like to mine its answer choices with sentimental favorites that appeal to our sense of decency or fairness. It's a tough world out there, though, and logic derives from the head, not the heart. Here is an example:

> Health professionals have argued that too much butter in a person's diet can cause the dangerous overdevelopment in the bloodstream of high-density lipoproteins that can clog arteries and put that person at risk of a heart attack. In South Korea, however, where per-capita butter consumption is almost non-existent, the incidence of heart attacks is no less than that in countries where butter is commonly served at every meal.

> Which of the following statements represents the most reliable conclusion that can be drawn from the information above?

> ○ Most people, if told of the potential risk of butter consumption, would willingly switch to margarine or some other butter substitute.
> ○ Despite arguments to the contrary, butter does not have a deleterious effect on the human heart.
> ○ Koreans avoid butter because they dislike the taste, not because of the health risk.
> ○ Butter consumption is probably not the only factor that can be linked to the incidence of heart attacks.
> ○ Other dairy products, such as cheese and yogurt, pose an equal threat to cardiovascular fitness.

Let's take a crack at the answer choices:

> ○ Most people, if told of the potential risk of butter consumption, would willingly switch to margarine or some other butter substitute.

Analysis: This is a heartstrings answer. We would like to think that the average person will give up something to preserve his health, but that's not necessarily the case. As much as we'd like to believe this, we don't know for a fact that it's true.

Decision: Eliminate it.

○ Despite arguments to the contrary, butter does not have a deleterious effect on the human heart.

Analysis: Here is a classic example of an answer choice that goes too far. We don't know that butter doesn't affect the heart *at all*. The Korean example suggests that there can be other causes of heart attacks, but it does not prove that butter is safe. Butter could still be as dangerous as the health officials say. Answer choices like this can be tricky because we humans tend to think in extremes. One example, however, does not prove an overall theory.

Decision: Move on.

○ Koreans avoid butter because they dislike the taste, not because of the health risk.

Analysis: Please. Is there any clue about this anywhere in the passage? Not even a hint.

Decision: Get rid of it.

○ Butter consumption is probably not the only factor that can be linked to the incidence of heart attack.

Analysis: Aha. We can defend this one. Butter may be dangerous to your bloodstream, yet Koreans (who don't eat any butter) are also getting heart attacks. That means that something else must be causing heart trouble among the Korean population.

Decision: Bingo.

○ Other dairy products, such as cheese and yogurt, pose an equal threat to cardiovascular fitness.

Analysis: Not even close. Here, the test writers are trying to appeal to some shred of sense that might lead you to believe that all dairy products are bad for you just because butter might be. But you're not about to fall for that, are you?

Decision: Nope.

Resolve/Explain Questions

A resolve/explain question asks you to explain a discrepancy or resolve two statements that don't seem to coexist well. Each resolve/explain question contains two seemingly contradictory facts, and the question will read something like the following:

- Which of the following, if true, contributes most to an **explanation** of how the department store's revenues tripled despite the closing of more than half its stores?

- Which of the following, if true, best resolves the contradiction described above?

- Which of the following statements, if true, would best **explain** the 1984 increase in paranoia?

Your job is to find the answer choice that shows that the facts aren't contradictory after all.

A month ago, the average price of a gallon of gasoline in Albemarle County rose 15 cents. Since then, however, each of the gas stations in Albemarle County has reported an increase of at least 20 percent in the aggregate number of gallons purchased.

Which of the following, if true, would best explain why so much more gasoline was purchased despite the steep price increase?

○ In an effort to fund a second refining facility nearby, the oil refinery that serves the majority of the gas stations in Albemarle County raised its prices.

○ A marketing strategy devised by a powerful environmentalist interest group has inspired many commuters who normally drive to work alone to organize car pools with coworkers.

○ A statewide strike of all commercial and commuter railway workers has brought all rail traffic to a halt.

○ Drivers are also purchasing more cans of heavy-grade oil, even though the price per can has remained virtually unchanged.

○ Almost no one who lives within Albemarle County also works within Albemarle County.

Straightforward, right? No conclusions, no assumptions, and none of that CPA stuff. Just a funny situation for you to reconcile: People are buying a lot more gas even though the price is higher. One of the answer choices explains this, and the rest don't.

◯ In an effort to fund a second refining facility nearby, the oil refinery that serves the majority of the gas stations in Albemarle County raised its prices.

Analysis: This might explain why the price is higher, but why are people buying more of it?

Decision: Eliminate it.

◯ A marketing strategy devised by a powerful environmentalist interest group has inspired many commuters who normally drive to work alone to organize car pools with coworkers.

Analysis: This one is no help whatsoever. If commuters have started car pooling, then it would follow logically that even less gasoline is being purchased. This choice is supposed to appeal to our heartstrings because we all perceive environmentalists to be enlightened protectors of our diseased planet. Yeah, whatever.

Decision: Nope.

◯ A statewide strike of all commercial and commuter railway workers has brought all rail traffic to a halt.

Analysis: It might seem irrelevant at first. After all, who cares about the railroads? But railroads function as an alternate form of transportation—especially commuter transportation. Therefore, it's feasible that commuters from Albemarle County are taking alternate gas-consuming forms of transport (such as cars or buses) to work.

Decision: Keep it.

◯ Drivers are also purchasing more cans of heavy-grade oil, even though the price per can has remained virtually unchanged.

Analysis: So people are buying oil, too. Well, oil and gasoline are both petroleum products, but this answer choice's usefulness ends there. This doesn't address the higher cost of gasoline or why the gas is flying into gas tanks.

Decision: No dice.

◯ Almost no one who lives within Albemarle County also works within Albemarle County.

Analysis: This is supposed to suggest to us that it's possible for residents of Albemarle County to get their gas elsewhere. It still doesn't explain why more gas is being bought.

Decision: Forget it. The best answer is (C).

OTHER POINTS TO CONSIDER

Keep these other points in mind as you develop your technique for analyzing arguments. Find as many practice problems as you can, and take note of the number of times each of these topics surfaces.

Watch for Extremes

One thing that is extremely important to the Process of Elimination on arguments questions is knowing when strong language is okay and when it's not. (Some examples of strong language are *only, must, never, always,* and similar words.) There are two question types that are particularly conducive to extremes and two that are not.

Weaken and strengthen questions look for the answer choice that will *most* weaken or strengthen the argument. Therefore, as long as an answer choice is relevant to the argument and does what it's supposed to do, the stronger the better. That doesn't mean that all correct answers on weaken and strengthen questions will have strong language; some, in fact, are quite mild and only weaken or strengthen the argument a little. But extremes are still good on those question types.

On **assumption and inference questions**, however, you want to be wary of strong language. Remember, the correct answer to an assumption question is something *necessary* to the argument. An answer choice with strong language may help the argument, but is it really necessary? Probably not. So watch out for extremes on assumption questions. Extremes are also dangerous on inference questions because most of us are tempted to push the arguments as far as we can, as long as they seem reasonable. But the key to inference questions is staying rigorously within the scope of the passages. Strong language usually takes that information too far, beyond what we can really infer. It's possible for an extreme answer to be correct on an inference question, but you had better have really good support for it.

Going to Extremes

For weaken/strengthen questions, the correct answer will probably use extreme language (though not always). But on assumption and inference questions, be wary of extreme language.

What Caused What?

The causal argument is common on the GMAT because its makeup fits so neatly in the CPA Model: A conclusion is deemed to be true *because* of a few premises.

When an argument asserts that A causes B, there are two common assumptions involved:

- There was no other cause for B.

- B wasn't a coincidence.

There are several dead giveaways for a causal argument, including phrases such as *because of*, *due to*, and *as a result*.

> Attendance at a local indoor health club has suffered in the last three months. One community leader believes that people have stayed away from the facility because it recently raised the price of a month-to-month membership by 35 percent.
>
> Which of the following, if true, would undermine the validity of the community leader's conclusion?

Each of the following two answer choices is a possible correct answer:

> ○ Due to a recent stretch of unseasonably warm weather, most people have taken to exercising outdoors.

This answer choice weakens the argument because it suggests an alternate reason why fewer people are going to the health club. Because it has been warm outside, it's possible that the weather (and not the higher membership prices) is keeping people away.

> ○ Committed to maintaining its profit margins, the health club decided to offset the decrease in the number of paying customers by increasing the price of membership to those who already belonged.

This one turns the causal relationship on its head. The community leader believes that the price increase caused the decrease in paying customers (A caused B) when, in fact, the decrease in customers caused the price increase (B caused A). Either of these is a valid way to undermine a causal relationship.

Statistics, Numbers, and Lies

Anyone who has ever had to crunch numbers knows that the shrewdest doctors can bend statistics to support any conclusion they want. There are two major points to know about when you're dealing with numbers. The first relates to conclusions that rely on some sort of survey or poll:

> When an argument is based on a sample, a survey, or statistical evidence, the assumption is that the people polled are representative of the whole or that the percentages are representative of the total populations.

It's a rather simple strategy—so simple, in fact, that questions like the one below have become more scarce lately:

> Employees of Drubb Corporation seem to be very pleased with the work that the company's board of directors is doing. Just last week, the majority of the company's secretaries signed a letter of support for the company's decision to announce a two-for-one stock split.

The author of this argument thinks that every employee likes the directors' new decision because the secretaries have expressed their support. The way to weaken the argument is to disprove the assumption that secretaries are just like all the other employees.

> ◯ As a result of a lawsuit that the board recently settled with the National Secretaries Union, each of the secretaries receives three times as many stock options as any other employee.

All this stuff about lawsuits might appear irrelevant, but it creates a reason why the secretaries are not representative of all employees (they're happier because they have more stock).

Math? In *This* Book?

The second statistical matter to learn about involves a little mathematical computation. Believe it or not, the test writers like to bring math into the Verbal section every once in a while because the numbers are likely to confuse you—especially if you're in the middle of a 75-minute Verbal section. Many math-related questions involve inferences.

> Country L used to import wheat from Country S because Country S's price per bale was the cheapest available. When Country S raised its price by 25 percent, however, Country L decided to transfer its business to Country D, which now boasted the best deal available.
>
> Which of the following, if true, would be best supported by the assertions above?
>
> ◯ The cost to harvest a bale of wheat in Country S increased by 25 percent.
> ◯ If Country S were to lower its price below Country D's price, then Country L would resume its import relationship with Country S.
> ◯ If Country L could somehow reduce the cost of producing domestic wheat by 25 percent, it wouldn't need to rely on any wheat imports.
> ◯ Country S and Country D do not import or export any wheat from each other.
> ◯ If Country D were to increase its price per bale of wheat by 25 percent, then a bale of wheat from Country S would once again be less expensive.

The test writers like to fill your head with alphabet soup to distract you from the task at hand, and it usually works. If you've done any math review with The Princeton Review, you know that one of our marquis techniques is to plug in real numbers for any variables. That technique works here as well.

○ The cost to harvest a bale of wheat in Country S increased by 25 percent.

Analysis: We'd all like to think that Country S has no profit motive and thus increased its price by the exact percent that its costs rose. But we don't know if that's true.

Decision: Good-bye.

○ If Country S were to lower its price below Country D's price, then Country L would resume its import relationship with Country S.

Analysis: This one looks tempting, because it's possible that Country S could be the cheapest again.

Decision: Keep it.

○ If Country L could somehow reduce the cost of producing domestic wheat by 25 percent, it wouldn't need to rely on any wheat imports.

Analysis: It's too extreme (*rely on any wheat imports?*). Besides, we have no information about domestic wheat production.

Decision: Sayonara.

○ Country S and Country D do not import or export any wheat from each other.

Analysis: This one is barely worth looking at. We have no clue whether Country S and Country D do any business together.

Decision: Eliminate it.

○ If Country D were to increase its price per bale of wheat by 25 percent, then a bale of wheat from Country S would once again be less expensive.

Analysis: Use numbers to bear this one out. Because we're dealing with percentages, let's say that Country S's price was $100, and it shot up to $125. Because Country D didn't have the best deal available but it does now, Country D's price must be somewhere between $100 and $125. If you take any number in that range and increase it by 25 percent, the result will be greater.

Decision: Choice (E) is the correct answer because the numbers back it up. But, you ask, what about (B)? Well, it's possible that Country S would be the cheapest again, but what if Country L found cheaper wheat someplace else? If Country S's price went from $100 to $125, and County D's price was $120, we can't assume that Country S would be the cheapest again if it lowered its price to $110. What if Country X sold wheat for $105? Thus (B) is not supported, and the answer is (E).

Arguing by Analogy

How many of you out there can relate to this scenario?

> **You:** Mom, will you let me stay up until 11 o'clock?

> **Mom:** Why should I let you stay up until 11 o'clock?

> **You:** Because Derek's mother lets him stay up until 11 o'clock!

Most 10-year-olds first learn to back up their logical positions by arguing by analogy: Something should be true about your family because it's true in Derek's family. It makes sense on the surface, but how does your mom respond to effectively kill your argument and send you to your room devastated?

> **Mom:** Well, I'm not Derek's mother.

You tried to make an argument by analogy, and your mom shot you down by refuting your assumption that all families are alike.

> When an argument is based on an analogy between two separate things, the assumption is that the two things are similar.

If you're asked to weaken an argument by analogy, look for an answer choice that indicates that the two things are different.

> Last month, the Hungarian embassy had to be emptied because of a perceived threat of a bomb in the building. Therefore, anyone who targets the Nigerian embassy next door will create similar chaos.
>
> Which of the following, if true, would most weaken the conclusion above?

The author concludes that life at the Nigerian embassy will be disrupted by a bomb threat because it happened at the Hungarian embassy. The author assumes that the two embassies will be equally affected because they are equally prepared.

Therefore, the correct answer might read something like this:

○ In response to the trouble at the Hungarian embassy, each of the other embassies on the block tightened security by doubling the number of watchmen who patrol the border of the property.

This answer choice asserts that the two embassies are different, so the chance that the two will be affected equally by a bomb threat is weakened. The argument isn't ruined, of course (after all, all the new guards could be blind or something), but you still have to scratch your head as to whether the argument is defensible.

EXCEPT Questions

Most people think that EXCEPT questions are the most difficult ones to work with, but that doesn't necessarily have to be the case. In fact, they're remarkably similar to regular questions; instead of four wrong answers and one correct one, there are four correct answers and one wrong one. Either way, one answer choice is supposed to stand out from the others.

The only difference is that you have to remember that you're working with an EXCEPT question. Too many students forget this in the heat of battle; in fact, many students don't even see the EXCEPT sitting right in front of them, even though it's right there in capital letters.

> To keep your focus, follow this technique:
>
> • Write the letters A through E on your scratch paper.
>
> • Work the problem as you always do.
>
> • Write "Yes" next to answer choices that answer the question properly, and "No" next to the one that doesn't.
>
> • Pick the choice with "No" next to it.

Let's say you're faced with a question like this, for example:

Each of the following is a state capital EXCEPT
○ Trenton
○ Sacramento
○ Tallahassee
○ Moscow
○ Columbus

Your scratch paper should look something like this:

A   Yes

B   Yes

C   Yes

D   No

E   Yes

Now you can pick (D).

PUTTING IT ALL TOGETHER

All right. We've covered just about everything you're likely to see and everything you'll need to know. Let's put the plan of attack into action as we analyze the practice argument from the beginning of the chapter.

> Scientists estimate that the cost of an Aerosonde, an unmanned airplane designed to collect atmospheric data during a transatlantic flight, is approximately $20,000. An ordinary weather balloon, by contrast, can collect virtually the same information for about $200. Therefore, weather balloons are clearly the more cost-efficient method for gathering information.
>
> Which of the following, if true, calls the above conclusion into question?
>
> ◯ Aerosondes are less costly than piloted planes and also do not put human life at risk.
> ◯ Politicians who have lobbied for federal funds to construct the Aerosonde are astonished at its in-flight agility.
> ◯ Weather balloons are subject to violent weather changes that can blow them miles off course.
> ◯ Aerosondes can be used over and over again, but weather balloons, because of their frailty, can only be used once.
> ◯ In the time it takes to launch an Aerosonde, it is possible to launch more than 100 weather balloons at once.

1. Read the question first and identify what type of question it is.

> Which of the following, if true, calls the above conclusion into question?

It's a weaken question. The CPA Model applies, so we should keep an eye out for the argument's conclusion.

2. Work the passage. Let's see what you've learned.

> Scientists estimate that the cost of an Aerosonde, an unmanned airplane designed to collect atmospheric data during a transatlantic flight, is approximately $20,000. An ordinary weather balloon, by contrast, can collect virtually the same information for about $200. Therefore, weather balloons are clearly the more cost-efficient method for gathering information.

This argument has three sentences. The last one is the argument's conclusion (again, *Therefore* is a dead giveaway):

> **Therefore,** weather balloons are clearly the more cost-efficient method for gathering information.

The author bases this conclusion on the two previous statements:

Premise 1: Scientists estimate the cost of an Aerosonde, an unmanned airplane designed to collect atmospheric data during a transatlantic flight, is approximately $20,000.

Premise 2: An ordinary weather balloon, by contrast, can collect virtually the same information for about $200.

<u>Loose Translation:</u> Weather balloons are a better deal than these new, high-tech weather planes because the balloons are much cheaper.

We're trying to weaken this argument, so our goal is to find an answer choice that suggests either that weather balloons are not a better deal or that the Aerosondes are more cost-efficient than the passage portrays them to be.

3. Predict what the correct answer should do. Then insert a prediction.

4. Use POE.

> ◯ Aerosondes are less costly than piloted planes and also do not put human life at risk.

Analysis: This makes a good point about aerosondes, but *piloted planes* are not the issue. There's no direct contrast with weather balloons, either. (Besides, it's possible to say the same things about weather balloons.)

Decision: Kill it.

○ Politicians who have lobbied for federal funds to construct the Aerosonde are astonished at its in-flight agility.

Analysis: Another answer choice that pulls at your heartstrings because it stresses one of the Aerosonde's good qualities, but is *agility* related to cost? Nope. This one's out of the scope as well.

Decision: See ya.

○ Weather balloons are subject to violent weather changes than can blow them miles off course.

Analysis: It tries to make itself attractive by taking a swipe at weather balloons, but it doesn't address the core issue: *cost*. Therefore, it's out of the scope.

Decision: Kill it.

○ Aerosondes can be used over and over again, but weather balloons, because of their frailty, can only be used once.

Analysis: Might seem irrelevant at first, but it does compare the Aerosonde to the weather balloon directly—something that no other answer choice has done yet.

Decision: Keep it.

○ In the time it takes to launch an Aerosonde, it is possible to launch more than 100 weather balloons at once.

Analysis: Also an attractive choice because the numbers seem to add up.

Decision: Let's say that you keep this one as well.

You're left with (D) and (E). Check the argument's parts again: The weather balloons are more cost-effective because they are one-hundredth as expensive. Choice (E) tries to lull you with numbers. The Aerosonde costs 100 times as much as a weather balloon, and you might want to pick this if you're seized by a panic. But this doesn't weaken the argument at all. If anything, it *strengthens* the argument by adding that in addition to being far less expensive, weather balloons are also a lot easier to launch.

You found a flaw in each of the other answer choices, so (D) must be the best choice just by POE. As it turns out, (D) does a good job of weakening the argument because it attacks a very important assumption: that cost equals *cost efficiency*. It's a subtle difference, but numbers like this are commonly confused. If the plane can be used over and over, as (D) asserts, then it might be true that the Aerosonde will ultimately be less expensive to use.

Note:

Here's a good point to recall the importance of not thinking in terms of extremes. If (D) is true, it must further be proved that the Aerosonde can fly 101 missions before it is more cost-effective than the weather balloon. However, the argument is indeed weakened.

Comprehensive Drill: Critical Reasoning

Take a stab at the following drill, and make special note of which arguments follow the CPA Model and which do not. Also, don't forget to read the question before you read the argument, and try to read the argument just once and summarize it in your head before you read the answer choices. Answers and explanations begin on page 154.

1. The Sports and Exhibition Authority has announced that the next election will feature a statewide referendum for the allotment of public funds to build a new football stadium in the state's capital city. Although the current facility is small and outdated, voters should reject this proposal because it stands to benefit only those who live in or near the capital at the expense of all of the state's taxpayers.

   Which of the following, if true, could supporters of the new stadium cite in response to the author's criticism?

   ○ A new facility will attract new retail businesses whose taxes will be used to fund statewide individual tax cuts.
   ○ The owner of the state's football franchise has threatened to move his team to another state across the country if a new stadium is not built.
   ○ During football season, the state's team plays only eight home games.
   ○ In each of the past five seasons, the football team has improved its record and increased its appeal among the state's football fans.
   ○ Five years ago, a neighboring state built a brand-new football stadium and successfully convinced an out-of-state team to relocate there.

2. A series of glitches within the satellite infrastructure of a cellular phone service company has resulted in service interruptions and several complaints from the company's clients. The company has responded by offering its clients free months of service and other rebates in order to keep its clients from changing to another service provider. Because of this new policy, the company's profits are destined to keep falling for years to come.

   Which of the following, if true, taken together with the information above, best supports the conclusion that the company's financial situation will only worsen as long as this new policy is in place?

   ○ Clients who experience technical difficulties with their cellular phones are unlikely to recommend the service to friends and business associates.
   ○ Because satellite technology and construction is still a relatively new industry, it's unwise to assume that every satellite will always work perfectly.
   ○ The money that the company passes on as rebates to its clients whose service has been interrupted had been previously budgeted to be spent on repairing the satellites.
   ○ In order to balance out the lost and forfeited revenue, the company will have to lay off at least 10 percent of its employees.
   ○ The company has no plans to launch any new satellites anytime soon.

3. Citing a year-long downward trend in global sales of personal computers, the CEO of Farmer Computer has announced that his company will shift much of its emphasis from PC production to corporate networking systems. Personal computers are now much more able to adapt to new networking software, but the software itself must be updated frequently.

Which of the following, if true, casts the most serious doubt onto this new strategy?

- ○ The Farmer brand name is well respected in the computer industry, but few industry analysts believe that Farmer will have the same success with networking.
- ○ Sales of Farmer PCs have increased dramatically over each of the past six quarters, and they show no signs of slowing down.
- ○ A slew of new competitors in the PC production business will inevitably result in widespread cost cutting to preserve market share.
- ○ Sales of cellular phones and other mobile communications are expanding at three times the rate of networking companies.
- ○ Two other companies have approached Farmer with the prospect of a three-way merger to form a dominant company that would own market share in the PC business.

4. Ms. S, an adoptive mother, recently read an article about a birth father who is suing the adoptive parents for custody of his child, who had been offered up for adoption without the birth father's permission. Ms. S adopted her child several years later through the same agency, but she should not be worried that her child's birth father will sue her for custody.

Which of the following, if discovered to be true, would lend the most support to the conclusion above?

- ○ The birth mother of Ms. S's child never informed the birth father that she was pregnant, so the birth father does not know of the child's existence.
- ○ In the last 20 years in the state in which Ms. S lives, adoptive parents have won 90 percent of the cases in which birth parents have sued for custody of an adopted child.
- ○ The adoption in the article was completed two months before a policy was instituted by the agency requiring the signatures of both birth parents on the paperwork releasing the child for adoption.
- ○ The birth father in the case described in the article was over the age of 18 at the time the adoption was completed.
- ○ Ms. S adopted one child through the agency mentioned in the article and another child through a lawyer specializing in adoptions.

5. Monique: Whenever I get depressed about the direction in which my life is going, I seem to receive another bit of horrible news. It's almost as if someone up there waits until I am at my most emotionally vulnerable and decides to make things worse.

The flaw in Monique's reasoning is the possibility that

○ the phrase "emotionally vulnerable" is difficult to quantify

○ Monique would feel better if she braced herself for bad news whenever she felt depressed

○ people deal with bad news in many different ways because some people are more stable than others

○ when Monique is emotionally vulnerable, the bad news she hears seems much more horrible than it actually is

○ her feelings of depression might be treatable if she sought professional counseling

6. A team of efficiency consultants conducted a study of Company X and found that 85 percent of its employees suffered a "midafternoon slump" between the hours of 2:00 p.m. and 4:00 p.m. During this slump, each employee's productivity went down an average of 30 percent. The consultants recommended, therefore, that management institute a policy encouraging employees to take their lunch breaks sometime between the hours of 2:00 p.m. and 4:00 p.m. because employees do not need to be productive as they eat lunch.

The consultants' conclusion relies on which of the following assumptions?

○ The consultants found no correlation between consumption of food and the feelings of lethargy experienced by the employees of Company X during the midafternoon slump.

○ Some of the employees of Company X do not eat breakfast until they arrive at the office at 9:00 a.m.

○ The consultants had seen the same slump phenomenon at Company P and had made the same recommendation to change the lunch hour.

○ Most of the employees of Company X expressed a preference to eat lunch sometime between the hours of 1:00 p.m. and 3:00 p.m.

○ The consultants also suggested adjusting the work schedules of half of the employees of Company X so that the employees would come in early in the morning and leave by 2:00 p.m.

7. The occurrence of schizophrenia in the general population is 1 percent. If one parent is schizophrenic, however, the incidence rises to 12 percent, and a child with two schizophrenic parents has a 45 percent chance of also suffering from the disease.

Which of the following can be most reasonably inferred from the passage above?

○ One's risk of developing schizophrenia is greater if one has a schizophrenic grandparent than if one has a grandparent with no diagnosed mental disease.

○ Early diagnosis of schizophrenia may reduce the severity of the impact of the disease on the patient's life.

○ One's risk of developing schizophrenia is higher if one has a full sibling with the disease.

○ Over the past 40 years, psychiatrists have advanced significantly in their understanding of the causes and treatments of schizophrenia.

○ A person's risk of developing schizophrenia is at least partially determined by genetic factors.

8. A poll has revealed that 95 percent of the residents of Essex County believe that the way to reduce violent crime is to build larger maximum-security prisons. When a referendum for the construction of a maximum-security prison in Essex County was added to the ballot the following November, however, the proposal was voted down by a three-to-one margin.

Which of the following, if true, forms the best basis for at least a partial explanation of the apparent discrepancy described above?

○ The threat of a life sentence in a maximum-security prison has been shown to be an adequate deterrent of violent crime.

○ The prison would have been constructed by a private company, and it would have been impossible for the county government to oversee the company's finances.

○ Fewer than half of the registered voters in Essex County voted.

○ Much of the substantial cost of the prison could have been offset by increasing the tolls required to cross the bridge over nearby Lake Essex.

○ Maximum-security prisons are a boon to the overall well-being of the state, but they also pose a considerable risk in the areas in which they are located.

9. Most doctors dismiss male pattern baldness as a problem of heredity. A new theory, however, postulates that baldness can also result from any number of external factors, such as a stressful urban lifestyle. Supporters of this new theory point to the fact that the incidence of baldness is almost twice as common among males who live in large cities as it is among those who live elsewhere.

Which of the following, if true, most seriously weakens the new theory described above?

○ Scientists have developed several drugs that halt baldness in men and can be taken internally.

○ Census reports show that most men who are born in large cities live almost their entire lives within the city of their birth in order to be near their families.

○ Most men do not develop male pattern baldness until they reach the age of 55, at which point their thoughts turn to pursuing a more restful lifestyle.

○ Men who have never lived in a large city are those least likely to develop male pattern baldness.

○ A fertility study determined that men who have developed male pattern baldness are less likely to marry and reproduce.

10. After several states negotiated a $195 billion settlement with the tobacco industry, State F used some of its money to create a youth-advocacy group whose antismoking advertising campaign was written entirely by high school-age students. The governor of State F has urged the state legislature to increase funding of this group because only teenagers know how to persuade other teenagers.

Which of the following, assuming that it could be carried out, would be most useful in order to evaluate the governor's desire to provide further funding to the youth-advocacy group?

○ Comparing the short-term effects of State F's antismoking campaign to the projected long-term success the campaign will probably enjoy

○ Breaking down the statistics for the decline of teen smoking into a month-by-month analysis and determining which months saw the steepest decreases

○ Comparing the decline in teen smoking in State F to the decline of teen smoking in other states that received money from the settlement and implemented advertising campaigns written by adults

○ Requiring that more adults be hired to supervise the group's finances

○ Comparing the aggregate number of smoking products bought the year before the group was set up to the number of smoking products bought during the year since the group was set up

11. Sport-utility vehicles have become extremely popular because of the robust and energetic image they project. Although these vehicles look sturdy, they are subject to only a small fraction of the safety standards the government imposes on ordinary passenger cars. Consequently, a high-impact collision involving both a passenger car and a sport-utility vehicle is much more likely to injure the occupants of the latter and not the former.

Each of the following serves to strengthen the conclusion above EXCEPT

○ those who design vehicles are inclined to make them safe only if government rules dictate that they must

○ sport-utility vehicles have a higher center of gravity, which makes them more susceptible to turning over in a collision

○ the government rigorously enforces its standards for maximum roof strength and impact resistance in all passenger cars

○ sport-utility vehicles are less aerodynamic than passenger cars, and this extra bulk hinders their ability to accelerate

○ people who drive sport-utility vehicles are often instilled with a false sense of security and therefore neglect to wear their seatbelts

12. In 1984, almost 2 percent of humans who were admitted to hospital emergency rooms after suffering a scorpion bite in the southwestern United States died from the attack. Ten years later, this figure had jumped to 4 percent. Clearly, the venom of the scorpion has become much more toxic to humans.

Which of the following statements, if true, most seriously weakens the above conclusion?

○ The scorpion population in the southwestern United States has remained steady since 1984.

○ There have been few innovations in the treatment of scorpion bites since 1984.

○ Most people who suffer scorpion bites are inexperienced hikers who are unaware of the best methods to avoid coming in contact with a scorpion.

○ Since 1984, people have learned that scorpion bites can be treated in the home as long as they are detected early.

○ People who survive one scorpion bite have a better than average chance of surviving a second bite.

13. At many universities in the United States, the average price of a used computer has risen dramatically. This rise has come about mostly because of increased demand from students entering college who need a computer but cannot afford to purchase a new one. In order to take advantage of this market, college seniors have been selling the computers that they have used throughout their college careers to incoming freshmen. This trend is sure to exert an upward pressure on the price of new computers as well.

To support a conclusion that the average price of a new computer will rise, it would be most important to establish which of the following?

○ The proliferation of e-mail and the Internet has made buying and selling used merchandise much easier.

○ Because most students need a computer to perform only basic duties, used computers are usually just as useful as new ones.

○ Most students who sell their used computers are inclined to replace them with new computers.

○ College seniors are more likely to wait until they secure employment before making any expensive purchases.

○ The majority of students who purchase new computers before entering college purchase another one before they graduate.

14. In order to help the most famine-stricken areas of the world, genetic engineers have proposed injecting certain animals with growth hormones, which increase the animals' ratio of meat to body fat. Those who oppose this plan are concerned that these hormones could cause health problems in the humans who eat the meat. A physician has defended the proposal, however, by asserting that humans can ingest as much as 15 milligrams of the hormones daily, and no animals would ever receive a dosage higher than 10 milligrams.

Which of the following statements, if true, would be of the most use to the plan's critics in response to the physician's claim?

○ Growth hormones occur naturally in many animals that are farmed for human consumption.

○ Each package of meat that had been treated with growth hormones would bear a label warning consumers of that fact.

○ Growth hormones are widely used among weight lifters who desire to build muscle mass in a brief period of time.

○ Some religions that are prevalent in famine-stricken countries have deemed that consumption of meat is sinful.

○ Growth hormones have been shown to cause sterility in certain animals.

15. In 1994, the most common eye-related disease from which Americans suffered was conjunctivitis, and glaucoma was a distant second.

Glaucoma is much more common among patients who are more than 50 years old than it is among those who are 50 or younger, but the incidence rate for conjunctivitis is the same for people of all ages.

The average age of all Americans is expected to exceed 50 by the year 2050.

Which of the following conclusions can be most properly drawn about eye-related diseases from the information given?

○ Conjunctivitis will remain the most common eye-related disease among Americans in 2050.
○ By the year 2050, glaucoma will overtake conjunctivitis as the most common eye-related disease.
○ More people will suffer from conjunctivitis in 2050 than did in 1994.
○ Most Americans will encounter either conjunctivitis or glaucoma by 2050.
○ The average age of Americans suffering from conjunctivitis will increase between 1994 and 2050.

16. Scientists previously believed that **human cells could divide an infinite number of times,** as long as the tissue harboring those cells remained perfectly healthy. However, **human spleen cells grown in an artificial, yet healthy, environment were shown to divide exactly twenty-four times** before they died off.

The bold phrases play which of the following roles in the argument?

○ The first phrase is the author's conclusion, and the second phrase provides an additional premise for that conclusion.
○ The first phrase states a theory, and the second phrase weakens that theory by providing a counterexample.
○ The second phrase clarifies an ambiguity that the first phrase neglects to address.
○ The first phrase asserts a possible phenomenon, and the second phrase offers a condition for that phenomenon to take place.
○ The second phrase provides evidence that the theory presented in the first phrase is incomplete.

17. Malcolm: I refuse to feel any contrition about failing to report all of my income on my income tax return last year. I have discussed this topic extensively with many friends, family members, and business associates, and it is clear to me that most Americans have bent the truth on their income tax returns at one time or another.

Luka: It is improper for you to rationalize your actions that way. Regardless of how often it occurs, an illegal deed is still illegal and should be punished.

Which of the following statements summarizes Luka's reasoning in response to Malcolm's admission?

- ◯ She questions the credibility of the sources whom Malcolm has consulted.
- ◯ She offers evidence that Malcolm's actions were much more severe than he perceived them to be.
- ◯ She demonstrates that Malcolm's rationalizations are based on insufficient evidence.
- ◯ She asserts that the frequency of a crime does not lessen its severity.
- ◯ She introduces the possibility that the moral convictions of different people can differ greatly.

18. At a certain investment bank that specializes in mergers and acquisitions, the highest percentage of potential deals that are never completed are those in which the bank's senior partner was the lead negotiator. Each of the senior partner's colleagues, however, states unequivocally that she is the most adept negotiator at the bank.

Which one of the following, if true, goes furthest toward showing that these two statements could both be correct?

- ◯ The current senior partner has a better record of success than her immediate predecessor did.
- ◯ Many of the junior partners were trained by the senior partner when they first joined the firm.
- ◯ The senior partner works only on potential deals that have the least chance of coming to fruition.
- ◯ The number of mergers in which the investment bank has been involved has declined slightly in each of the past three years.
- ◯ The senior partner was chosen by the board of directors of the bank's parent company, a large publishing conglomerate.

19. Economists estimate that the average median income per household has remained stagnant over the past ten years. Paradoxically, however, consumers enjoy more purchasing power now than they did a decade ago.

Which of the following, if true, helps reconcile these two seemingly contradictory statements?

○ There has been a surge of job creation over the past ten years, but the average salary of these jobs is considerably less than in the decade before.

○ The economists' data were weighted toward urban areas, where consumers have more purchasing options.

○ Over the past decade, the number of people constituting a typical household has fallen from 3.0 to 2.6.

○ Inflation has remained constant over the past ten years.

○ The last decade has seen a sharp rise in the number of legal immigrants, most of whom are willing to work the same jobs for less money.

20. Social anthropologists argue that a culture can only progress when the natives of that culture take the initiative to advance their nation themselves, independent of outside influence. Non-natives should be free to dispense valuable advice, when appropriate, but a culture cannot truly evolve if it is merely dragged forward by external forces. Therefore, if one considers labor unions as cultural institutions, it must be true that _____.

Which of the following best completes the last sentence of the passage?

○ labor unions must be truly autonomous in order to advance themselves

○ some labor unions need more independence than others do, depending on the line of work its members are engaged in

○ labor officials need to fashion their goals so that each union member can retain a sense of independence

○ the counsel of consultants and other non-members is rarely helpful when a union is trying to evolve

○ the more independent a labor union is, the more progress it will make

21. Movies that are rated "R" usually dramatize scenes of extreme violence and are thus restricted to children aged 17 or older. When a group of 15-year-olds who have been allowed to view a violent R-rated movie interacts with another group of 15-year-olds who have not seen the movie, the group that has seen the violent movie commits more violent acts than do the teenagers who have not seen the movie. Therefore, the quantity of violent acts among 15-year-olds can be curbed dramatically if they are not permitted to view R-rated movies.

The argument above relies on which of the following assumptions?

○ The age at which teenagers are allowed to view R-rated movies should be lowered from 17 to 15.

○ Parents are accountable for the violent acts their children commit.

○ The degree of violence inflicted on one group by another is a subjective consideration.

○ The 15-year-olds in the two groups mentioned above came from very similar socioeconomic backgrounds.

○ The 15-year-olds in the second group indicated a strong desire to view the R-rated movie.

22. Community activist: "The multi-purpose stadium that you plan to build in the most densely populated area of town will cause the neighborhood great harm. Most of the people attending the stadium's events will arrive by car, thus adding to the area's already alarming traffic problem."

Real estate developer: "Traffic around the new stadium will not get any worse because more than three-fourths of the area residents we interviewed indicated that they would move away if the stadium were built."

The answer to which of the following questions will most likely yield significant information that would help to evaluate the developer's rebuttal?

⬭ How many professional sports franchises will use the new stadium?

⬭ Is the municipal government considering a carpooling law for the region surrounding the stadium?

⬭ Does the developer plan to build parking garages to accommodate the stadium's patrons?

⬭ Why are so many area residents planning to move out of the neighborhood?

⬭ What percent of the area's residents own cars?

23. Among the 17 states in which the BusyBank brokerage house conducts business, Rhode Island was home to the branches that exhibited the greatest percent increase in overall statewide commissions. This achievement is especially surprising because Rhode Island has the fewest branches and the lowest commissions of any state in BusyBank's network.

The degree of surprise expressed over the above results is unfounded because

⬭ proficiency can improve if efforts are concentrated in smaller regions

⬭ a home office should remain apprised of its satellites' day-to-day operations

⬭ it is improper to assume that a small area must have the fewest branches in it

⬭ it is unreasonable to expect that a figure cannot experience a large percentage increase solely because that figure is the smallest of a group

⬭ a low figure, by definition, exhibits the greatest potential for improvement

DRILL ANSWERS AND EXPLANATIONS

Translating Arguments Drill

Here are examples of how the arguments could be translated, but remember there is no absolute correct answer.

1. People who live in farm country might actually be better consumers to target than city folk because farmers' costs are a lot less, and they have a lot of extra money to throw around.

2. The city has suggested selling off some of its rebuilding projects to raise cash, but some people don't like the idea because London did it and their commuter trains are lousy as a result.

3. Don't trust the big banks when they rate an investment opportunity because they might just be trying to boost their own stock holdings.

4. Buying ads during the Super Bowl is no longer worth it because the teams with the most fans (and the most viewers) currently stink and fewer people are watching.

5. During economic booms, the number of kids who want to go to college goes up. The number applying to graduate programs goes down, though, because adults want to work during the best economic times.

6. Bacteria (or infections) that people get are becoming too strong to be killed off by usual drugs, so drug companies have to spend a lot of dough developing new drugs to kill off the new bugs.

7. Avoiding paying your taxes is dumb because the government will only raise taxes so that you'll have to pay more later. Also, the government will be really upset when it finds you.

8. Lots of people think that ads for alcohol make kids drink too much and break the law. There are lots of booze ads in France, though, and they don't have as many booze-related problems as the United States does.

9. This furniture collector and expert says a lot of old desks that are supposed to be antiques are actually all a bunch of fakes.

Comprehensive Drill: Critical Reasoning

1.   **A**   The author of the argument doesn't support the new football stadium because everyone will pay for it and only a few will reap the benefits. Therefore, you want to find an answer choice like (A), which shows the new stadium will actually benefit more people. Choice (B) tugs at your heartstrings because it seems like a good reason to build a new stadium, but it doesn't address the issue of benefits to the few rather than to everyone. Neither does (C), (D), or (E); if anything, (C) is another reason not to build the stadium, and (D) and (E) are irrelevant.

2.   **C**   The company hopes to keep its clients from leaving by giving them money to stay. If this money, however, is earmarked for solving the problem at its source by fixing the satellites, as (C) stipulates, then the satellites will never be repaired, clients will keep complaining, and the company will keep paying them off. The cycle is doomed to continue indefinitely. Choices (A) and (D) might have a negative impact on sales, but neither addresses the premise that the company is paying the customers to stay loyal. It's difficult to determine (B)'s effect on the argument, because we don't know if the company's problems are normal or worse than normal. And because the company might not need to launch any more satellites, (E) is irrelevant.

3.   **B**   Among the answer choices, you're looking for the best reason for Farmer to abandon its new ideas and keep making personal computers. The company's premise is a year-long downward trend in global sales, but (B) says that Farmer is doing well despite the global downward shift. Therefore, it should keep doing what it does well. Choice (A) is a compelling choice, but the analysts could be wrong. Choice (C) also appears negative, but you can cut prices and still make profits. Choice (D) is irrelevant because we don't know if Farmer has anything to do with cell phones. The merger mentioned in (E) wouldn't be worth much if the PC market were declining; in order for the merger to be worthwhile, we'd need to know that global PC sales will rebound.

4.   **C**   You're looking for the best reason why Ms. S should not be worried, and (C) provides it. The new policy that the adoption agency has put into place requires that all adoptions be approved by the birth father, so he has signed away his right to sue for custody. If (A) and (B) are true, then the father could still sue if he wanted. Choices (D) and (E) are irrelevant because age was never mentioned as an issue, and neither was the number of children that Ms. S has adopted.

5.   **D**   This argument relies on a causal assumption that her fits of depression cause her to receive horrible news. She assumes that this causal link is the work of someone up there, but it's possible that there is an alternate cause: her own perceptions. Her depression might make her believe that any new problems are worse than they actually are. Choice (A) is not helpful because the degree of her emotional vulnerability isn't at issue. Choices (B) and (E) don't address the causal link either. Choice (C) is way beyond the scope because it's too general.

6.   **A**   The consultants think that the company's employees lose productivity between 2:00 P.M. and 4:00 P.M., so that is the best time for them to eat lunch. The consultants assume, therefore, that lunch and the "slump" are unrelated. If (A) were false, and eating lunch caused this "slump," then it

wouldn't matter when the employees ate lunch, and the conclusion would be worthless. Breakfast is irrelevant, so (B) is out. Choice (C) is a heartstring choice that argues by analogy, but we don't know how different (or similar) Companies X and P are. You can also eliminate (D) and (E) because the employees' preferences and any other suggestions are out of the scope.

7. **E**   As in any inference question, your job is to ask yourself, "What do I absolutely know is true?" The data suggest that a family history of schizophrenia greatly increased the chance that a child will have the disease, so it makes sense that heredity is at least partially determined by genetic factors. Choice (E) is a nice choice because it's so weak. It doesn't say much at all, so it's hard to argue against. Choice (A) might seem attractive, but it says a grandparent with no diagnosed mental disease; what about the other three grandparents? Choice (B) is a heartstring choice because it makes sense in our minds, but it's never mentioned in the argument. Choice (C) is also out of the scope. We know nothing about medical advances, so (D) is out.

8. **E**   This is a paradox question; you have to figure out why people want prisons to be built but don't want them near their homes. Once you boil down the question like this, you'll probably realize that the people of Essex County are suffering from a classic case of NIMBY (Not In My Back Yard). Choice (E) expresses this best; prisons help the whole state, but they threaten the people who live near them. Choice (A) explains why they like prisons, but we don't know why the referendum was defeated. Choice (B) explains why the prison was voted down, but it doesn't address why the folks like prisons. Choice (C) is in the right ballpark, but we don't know whether the people who voted are representative of the whole. Choice (D) doesn't help to explain anything because the cost of the prison is not at issue.

9. **B**   The conclusion of this weaken argument is that baldness is caused by external factors (and not due to heredity), and it states that there are more bald guys in big cities. Choice (B) turns this premise on its head by saying that many bald guys in cities are related to other bald guys in the same city, so the cause might be heredity after all. Treating baldness is utterly irrelevant, so you can get rid of (A). Choice (C) is too general because it talks about all men rather than just those who live in big cities. Choice (D) strengthens the argument by saying that guys who don't live in cities don't go bald. Choice (E) also lessens the chance that baldness is hereditary.

10. **C**   The governor says that the kids are the difference because only kids can talk to kids. Therefore, the best way to determine if the ad campaigns written by kids were successful is to compare State F to other states that didn't hire kids to write the campaigns. If kids' work has had a greater impact than adults' work has, then the kids should continue to get funding. Choices (A) and (B) are wrong because they don't address whether kids should write the ad campaigns. Choice (D) has no impact on the creative aspect of the campaigns, so it's out of the scope. And (E) isn't helpful because the campaign was set up to reduce teen smoking, not all smoking. Adult smokers may have been unaffected.

11. **D**   Before we discuss the answer to this strengthen EXCEPT question, it's important to make a point: Four of the answer choices strengthen the argument, and one does not. That doesn't necessarily mean that this fifth choice weakens the argument. It just means that it doesn't strengthen it (it could be out of the scope). The argument says that people who drive SUVs are more likely to be in-

jured in a car wreck, and (B), (C), and (E) strengthen the idea by asserting either that cars are safer or that SUVs are more dangerous. Choice (D) is irrelevant (and therefore the best answer) because we don't know if a lack of acceleration makes a car any less safe to drive. Choice (A) strengthens because the argument says that SUVs don't have as many safety standards; thus, SUV designers will cut corners if they can.

12.   D   You want to support the idea that scorpion venom isn't any more dangerous than it was in 1984, and there is some tricky math involved. The percentage of scorpion bite victims who go to the hospital and then die has increased, but it's possible that people have learned to treat the bites at home and that hospitals receive only the most severe cases. Let's plug in some numbers: In 1984, 100 people came to the hospital with scorpion bites, and two died. In 1994, let's say that 100 people were stung, but 50 of the victims treated their wounds at home and the other 50 came to the hospital (two of whom died). The statistics are the same, but the percent of hospital cases who die increases because there were fewer hospital cases in the first place. Each of the answer choices besides (D) is irrelevant.

13.   C   This is a well-disguised assumption question because the conclusion that prices of new computers will go up relies on (C). In order for new computers to increase in price as much as used computers, it must be true that new computers are being bought at about the same rate as used computers. Choice (C) fills the gap in the argument's logic. Choices (A) and (B) might help explain why the market for used computers has gotten larger, but they don't address the commensurate rise in new computer prices. At first glance, (E) looks as though it might help; however, it doesn't link used computers to new computers like (C) does. Choice (D) is too general, and the issue is whether seniors will buy new computers, not how long they'll wait to buy them.

14.   A   Watch out for the convoluted nature of this question: You want to support the critics, so you want to weaken the physician's claim and find evidence that injecting growth hormones is dangerous. The physician says that no animal will be injected with a harmful dose of growth hormones, and he assumes that there aren't any growth hormones already present in animals. If (A) is true, then the hormone injections can be harmful. Warning labels don't affect the health value of growth hormones, so (B) is out. Choice (C) might help build muscle in humans, but we don't know if it's harmful. If (D) is true, then people are less likely to eat the meat that is injected with the growth hormones; but that doesn't address whether the meat is safe. Choice (E) is irrelevant because the issue at hand is whether the growth hormones are harmful to humans, not whether they are harmful to animals.

15.   E   Let's paraphrase the three points of this inference question: (1) conjunctivitis (or pinkeye, for those of you who want to know) was more common than glaucoma; (2) glaucoma affects older people, but conjunctivitis affects everyone; and (3) people are getting older. From this information, we know that because the average age of Americans will rise, then the average age of pinkeye sufferers will also rise; (E) is the best choice. People have better success on this problem by ruling out the alternatives. Choices (A) and (B) are opposites of each other. We don't know which disease will be more common, so they're both out. Choice (C) is also tempting, but we don't know if it will be the case. What if some new wonder drug is invented? And we most certainly know nothing about (D); most Americans is awfully extreme.

16. **B** The words *previously believed* prior to the first bolded phrase indicate that it is an old theory that is about to be supplanted by new information. The second phrase provides a piece of information that indicates that the first theory is unlikely to be true, at least not for all human cell types (this is your counterexample). Note the word *however*, which prefaces contrasting information, prior to the second bolded phrase.

17. **D** Malcolm states that he doesn't feel guilty about cheating on his income taxes because everybody does it. Luka says that his rationalization doesn't cut it; a crime is a crime is a crime (that's not a typo—it's just in there for emphasis), and it doesn't matter how many people commit that crime. Choice (D) captures this idea best. She never assails Malcolm's credibility or his perception of the crime (he knows it's bad); eliminate (A) and (B). She also doesn't say that Malcolm didn't talk to enough people, so you can eliminate (C). Choice (E) might be true in general (watch out for those heartstrings!), but it's not what Luka says.

18. **C** The senior partner has a bad track record with mergers, but her colleagues still believe that she's a real whiz. If (C) is true, then it makes sense that many of the deals the senior partner worked on were doomed to fail, regardless of who worked on them. Therefore, it's still possible that the senior partner is a good negotiator. Choice (A) is wrong because her predecessor's work is not relevant to the discussion. Choice (B) might explain why the junior partners respect her, but we don't know that for sure. They may have disliked her teaching technique. Choice (D) is also irrelevant because the issue revolves around percentages, not actual numbers. The best chance that (E) has is that the board of directors doesn't know much about investment banking and thus promoted someone who is incompetent. Then why do the junior partners like her so much?

19. **C** The key distinction is between households and consumers. If there are fewer people in a household, yet that household's income has remained about the same (that is, remained stagnant), then it stands to reason that each of the consumers within that household has more money to spend. This is an excellent example of why looking for shifts in language is so important to understanding arguments. Noticing the shift from "households" to "consumers" is the key to this question. Choice (A) might explain why income per household is about the same, but it doesn't explain why consumers can purchase more. Choice (D) is no help, because it doesn't explain why consumers have more purchasing power. If inflation has been steady for ten years and their incomes have been stagnant, they should have less purchasing power, not more. Choice (B) is out because the location where the information was gathered doesn't explain the paradox, and the number of purchasing options is irrelevant. Choice (E) may partly explain why incomes are stagnant—because immigrants are willing to work for less money—but it doesn't explain why consumers have more purchasing power.

20. **A** The argument's main idea is that advancement relies on internal autonomy rather than external influence. The topic of the argument is culture, and the last sentence refers to labor unions as examples of culture. Therefore, to argue that labor unions must rule themselves in order to grow is consistent with the argument's overall message. Choice (B) is out because the particular line of work of any union is irrelevant. Choice (C) is also off the mark because a sense of independence doesn't necessarily equate to actual independence. Choice (D) is out because the argument explicitly allows that

counsel from the outside can be valuable—as long as it accompanies forces from within the unions themselves. Choice (E) may seem to follow logically, but there is no actual support for the proposition that greater independence creates greater progress. Just because something is necessary to achieve a result doesn't mean that more of that thing will achieve more of the result.

21. **D** This is a causal argument because the author is trying to argue that the R-rated movie directly caused the violent acts of the 15-year-olds who say it. The fundamental assumption of a causal argument is that there is no other cause, no other explanation of the behavior. Therefore, the argument must be assuming that seeing the movie was the only difference between the two groups. Everything else—including the students' socioeconomic backgrounds—had to be the same between both groups. Therefore, (D) is the best response. Choice (A) is out because there is no call for lowering the age at which kids can see R-rated movies; in fact, the argument suggests that younger kids seeing these movies is a bad thing. Choice (B) is out because it doesn't make any distinction between the two groups to explain their different responses, and parental accountability is irrelevant to this argument. Choice (C) may be true, but it is not something assumed by this argument. The argument assumes that violence can be measured clinically, so if (C) were true, then the argument would be weakened. Choice (E) is out because desire among the kids to see the movie doesn't change the fact that they didn't see it.

22. **E** The developer assumes that the departure of car-owning residents, who currently contribute to the area's traffic problems, will offset all the new cars destined to arrive. However, if it were discovered that those who departed didn't have cars to take with them, then their departure would not ease the traffic problem. Therefore, the percentage of residents who own cars would be a helpful thing to know in order to evaluate the developer's rebuttal. Choice (A) might seem reasonable, but only in the unlikely event that the answer is "zero." Besides, it does not address the developer's core point that residents will leave the area. Choice (B) might pull at your heartstrings, but whether or not a carpooling law is being considered is irrelevant. The developer's argument is about residents moving away, not about better traffic management. Choice (C) is bad for the same reason. The argument is about residents moving away, not about whether we'll have enough parking capacity to handle more cars. Choice (D) is wrong because the reasons for leaving are irrelevant; it's only important that residents go—and take their cars with them.

23. **D** Here's a little of that math that occasionally creeps into the Verbal section. The great thing about "percent increase" is that it makes the largest and smallest quantities comparable. So just because a number is low doesn't mean it can't rise in an impressive manner. Choice (A) is out because we don't know anything about why the Rhode Island operations saw such large gains, and furthermore, proficiency could easily improve in large regions as well. Choice (B) is silly because it doesn't address the inherent flaw of the argument—the assumption that small numbers can't rise dramatically on a percent basis. Choice (C) can go because we're not assuming that Rhode Island has the fewest branches; we know it because we were told so. Choice (E) is wrong because a low figure is certainly not defined by the ability to improve more than a large one. There's no way to know in advance which one will improve more, especially when considered on a percentage basis.

Chapter 4
Analytical
Writing
Assessment

IT'S THE "WRITE" TIME

So far we've covered how to read all the diverse and convoluted verbal material on the GMAT. Now it's your turn to do the writing.

Unfortunately, it's not in your best interest to force the test writers to read the same dense, uninteresting dreck that you have to read on the GMAT. Your writing needs to be all that passages on the GMAT are not: interesting, concise, and enjoyable to read.

This chapter is dedicated to helping you take on that sense of clarity, but let's not kid ourselves. Reading this book over a three-week period isn't going to turn you into a Vladimir Nabokov. What you can learn, however, is how to make your writing more pleasant for the many essay graders and admissions officers who will grade it later.

What was said in the Introduction about timing still applies; you should always learn something new without the added pressure of a time limit. This chapter will start with the basics of better writing; after a lot of practice, you'll be better acquainted with your new skills and you'll be able to use them better in a more improvisational manner. (In other words, you'll do better on the Analytical Writing Assessment essay.)

Read More!

Writing better comes from a better appreciation of the process and from better acquaintance with the best writing you can find. If you're a native English speaker, you learned to speak English not by reading a textbook, but by mimicking whoever raised you. Mimicry is still the best way to learn any new language (to which anyone who has spent any time as an exchange student will attest) as well as to improve your grasp on the language you currently speak.

Read More, Write Better

If you read more, you'll gain a better appreciation for the written word and, in turn, be able to mimic professional styles in your own writing.

So as you prepare to tell the world about yourself, spend as much extra time as you can reading the work of professional writers. Sources of the best reading material include:

- **Newspapers:** You'll want what you write on your applications to have the same formal character that most daily newspapers project. Granted, you'll want your writing style to have a bit more flair than the choppy, no-nonsense style of basic print journalism, but it's still an excellent example of writing that states its case once and moves on. (More on that later.)

- **Magazines:** You probably have a few favorite weeklies and monthlies, so be sure to read them before you bundle them all up for recycling. If you're feeling ambitious, buy a few copies of the more eggheady periodicals, such as *The Economist* (which, despite its misleading title, is not just about the economy).

- **Books:** If you're one of the lucky ones who have enough time to read books for pleasure (or you've just got enough self-discipline to turn off the TV), both fiction and nonfiction are wonderful ways to absorb various writing styles. Bear in mind, though, that some fiction can be wacky; your application writing should take on a more straightforward demeanor.

If you make the time to read more, you don't have to keep telling yourself, "Absorb the style. Absorb the style. Must learn to write better. Absorb. Absorb." At the risk of sounding new-age, your own writing style will evolve organically as long as you keep practicing.

YOUR APPROACH TO WRITING

If you're like most people about to embark on the GMAT/MBA experience, then:

- You haven't written much of anything since you graduated from college.

- The prospect of having to do all that writing on your applications either annoys or petrifies you. These are normal emotions, especially if you don't consider yourself much of a writer and are especially intimidated by the tyranny of the blank computer screen.

> You can begin to derive a little comfort from writing if you start to think of it as less of a burden and more of an opportunity to tell your readers about who you are and how you think.

Once you can adopt a more optimistic attitude toward arranging words on the page, you'll be surprised how your whole viewpoint will change for the better. Writing will become less work and more interesting. Of course, any several-step program worth a plugged nickel needs to have some sort of catchy mnemonic title for maximum effect. With that in mind, we give you...

THE FIVE F'S

Here's a basic five-step approach to formulating your thoughts and getting them on paper. No one expects you to get it all right the first time; the best essays, in fact, are the result of many drafts and rewrites. So find yourself a desk in a quiet, well-lit space, and get started.

Step 1: Free-Think

Brainstorming

This technique is a great way to get all of your ideas down on the page in an informal way.

Once you have your topic, start brainstorming. Let your mind generate ideas that you might want to incorporate into your essay, write them all down, and *don't censor anything*. You'll have plenty of time later to decide which ideas will fit into your overall theme and which ones are irrelevant.

Step 2: Form an Outline

To keep your essay from reading like a transcript of your stream of consciousness, you have to create an outline of what you're about to say. Organized essays are infinitely more pleasant to read, and essay readers will pick up on your sense of structure right away.

Now is your chance to choose among your brainstormed ideas. Organize them with some sense of order, and discard any of those that don't seem to fit in. This seems like an abstract practice, but you'll develop a feel for it.

Step 3: Flesh It Out

Most of us think in conversational English, not formal English. So why make it harder for yourself? Once you've got your outline, start writing as if you're explaining your thesis to a friend. You might even find that making an audio recording of your ideas (most smart phones and computers have a recording feature or app) is helpful; you can transcribe it later. Expressing your thoughts informally speeds the creative process and keeps your ideas more genuine.

Step 4: Formalize It

In Chapter 3, we talked about turning formal English into conversational English as you read. As you write, you should follow the same process, but in reverse. When you feel as though your essay's content is complete, let your formal style take over and turn your thoughts into a more polished piece of writing.

Step 5: Fine-Tune It

This is where the reviews and rewrites figure in. After you've written your first draft, enlist the opinions of people you trust. These people don't necessarily have to be superstar writers; in fact, the opinion of an average person is a better indicator of how well you expressed your points.

As you revise your essay, you should also keep an eye out for these basic style points that form the backbone of competent writing. They're not that complicated, and they'll go far to help you turn a mediocre piece into a solid effort.

STYLE POINTS

No person has the right to tell you which writing style to develop because how you write derives from who you are. The term style is hard to define; it could involve all of the points we're about to discuss, or none of them. Style is the difference between "It was the best of times, it was the worst of times" and "Times were great, but they were bad, too."

Your own style will evolve as you practice, but there are a few basic do's and don'ts that will increase an essay's value in the eyes of the reader.

The Elements of Style

Before you write a thing, get a copy of Strunk & White's *The Elements of Style*. *White* is E. B. White, who authored such children's books as *Charlotte's Web* and *Stuart Little* and was a contributor to *The New Yorker* for some 50 years. *Strunk* is Will Strunk Jr., White's English professor at Cornell. This little book is a brilliant source of information about proper grammar and word usage, and it extols above all else the virtue of brevity.

Let Every Word Tell

No primer on the virtues of writing is complete without some pompous Shakespearean quote, so here's one that's especially relevant. As Polonius told Claudius in *Hamlet*, "brevity is the soul of wit."

Pointless repetition drags too many essays into the morass of mediocrity. If you've made your point, don't linger on it. You'll be tempted to make it again, and you'll weaken your message. Many students make this mistake, especially during the AWA, if they can't think of anything else to say. If this happens, challenge yourself to come up with another supporting point. In his little book, Will Strunk voiced it this way:

> Vigorous writing is concise. A sentence should contain no unnecessary words, a paragraph no unnecessary sentences, for the same reason that a drawing should have no unnecessary lines and a machine no unnecessary parts. This requires not that the writer make all his sentences short, or that he avoid all detail and treat his subjects only in outline, but that every word tell.

Economic use of words is also important on your application essays if you've typed more than 1,000 words and you've been limited to 500. Should this happen, look for ideas that can be expressed in fewer words and eliminate the stuff that you don't need.

Word Variety

You don't have to have an encyclopedic vocabulary to vary your choice of words. And no one's asking you to study a thesaurus (although it's a good writing tool to have on hand). But adding a synonym now and then will help you avoid paragraphs like this:

> Communication is as important as creativity because no idea is worth anything unless it can be communicated to someone else. Communication starts at an early age, when we first learn to communicate with our parents. And let us not forget the quality of communication; an idea that is poorly communicated is not worth much more than one that is not communicated at all.

Without being too florid in your word choice, you can make a few strategic substitutions and turn that paragraph into this one:

> Communication is as important as creativity because no idea is worth anything unless **someone can convey it** to someone else. Communication starts at an early age, when we first learn to **talk** with our parents. And let us not forget the quality of communication; an idea that is poorly **expressed** is not worth much more than one that is not **expressed** at all.

It's okay to repeat a word once or twice within the same paragraph, especially a word like *communication* that has few appropriate synonyms. And it's also a good idea to use it twice in the same sentence (like *expressed* in the last sentence) for the sake of parallelism. But if you use the same word over and over and over and over and over (like now, for instance), your reader will likely be unimpressed.

Sentence Variety

As you write more, you'll also develop an appreciation for good rhythm. A paragraph that contains only identically constructed sentences sounds monotonous:

> The North Atlantic Treaty Organization's days are numbered. None of the group's 16 members can agree on the alliance's purpose. They also don't know how much power they have. NATO has been effective in the past. People are not convinced that previous triumphs merit more money.

See how dull and robotic that sounds? With some more descriptive words and a few connectors here and there, though, you can construct a paragraph with sentences that have different constructions and thus are more pleasant to read:

> The days of the North Atlantic Treaty Organization are numbered because none of the group's 16 members can agree on the alliance's purpose or the degree of power it can wield over transgressors. No matter how effective NATO has been in the past, few people (especially Americans) are convinced that previous successes merit further financing.

No matter how sophisticated the sentence structure is, you can always overdo a good thing:

> Although the general public fears genetically modified organisms, they serve a great purpose. Some scientists assert that these organisms are dangerous, but there is no tangible proof of this. Despite urgings that such organisms require less in terms of pesticides and herbicides to survive, newspapers print stories that scare readers…

Each sentence has a nice complex rhythm to it, but the rhythm of sentences is very similar. Therefore, you're not going to score too many style points here.

Distinguish Yourself

You may have heard stories about people who submit outlandish essays and are accepted to all the schools they want. One of the most circulated stories involves an essay question like this: "If you could conjure anyone, living or dead, real or fictional, to sit next to you on a first-class, nonstop flight from New York to Tokyo, who would it be and why?" One waggish applicant apparently answered that he'd prefer the seat to be left empty so that he could get some sleep and not feel compelled to chat the whole time.

Whether this actually happened is the subject of passionate debate, but there is truth to the idea that you don't always have to color within the lines. Remember the plight of the AWA readers: eight-hour shifts, three minutes per essay. And business school admissions people don't have it much better. If you can make your essays stand out (in a positive way, that is) from the thousands that are written each year, you'll definitely benefit.

There is a terribly insidious viewpoint among MBA applicants that you have to write what the readers want to hear. Too many students do just that, resulting in thousands and thousands of carbon copies of platitudes. Essays are your opportunity to advertise who you are; if you've got a sense of humor, show it off!

> When writing your essay, concentrate on what you want to say, not on what you think the reader wants to read.

Feel the Burn!

Your writing ability is a lot like a muscle. If you use it often and keep in shape, your ability and endurance will improve, but in disuse it will atrophy and wither. If you're preparing to take the GMAT on your own, make sure you write at least two essays per week. (GMAC's *The Official Guide for GMAT® Review* is jammed with essay topics, so you can spread them out over as long a period as you would like.) After a month or so, compare your most recent essays to the ones from the beginning. If you've kept up a brisk writing regimen, you should see improvements that you didn't even know were happening.

Two Is the Magic Number

If you're applying to business school, you should try to write at least two essays per week to practice.

THE ESSAY

The first thing you will be asked to do on the GMAT is to write an essay using a word-processing program. You will have 30 minutes for the essay. You will not be given the topic in advance, or even a choice of topics. (However, as we just mentioned, you can download a list of current topics from GMAC's website by clicking on the link for the Analytical Writing Assessment section.) The AWA is an Analysis of an Argument. The AWA appears first for a reason. The test writers know that taking a four-hour standardized exam can turn your brain to oatmeal. Therefore, it wants to give you the chance to write your essay when you're at your freshest.

How the AWA Works

The word-processing program used for the AWA is a bare-bones version of any program with which you may be familiar. It's basic, but it does have the only three functions you'll need: cut, paste, and undo. You can practice your word-processing skills in any standard software program (such as Microsoft Word) or use the essay portion of the GMATPrep® software.

The screen you'll see on your monitor looks like this:

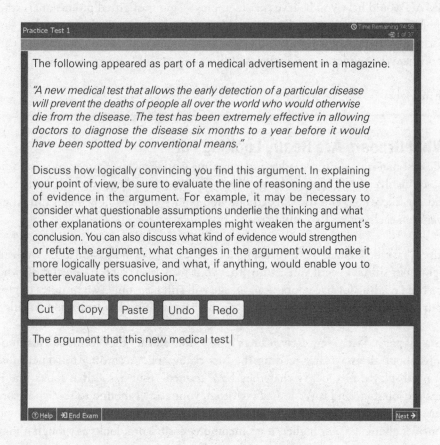

The statement for you to assess will appear at the top of the screen, followed by the instructions. Just type in your response and submit it within the 30-minute time limit you have for the essay.

How the AWA Is Scored

The AWA is scored separately, and you will receive this score along with your official score report from GMAC. Essays have two readers, one of which may be an automated essay-scoring engine, and are scored on a scale from 0 to 6, in half-point increments. The average of the two scores is your final score. If the two scores differ by more than a point, a third reader evaluates the essay to determine the final score.

Essay readers look for the following qualities in an exemplary essay response:

- a fully developed position based on insightful reasons and/or persuasive examples

- well-organized ideas

- superior control of language, diction, and syntactic variety

GMAC would have you believe that it employs legions of gifted professionals who carefully pore over all the AWA essays. After all, only the most educated palate can distinguish fine wine from jug wine, and only a seasoned veteran wordsmith can appreciate the subtleties and nuances of fine prose.

Yeah, right.

What Graders Are Really Looking For

The vast majority of essay graders are part-time workers whose careers at least indirectly involve the field of writing. Most of them are college teaching assistants and the like who could use the extra money. And you know how much time they spend on each essay? Two minutes.

Yup. That's it. Graders have to read some 30 essays per hour, and they work in eight-hour shifts. Even if you assume that your reader isn't a bleary-eyed mess who has been reading for five hours straight, she will still have only two minutes to give your essay a quick skim to determine your writing style and organizational skills.

As a matter of fact, a few essay readers have admitted that they formulate assumptions about an essay after reading the first paragraph. According to some, most essays display a mediocrity that they have termed "four-ness." If it looks like it gets the job done and isn't too badly written, your essay is bound to receive a score between 4 and 5. If the essay makes a wonderful first impression, the grader will consider giving it a 5 or higher; if it's incomprehensible or it looks as though it may have been written by a monkey, you'll get a 2 or worse.

Because of the short time span for review, readers are really looking for an essay that:

- is long enough to look thorough

- doesn't ramble aimlessly

- addresses the question and supplies good supporting points

- is easy and interesting to read quickly

As you might imagine, there are ways to make sure your readers see what they're looking for right away.

GENERAL ESSAY TIPS

There are many secrets for success on the AWA regardless of the subject matter. Here are some overall tips for how to get a high score on the essay.

1. Brush Up on Your Typing

Before the GMAT was computer-based, all AWA essays were handwritten in pencil, and business schools received reduced-size photocopies of every essay. Needless to say, reading these was a real hassle—especially when you consider the limited time graders have to make heads or tails of what you're trying to say. In fact, some graders have admitted that GMAT takers could score points just by making their essays neat enough to be read easily.

All essays are now composed at the keyboard, so handwriting is no longer an issue. (This makes the AWA readers happy.) If you can't type well on a standard QWERTY keyboard, now is the time to learn. Writing under pressure is tense enough; you don't want to add to the headache by hunting around for the right letter. And remember that your essay will also be checked for spelling mistakes (which doesn't seem fair because the writing software doesn't have spellcheck). These mistakes are not supposed to affect your grade, but you will be penalized if your misspellings are so numerous as to make your essay too difficult to read.

If you can type the following in about 15 seconds without looking at your keyboard, you'll do just fine:

```
The quick brown fox jumps over the lazy dog.
```

This sentence is well known to anyone who has taken a touch-typing class, because it contains all 26 letters in the alphabet. If you have access to a computer, use it when you practice writing essays. You'll be better prepared for the real thing.

2. Follow the First Two F's—Free-Think and Form an Outline

You don't have time for a lot of revision and polishing, but the first two F's from the previous chapter are still important on the AWA because organization is so crucial. You get 30 minutes to write the essay; spend the first ten minutes or so thinking about what you'll say and how you're going to say it. Read the essay topic once or twice and start thinking of pertinent thoughts. No matter how stupid they might seem at first glance, *don't censor anything*.

Brainstorming is also helpful if you read the topic and have absolutely no idea how you feel about it. Given the stress of the process, it's rather common for a student to draw a complete blank and have a panic attack. If this happens, get a hold of yourself. (Sure, that's easy to say now.) Once you get a few ideas out of your head and onto your scratch paper, you'll have a better chance of formulating an opinion that you can discuss in a few paragraphs.

Then comes the outline, which is the most significant element in an essay's creation. If you spend the time to stitch all the elements into a viable structure, the essay will be much easier to compose. And because graders love organization and have so little time to look for it, make life easy for them. Every introduction you write should contain a sentence that looks something like the following:

```
I believe that [insert thesis here] for the following [insert number
here] reasons.
```

Once your reader sees that, she knows you took the time to organize your thoughts before you started typing. This structure jumps out at the reader right away, and it makes a good impression. You can make your outline even easier to follow by numbering your supporting points paragraph by paragraph, like this:

Last sentence of intro paragraph:

```
Pittsburgh, Pennsylvania, is the best place in the world
to live for the following three reasons.
```

First sentence of paragraph 2:

```
First, Pittsburgh boasts the cultural opportunities of a
big city like Chicago or New York, but it maintains the
charm of a much smaller community.
```

First sentence of paragraph 3:

```
Second, Pittsburgh's climate features the variety of
all four seasons, but its unique geographical position
helps temper the Midwest's bitter winters and keeps it
mild in the summer.
```

First sentence of paragraph 4:

```
And finally, Pittsburgh's small market keeps its sports
teams from signing obnoxious, overpriced athletes who fa-
vor wealth over the game they play.
```

3. Go for the Bookends First

The paragraphs that will make the biggest impression on your AWA reader are the first and last—affectionately known as the bookends. Because you have to use a word processor, why not use it to its greatest advantage? Most students start out okay on essays, but they tend to finish hurriedly when they see the time dwindling. Starting out with the bookends ensures that your essay will finish strong (especially if you take the time to read the whole thing at the end—see tip 10). If you can knock your reader's socks off with a strong introduction and conclusion, these paragraphs will stick in the reader's mind as she calculates your grade.

Leave a Lasting Impression

The first and last paragraphs of your essay are crucial, because they're the ones the essay readers are most likely to remember.

There is a saying that the easiest way to walk a straight line is to keep your eyes fixed on a faraway object on the horizon and walk toward it. That's the case with essays as well. If you know what you're going to conclude before you start typing, your essay will be much more cohesive. You would be surprised at the percentage of writers who just start typing and rambling when the timer for the AWA starts, hoping that their theses will make more sense as time elapses.

4. Acknowledge the Other Side

Your stance on a particular subject becomes much more compelling if you show an understanding for how supporters of the other side of the subject feel. This illustrates that you've considered both approaches to an issue (whether or not you actually have) and can talk about the subject in an informed manner.

Use of this technique will involve some contrary trigger words, like the following:

```
Macro-Pute should be congratulated for the overwhelming
success that its operating system enjoys, but there
are four reasons why its monopolistic practices should be
curbed.

Although Madonna has millions of devoted fans worldwide,
I believe that her music heralds the end of Western civi-
lization as we know it for the following ten reasons.

While many analysts blame North Korea for the current
standoff with its neighbor to the south, people should not
be so quick to exculpate South Korea.
```

Once you have referred to those who don't share your opinion, however, don't spend any more time defending them. Your primary goal is to support your opinion, and time is limited.

5. Refer to Books and/or Current Events

As mentioned earlier, reading a lot is a great way to help you write better. But keeping up with your reading has a dual purpose. If you use current events or literary references in your writing, (1) you have many new premises on which to rely and (2) your readers will value your opinions all the more because you'll appear well read.

6. Aim for Length

Readers can't help themselves. If they look at an essay that's short, they will assume (subconsciously or otherwise) that the thesis is inadequately developed. Right away, your ceiling will be lowered to a maximum score of 4. On the other hand, if you go on and on with no concern for brevity or conciseness, your essay will appear verbose and rambling. Neither too short nor too long is what will get you a high score. Your goal should be to write at least four or five good-sized paragraphs. With practice this target will become easier to achieve.

Remember:
The directions ask you to support your conclusion based on experience, observations, or reading. The Analysis of Argument essay is concerned with how you analyze the information that they have given you.

7. Cater to a Short Attention Span

If you've had any experience writing essays in high school and college, you know that one of the best ways to make an essay look longer is to use lots of paragraphs. Padding your essay's length has a dual effect, though—it also makes the essay easier to read. Think of reading comprehension passages; each new paragraph offers you a chance to rest before you begin reading again. Look at these two short passages:

Passage 1:

To the north of Massachusetts, most of what is now New Hampshire and Maine was granted in 1622 by the Council for New England to Sir Ferdinando Gorges and Captain John Mason and their associates. In 1629, Gorges and Mason divided their territory at the Piscataqua River; Mason took the southern side, which he named New Hampshire. The first settlement appeared at Rye in 1623, the same year as the genesis of what would become the Massachusetts Bay Colony. It remains uncertain whether Rye was deserted or merged into another colony founded at nearby Strawberry Bank, which was later renamed Portsmouth. In the 1630s, Puritan immigrants began filtering in, and in 1638 the Rev. John Wheelwright founded Exeter. Maine consisted of a few scattered and small settlements. Most of these were fishing villages centered around the main commercial hub of York. Like each of the other offshoots of Massachusetts, the Maine territory lacked a charter and maintained its autocracy until 1691, when Maine was officially incorporated into Massachusetts.

Compare

Which passage is easier to read?

Passage 2:

To the north of Massachusetts, most of what is now New Hampshire and Maine was granted in 1622 by the Council for New England to Sir Ferdinando Gorges and Captain John Mason and their associates. In 1629, Gorges and Mason divided their territory at the Piscataqua River; Mason took the southern side, which he named New Hampshire.

The first settlement in New Hampshire appeared at Rye in 1623, the same year as the genesis of what would become the Massachusetts Bay Colony. It remains uncertain whether Rye was deserted or merged into another colony founded at nearby Strawberry Bank, which was later renamed Portsmouth. In the 1630s, Puritan immigrants began filtering in, and in 1638 the Rev. John Wheelwright founded Exeter.

Maine consisted of a few scattered and small settlements. Most of these were fishing villages centered around the main commercial hub of York. Like each of the other offshoots of Massachusetts, the Maine territory lacked a charter and maintained its autocracy until 1691, when Maine was officially incorporated into Massachusetts.

Breaking a passage up into paragraphs makes the text look less immense and ponderous, and the same goes for your essay. It also makes the very important impression that you're not likely to repeat yourself as you make your points.

8. Say It Once and Move On

The most common trap into which the average essay writer falls is repetition. It may be because you could only think of one pertinent thought and figured you'd do your best to string it out until it looked long enough. This is akin to adding water to soup so that it will feed more people. All you have is just a big vat of watery soup.

More often, repetition comes from the stress of the time limit. Once you decide that you have a good point to make, you want to emphasize it by saying it again, only in different words. (Some writers don't even bother to change the words, and that's an even worse transgression.) Don't do this.

9. Be Resolute

Your job as a writer is to compel your reader to share your beliefs. Therefore, it's very important not to use wishy-washy words. If you don't seem convinced of your viewpoint, how can you persuade others?

The best examples of well-written, compelling essays are in your local paper's opinion page. Each of the writers who appear there is a professional writer whose job it is to sway you to his or her way of thinking. A lead editorial in a newspaper might read something like this:

> Despite arguments that the flaws in the maritime treaty have been remedied, the president should in no way endorse the newest version. The Navy and the U.S. shipping industry support its ratification because it brings order to the nebulous business of navigational rights in international waters. This codification would be more than offset, however, by the morass of bureaucracy it would cause in the effort to bring fishing rights, deep-sea mining, and global pollution under the control of one supra-national governing body. If the treaty reaches the president's desk, he should refuse to sign it.

After you've read this paragraph, there's no doubt of the author's viewpoint. Your writing should be just as sure of itself. Therefore, minimize the use of words such as

Don't Be Wishy-Washy

Be assertive in your writing and make your points clear. Instead of writing "This might be a problem," write "This *is* a problem."

would, might, and *possibly,* and replace them with stronger words such as *is* and *will.* Don't worry; you won't lose points for sounding too liberal or too conservative.

WRONG

This *would be* a major problem…

Single mothers *might* benefit from lower taxes…

Stock prices *are possibly* too overvalued…

RIGHT

This *is* a major problem…

Single mothers *will* benefit from lower taxes…

Stock prices *are* too overvalued…

---

10. Save Time for a Final Read

Finally, even though the computer gives you 30 minutes to create literary magic, you really should use only 28 or so. As you practice these essays, you may notice that you lose flow if you work on different parts of your essay at different times. Ideally, you should save a couple of minutes to give your essay a final read-through looking for typos, grammatical glitches, and any other stuff that doesn't make any sense.

Feel the Burn (Again)!

There is some practice material in this chapter, but it's also helpful to go right to the source for practice essay topics. In the back of GMAC's *Official Guide,* as well as on the GMAC website, you will find a list of essay topics. If you want to keep up steady improvement, make yourself write at least two essays per week. To keep things as spontaneous as possible, open up to a page of topics, close your eyes, and point to one. Then, set the timer for 30 minutes and start typing.

The best way to gauge your improvement is to pair up with another student. Write your essays and then swap them with your partner's, and give each other frank criticism (positive and negative).

And by all means, be patient! If you're not used to writing very often, it might take a while before your essays show a lot of improvement. If you keep practicing and you have a friend or colleague who is willing to work with you, you will get better. If you feel as though you're not making much progress, go back and read the suggestions for becoming a better writer and try to find some inspiration there.

If All Else Fails

As mentioned at the beginning of this chapter, the AWA is not going to keep you out of business school. The AWA essay is indeed another tool to help business schools evaluate your verbal skills, but no admissions officer will look at a GMAT report sheet and think: "Hmm. This applicant looks perfect for our program. Too bad about that 3.5 on the AWA."

The AWA is not worth fretting over. Just take your time, do the best you can, and use the first 30 minutes of the GMAT to get ready for the rest of the exam (which is much more important). With that in mind, let's look at some specific techniques.

ANALYSIS OF AN ARGUMENT

Analyzing arguments on the AWA is a much different exercise that is closely related to answering the multiple-choice critical reasoning questions. (If you haven't yet read that chapter, you might want to do that now. Many of the terms we'll refer to here are discussed there in much greater detail.)

For your Analysis of an Argument essay, you'll be shown an author's conclusion and one or two premises on which the conclusion is based. The instructions for the Argument essay will always look like this:

> Discuss how logically convincing you find this argument. In explaining your point of view, be sure to evaluate the line of reasoning and use of evidence in the argument. For example, it may be necessary to consider what questionable assumptions underlie the thinking and what other explanations or counterexamples might weaken the argument's conclusion. You can also discuss what kind of evidence would strengthen or refute the argument, what changes in the argument would make it more logically persuasive, and what, if anything, would enable you to better evaluate its conclusion.

Now that you've read these once, don't bother ever reading them again. You'll waste valuable time.

WHAT THE DIRECTIONS MEAN

Your job is to assess whether the logic the author uses to arrive at his conclusion is valid based on the following criteria:

- Do the premises he cites support the conclusion adequately?

- Are the assumptions he relies on valid?

- Is it possible to interpret the premises a different way and arrive at a different conclusion?

- What other information is missing?

That's it. It's just like using the CPA Model. And there's one very important thing to remember about the Argument essay: *Your opinion of the author's conclusion is utterly irrelevant.* It's not so much what he says; it's how he says it. For example, here is a stripped-down version of a student essay for an AWA Argument:

> The superintendent of a large residential property indicated that the termite problem has been brought under control because he has sprayed the basement.

WRONG

> The author is correct to condemn the increase in the termite population of most American urban centers. These vermin have plagued humans for centuries, spreading disease and making the world we leave for our children into a dirty, disgusting ball of filth. Traps should be set in every square foot of every building on the planet in order to stem the tide of this reign of terror…

RIGHT

> The superintendent's conclusion that he has solved the termite problem in his building is flawed because it relies on the dubious assumption that all the termites in the building are in the basement. Further, the super assumes that the termites will not somehow recognize the spray and avoid it. And we also don't know whether the spray will always work properly…

The first ("Wrong") response is inappropriate here. Your reader doesn't care what you think about termite control. He wants you to assess the way in which the author arrives at the conclusion. The second ("Right") response fits the bill; the writer asserts that the author's concluding statement is not defensible because the assumptions are dubious.

There's Always Something Wrong

Regardless of what the argument says, your essay can never begin like this:

```
The author's conclusion is completely valid in every
way. I came away from her argument completely convinced
of its authenticity as a piece of rock-solid logic…
```

The AWA Arguments are terse little statements with at most two or three supporting points. There's no way that anyone could come to an unassailable conclusion with so few premises. In fact, you can start out every Argument essay you ever write with a sentence along these lines:

```
The author has come to a faulty conclusion that [insert con-
clusion here] because she relies on X premises that are
insufficient and Y assumptions that are dubious at best.
```

Some arguments will seem plausible at first, and you will be tempted to agree with the author at some point. It's still okay to acknowledge whatever good points the author makes, but look hard for the holes in the logic. The author always misses something, and your overall tone should be negative. Let's look at a few sample topics:

Argument 1:

> *The following appeared in a newspaper editorial.*
>
> *The global entertainment company Zipney has signed an agree-
> ment with the government of the eastern European county of
> Magdania to build a Zipneyland theme park there within the
> next five years. Because Zipneyland parks in Los Angeles and
> London attract between three and six million tourists per year,
> the years of waning tourism in Magdania are clearly over.*

Problems: Here's a classic "argument by analogy" in which the items being compared are not necessarily comparable. The author assumes that the Magdanian Zipneyland will attract the same number of tourists as those in London and Los Angeles, but that's not necessarily true. London and L.A. are big tourist hubs already; what if Magdania doesn't have the same appeal? Magdania is in eastern Europe, an area that might not espouse Western culture as well as the other two cities do.

There's also the issue of the quality of the park. Will it be exactly the same as the other two? Have Zipney's revenues stayed strong, or has a backlash against the Zipney-fication of society pared profits enough so that Zipney will cut a few corners here and there?

Argument 2:

The following appeared in a campus newsletter.

For years, student activists have been campaigning for a two-day fall break in October to give students a chance to relax and catch up with their studies. This year, the administration will institute such a break for the first time, occurring on the Thursday and Friday before Halloween. Given the activists' success, their desire to have fall break extended to a full week will certainly be fulfilled.

Problems: The author assumes that the fall break was instituted because of the activism, but we don't know if that's true. To weaken a causal argument, suggest an alternate cause: Maybe the fall break was a monetary decision, or perhaps the faculty finally decided that they wanted the break as well. If the students didn't bring about the break in the first place, they probably won't be able to extend it.

Even if the causal relationship does exist, the author also assumes that you can get whatever you want as long as you push for it. The administration might feel as though two days is fine but that a week is too long an interruption. Is there a spring break? There might be some provision in the school's charter that prohibits more than one week-long break per year.

Argument 3:

The following appeared in a finance magazine.

At the annual SpoonCorp shareholders' meeting in Alaska this year, several shareholders expressed their objection to the company's imminent merger with archrival LadleWorks. Because these individuals own only a collective 15 percent of the company's stock, SpoonCorp's board of directors should go ahead with the merger as planned.

Problems: Here's where the test writers like to sway us with numbers. The author assumes that the other 85 percent of the shareholders support this merger. We don't know if that's true. The other shareholders might not have been able to come to the meeting; the Alaskan site might have been too remote. It's also possible that the objectors may have been sent as representatives of those people who couldn't come. Thus, the 15 percent figure is misleading.

It's the Author's Fault

Notice that in the analysis of all three arguments, the problem was the author and his logic, not his conclusion. Your job is to tear the author apart. Problems the author will usually display include the following:

- insufficient premises

- missing premises

- wrong assumptions

- supporting data that need to be clarified

Making the author the culpable party keeps your attention on his logic and prevents you from addressing the conclusion itself.

Don't Forget the Context Line!

The first line you read when your essay begins is a reference to the publication in which the argument appeared:

- *The following appeared as part of a memorandum to all members of an exclusive club.*

- *The following is an excerpt from the promotional literature for a new video game.*

- *The following appeared in the editorial section of an entertainment magazine.*

Most people gloss right over this piece of information and jump right into the question, and that's a mistake. The test writers like to disguise this line as a throwaway introduction, but the source of the argument can often be as important as the argument itself. You might find an author's statement that predicts the outcome of an election very persuasive until you look up and realize that the writer is marketing director at a dog food company. What evidence is there that someone who hawks Rover's dinner knows anything about politics? That's the sort of thing you want to address in your essay.

Practice AWA Argument Essays

Try writing answers to each of these five Argument essays. There are no "right" answers, obviously. Show your responses to someone whose opinion you respect. By following the tips we've outlined in this chapter, you are sure to do well.

A. *The following appeared in an American medical journal.*

   A new study has shown that cardiac patients can reduce their chances of heart attacks by taking a reduced-potency aspirin pill once per day. Therefore, now would be a good time to invest in Malatet Pharmaceutical Corp., which happens to be Europe's largest producer of reduced-potency aspirin.

   Discuss how logically convincing you find this argument. In explaining your point of view, be sure to evaluate the line of reasoning and use of evidence in the argument. For example, it may be necessary to consider what questionable assumptions underlie the thinking and what other explanations or counterexamples might weaken the argument's conclusion. You can also discuss what kind of evidence would strengthen or refute the argument, what changes in the argument would make it more logically persuasive, and what, if anything, would enable you to better evaluate its conclusion.

B. *The following appeared in a media trade paper.*

   The average person who is 54 years of age or older watches about 38 hours of TV per week, while people between the ages of 18 and 54 watch only 21 hours per week. Because the American population is aging rapidly, advertisers would be better served to target their marketing to an older audience.

   Discuss how logically convincing…

C. *The following appeared in a promotional flyer.*

   In the three years since President Bilkus has been in office, the number of violent crimes in urban areas has decreased by 35 percent. During the administration of President Bilkus's predecessor, crime rose at an average rate of 10 percent per year. Thus, Americans who want to see crime reduced even further should vote to re-elect President Bilkus this fall.

   Discuss how logically convincing…

D. *The following appeared in an internal memo of a small Internet company.*

   When Alice's Restaurant started making its waiters and busboys wear uniforms, employee tardiness decreased and tips increased. Thus, our productivity will rise if we impose a dress code on our employees.

   Discuss how logically convincing…

E. *The following appeared in a shareholder's prospectus of a large, man-ufacturing conglomerate.*

Since 1980, golf courses have provided land developers with the most consistent source of revenue. Therefore, our company should trans-form the 200 acres of lakeside wilderness into a golf course.

Discuss how logically convincing…

The Good, the Bad, and the Ugly

Let's revisit the first argument topic and assess some sample responses. Here's the argument again:

The following appeared in an American medical journal.

A new study has shown that cardiac patients can reduce their chance of heart attacks by taking a reduced-potency aspirin pill once per day. Therefore, now would be a good time to invest in Malatet Phar-maceutical Corp., which happens to be Europe's largest producer of reduced-potency aspirin.

Discuss how logically convincing…

Response 1:

This argument is poorly arranged. It uses assumptions and premises that are not useful and is therefore not very strong.

For example, how do we know that this study is a good one? Maybe the scientists didn't know what they were doing and their information is incorrect. After all, people are capable of making mistakes and experiment-ing is always subject to margins of error. It's not a good idea to believe this argument until you get to know more about the scientists and the other work that they have done. It is important to know that they have histories of excellence in their fields and are able to determine when the tests they have performed are accu-rate. There have been many examples in the past of scientific failures, and this could be another one.

Also, it is important to know about "reduced-potency" aspirin. We need to know how "reduced" the potency is and test it with aspirin that is more po-tent. Is it possible for a "high-potency" aspirin to have an even better effect? Because if the company makes "reduced potency" aspirin but not "high-potency" aspirin, the company could be in trouble.

In conclusion, this argument cant be a good one because we don't know if the study was propery conducted and that "high-potency" aspirn isn't better for you.

Assessment: Frankly, this person didn't have much to say, and it shows. From the get-go, it's clear that this writer was floundering around looking for a point to make. It happens sometimes. You read a topic, think to yourself that you have no idea what to write, and panic quickly sets in. Unfortunately, essay readers can detect this a mile away, and they don't have to read much to know that there isn't much content here. The lack of word variety is a problem (some form of the word *potent* appears six times in the third paragraph), and the misspellings toward the end make it obvious that the writer ran out of time. This one gets a 3 at best.

The best way to guard against brain power outages like this one is to practice as many essays as you can. You develop a way to get at least something interesting on the page in the half hour you've been given. Also, remember that a half hour is a long time. (If you're unconvinced, sit on the floor and do absolutely nothing for a half an hour.) If at first you draw a blank, be patient with yourself and try not to freak out. If you relax, something will probably come to you, and you'll be able to salvage your efforts.

Response 2:

Human behavior tells us that this argument is flawed on many levels because it relies so much on assumptions about how people will react to the news of this new study. There is an announcement that a weaker form of aspirin can guard against heart disease, and right away we are to believe that Malatet Pharmaceuticals will make a lot of money. This author forgets that reduced-potency aspirin won't be successful unless people trust the product and buy it over and over again. We humans are suspicious by nature, and it takes a lot to win over our trust when it comes to what we put in our bodies. What do we know about this Malatet company? It obviously chose a clever name because *mal a la tete* means "headache" in French, but that isn't enough. Humans need and appreciate humor in life, but we need more than just whimsy from drug companies because our health is serious business. First, Malatet has to persuade us to buy its products, and then to buy its stock. Both are a tall order by themselves; together, it is an even more formidable challenge. The author also assumes that when we buy the aspirin, we will actually have the self-discipline to take it regularly. Humans can be lazy and forgetful, and this aspirin is unlikely to have the effect it portrays itself to have if no one bothers to take it. It's impossible to trust this argument. The fact that Malatet is a European company is also especially deceptive because Americans often associate Europe with cutting-edge medicinal professionals, especially for its prowess among Swiss neurosurgeons. It is tempting to group this company with the many other fine European institutions, but sometimes the exception does not prove the rule. We humans must be alert and not jump to any unlikely conclusions.

Assessment: Well, now. This person clearly has a few mistrust issues. The subject matter that this writer has chosen might seem a little weird, but there are a few grains of sense within. For example, it is true that people might not be inclined to start taking aspirin as a preventative medicine just because of a new study. The word has to get out that it's safe, and then people have to decide that it's an important thing to do.

The main problem with this essay is that it's all one paragraph, and it falls at the feet of the reader with a large, ponderous thud. If this writer had chosen to break the essay up into smaller paragraphs, he might have scored a few points for originality. But most of the essay is off on its own tangent, it doesn't appear very organized, and the reader will resent the lack of paragraph structure. Depending on the reader's mood, the score will fall somewhere between 3 and 4.

Response 3:

This argument urging investors to start buying shares of Malatet Pharmaceutical is unpersuasive because it relies on too many assumptions that aren't necessarily true. There are three areas that merit further explanation before this author should receive any degree of credibility.

My first problem with this argument is the author's enthusiasm for the company just because it's the market leader in one product. Is it ahead of the game because it's the best, or are its competitors likely to overtake it once they hear about this new study? The author could enhance his position by showing that the company is managed well and will stay on top if the market for reduced-potency aspirin grows.

This brings me to my second point: the market itself. The author says that Malatet is the largest maker of reduced potency aspirin in Europe, but we know nothing about Europe's relationship with the global market. Before we can send Malatet any money, we need to know if its business extends to larger markets in North America or Asia. If there are competitors in these areas with whom Malatet cannot compete, then it's unlikely that Malatet will enjoy any long-term growth. I would also like to know how big the European market is and how many European competitors there are. If Malatet is virtually unchallenged in its field, I'll invest; if there's another company breathing down Malatet's neck, then I'll probably pass.

Finally, I take issue with the source of this article, which appeared in a medical journal. I can see how this publication would know about medicine, but do its editors know anything about investing? Any evidence that this journal has shown some financial acumen in the past would strengthen this argument greatly.

There are just too many holes in this argument, so it is
difficult to take the author seriously. Unless some further evidence surfaces in each of the three areas described above, the premises that are presented are insufficient proof that the conclusion is viable.

Assessment: This is the argument you want to write. It is organized well, it
describes three problems the argument has and describes them in detail, and it
suggests ways to make the argument more sound. The grammar is good, the word
choice is variant and expressive, and the tone is firm and resolute. This writer also
makes good use of the context line by asserting that medical journalism and stock-
picking aren't related.

There are a few minor points to add because no essay is perfect. There are some
people who will tell you not to write in the first person as this person did, and he
mixes up his I's and his we's. But if you can crank out an argument essay like this,
you won't have much of a problem getting a 5.5 or a 6.

Chapter 5
Integrated
Reasoning

In 2012, the GMAT gained a new section called Integrated Reasoning. This chapter reviews the basics of the new section, including a run down on all four new question types. We've also included a chapter that explains some strategies that will help you handle these questions. Finally, this book includes two complete Integrated Reasoning sections with explanations so that you can practice.

MEET THE INTEGRATED REASONING SECTION

The Integrated Reasoning section is 30 minutes long. You'll see it as the second section of your test. Officially, there are only 12 questions, which sounds pretty great. However, most of those questions have multiple parts. So, for example, a Table Analysis question—one of the new question types we'll discuss—usually has three statements that you need to evaluate. So, your answer to the question really consists of three separate responses. For the entire section, you'll actually need to select approximately 28 different responses.

Integrated Reasoning Is Not Adaptive

Unlike the Math and Verbal sections, the Integrated Reasoning section is not adaptive. So, you won't see harder questions if you keep answering questions correctly. That's good news because it means that you'll more easily be able to focus your attention on the current question rather than worrying whether you got the previous question right!

Test writers refer to non-adaptive sections as linear. Pacing for a linear section is different from the pacing that we reviewed for the adaptive Math and Verbal sections.

For Integrated Reasoning, pacing is motivated by two general principles.

Pacing Guidelines

1. Work the easier parts of each question first. As you'll see, many Integrated Reasoning questions call for more than one response per question. Work the easier parts of each question first.

2. Don't get stubborn. With so many questions to answer in only 30 minutes, the Integrated Reasoning section can seem very fast paced. Spending too much time on one question means that you may not get to see all of the questions. Sometimes it's best to guess and move on.

Integrated Reasoning Scores

The Integrated Reasoning section is scored on a scale from 1 to 8 in one-point increments. While GMAC has not released too many details about the way in which they calculate the score for this section of the test, there are two key facts to keep in mind.

- **Scoring is all or nothing.** Most Integrated Reasoning questions include multiple parts. To get credit for the question, you must select the correct response for each part. For example, Table Analysis questions generally include three statements that you must evaluate. If you select the wrong response for even one of these statements, you get no credit for the entire question.

- **There are experimental questions.** GMAC has stated that the Integrated Reasoning section contains experimental questions that do not count toward your score. They have not, however, stated how many experimental questions there are in the section. It's likely that two or three of the twelve questions in the section are experimental. If you find a question particularly difficult or time-consuming, it is worthwhile to remember that the question could be experimental.

To score the section, GMAC first calculates a raw score. You get one point for each non-experimental question that you get completely correct. Then, your raw score is converted to the 1 to 8 Integrated Reasoning scaled score.

There's a Calculator

There's an onscreen calculator available for the Integrated Reasoning section. The calculator is not available, however, for the Math section. For the Math section, you still need to perform any necessary calculations by hand.

The calculator for the Integrated Reasoning section is relatively basic. There are buttons to perform the four standard operations: addition, subtraction, multiplication, and division. In addition, buttons to take a square root, find a percent, and take a reciprocal round out the available functions. There are also buttons to store and recall a value in the calculator's memory.

Use a Calculator

You are allowed to use a calculator for all Integrated Reasoning questions.

To use the calculator, you'll need to open it by clicking on the 'calculator' button in the upper left corner of your screen. The calculator will generally open in the middle of your screen but you can move it around so that you can see the text of the problem or the numbers on any charts or graphs that are part of the question. You can enter a number into the calculator either by clicking on the onscreen number buttons or by typing the number using the keyboard.

Here's what the calculator looks like:

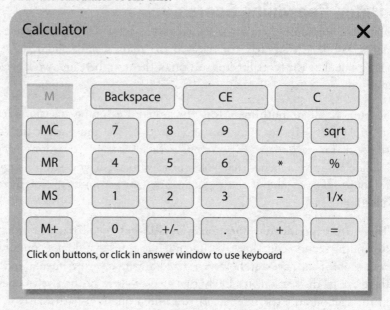

For the most part, the keys on the onscreen calculator work as you might expect. However, a few keys may not work as expected. Oddly enough, that's particularly true if you are used to using a more sophisticated calculator. So, here are few tips about using some of the calculator keys:

MC	MC is the memory clear key. Use this key to wipe out any values that you have stored in the calculator's memory.
MR	MR is the memory recall key. Use this key to return any value that you have stored in the memory to the calculation area. For example, if you want to divide the number currently on your screen by the number in the memory, you would enter the key sequence / MR =.
MS	MS is the memory store key. Use this key to store the number currently on the screen in the calculator's memory.
M+	M+ is the memory addition key. Use this key to add the current onscreen number to the number in the calculator's memory. For example, if 2 is stored in the calculator's memory and 3 is on screen, then clicking M+ will result in 5 being stored in the calculator's memory.
Backspace	Backspace is used to clear the last digit entered. Use this key to correct mistakes when entering numbers without clearing the entire number. For example, if you entered 23 but meant to enter 25, click backspace then enter 5.

CE CE is the clear entry button. Use this button to correct a mistake when entering a longer calculation without starting over. For example, suppose you entered 2*3+5 but you meant to enter 2*3+9. If you click on CE right after you enter 5, your screen will show 6, the result of 2*3, and you can now enter +9= to finish your intended calculation.

C C is the clear key. Use this key when you want to start a calculation over. In our previous example, if you click C after you enter 5, the intermediate result, 6, is not retained.

sqrt sqrt is the square root key. Click this key after you enter the number for which you want to take the square root. For example, if you enter 4 sqrt, the result 2 will display on your screen.

% % is the key used to take a percentage without entering a decimal. For example, if you want to take 20% of 400, enter 400*20%. The result 80 will now show on your screen. Note that you do not need to enter = after you click %.

1/x 1/x is used to take a reciprocal. Click this key after you enter the number for which you want to take the reciprocal. For example, the keystrokes 2 followed by 1/x produces the result 0.5 on your screen. Again, note that you do not need to enter = after you click 1/x.

Be sure that you thoroughly understand the way the keys for the onscreen calculator work so as to avoid errors and wasted time when you take your GMAT.

THE QUESTION TYPES

There are four question types in the Integrated Reasoning section. While some of these questions test critical reasoning skills similar to those tested on the Verbal section, these question types are also used to test the same type of content that is tested in the Math section. So, expect to calculate percents and averages. You'll also be asked to make a lot of inferences based on the data presented in the various charts, graphs, and tables that accompany the questions. So, the format of these questions may take some getting used to but the content will probably seem familiar.

Let's take a more detailed look at each of the new question types.

Calculator Practice Tip
When you practice for the Integrated Reasoning section, use a calculator similar to the calculator provided by GMAC. If you are doing online practice, use the onscreen calculator. If you are working problems from this book, use a basic calculator rather than that fancy calculator that you might still have from your high school or college math classes.

Table Analysis

Table Analysis questions present data in a table. If you've ever seen a spreadsheet—and really, who hasn't?—you'll feel right at home. Most tables have 5 to 10 columns and anywhere from 6 to 25 rows. You'll be able to sort the data in the table by each column heading. The sort function is fairly basic, however. If you're used to being able to sort first by a column such as state and then a column such as city to produce an alphabetical list of cities by state, you can't do that sort of sorting for these questions. You can sort only one column at a time.

Answers for This Question

We'll discuss how you can solve this Table Analysis question—including which strategies you can apply—in our second chapter devoted to the Integrated Reasoning section.

Here's what a Table Analysis question looks like:

Sort By   [Select...   ▼]   **1**

National Park		Visitors			Area	
Name	State	Number	% change	Rank	Acres	Rank
Grand Canyon	AZ	4,388,386	0.9	2	1,217,403	11
Yosemite	CA	3,901,408	4.4	3	791,266	16
Yellowstone	WY	3,640,185	10.5	4	2,219,791	8
Rocky Mtn.	CO	2,955,821	4.7	5	265,828	26
Zion	UT	2,665,972	-2.5	8	145,598	35
Acadia	ME	2,504,208	12.4	9	47,390	47
Bryce	UT	1,285,492	5.7	15	35,835	50
Arches	UT	1,014,405	1.8	19	76,519	42
Badlands	SD	977,778	4.7	22	242,756	28
Mesa Verde	CO	559,712	1.7	30	52,122	46
Canyonlands	UT	435,908	-0.1	36	337,598	23

The table above gives information for 2010 on total visitors and total acreage for 11 U.S. National Parks. In addition to the numbers of total visitors and total acreage for each National Park, the table also provides the percent increase or decrease over the total visitors for 2009 and the rank of the National Park for total visitors and total acreage in 2010. **4**

Each column of the table can be **2** sorted in ascending order by clicking on the Select button above the table and choosing, from the drop-down menu, the heading of the column on which you want the table to be sorted.

Consider each of the following **3** statements about these National Parks. For each statement, indicate whether the statement is true or false, based on the information provided in the table.

True False **5**
○ ○ The park that experienced the greatest percent increase in visitors from 2009 to 2010 also had the least total acreage.

○ ○ The park with the median rank by the number of visitors is larger than only one other park by acreage.

○ ○ Exactly 20% of the parks with ranks less than 40 by acreage and showing positive growth in visitors were in Utah (UT).

○ ○ The total number of visitors at Arches in 2009 was less than 1,000,000.

One thing you won't see on your screen when you take the Integrated Reasoning section are the circled numbers. We've added those so we can talk about different parts of a Table Analysis question. Here's what each circled number represents:

1   This is the Sort By drop-down box. When opened, you'll see all the different ways that you can sort the data in the table. In this table, for example, the possibilities are National Park Name, National Park State, Visitors Number, Visitors % change, Visitors Rank, Area Acreage, and Area Rank. You can always sort by every column.

2 These are the standard directions for a Table Analysis question. These directions are the same for every Table Analysis question. So, once you've read these directions once, you don't really need to bother reading them again.

3 These lines are additional directions. These additional directions are slightly tailored to the question. However, they'll always tell you to base your answers on the information in the table. They always tell you which type of evaluation you are to make for each statement: true / false, yes / no, agree / disagree, and so on. Again, you can probably get by without reading these most of the time.

4 These lines explain the table. Mostly, this information will recap the column headings from the table. Occasionally, you can learn some additional information by reading this explanatory text. For example, the explanatory text for this table states that the Visitors Number column is for 2010 and that % change column shows the change from 2009 to 2010.

5 These statements are the questions. Typically, there are four statements and you need to evaluate and select an answer for each. The good news is that you can answer these in any order. However, if you try to move to the next question without selecting a response for one or more statements, a pop up window opens to inform you that you have not selected an answer for all statements. You cannot leave any part of the question blank.

Read What You Need When You Need It

You may not need to read the explanatory information about the table (number 4) to evaluate the statements. You should study the column headings first. If you understand those, go straight to the statements. You can always go back and read the explanatory information if you need to.

If you've read through the statements, you may have noticed that the questions asked you to do things such as calculate a percentage or find a median. That's typical for Table Analysis questions. You've probably also realized just how helpful the sorting function can be in answering some questions.

Graphics Interpretation

Graphics Interpretation questions give you one chart, graph, or image and ask you to answer two questions based on that information. The questions are statements that include one drop-down box. You select your answer from the drop-down box to complete the statement.

Here's an example of a Graphics Interpretation question:

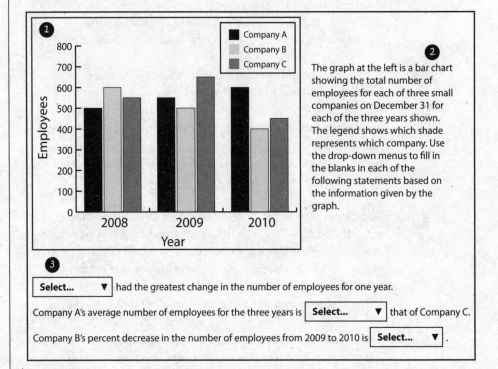

The graph at the left is a bar chart showing the total number of employees for each of three small companies on December 31 for each of the three years shown. The legend shows which shade represents which company. Use the drop-down menus to fill in the blanks in each of the following statements based on the information given by the graph.

3 Select... ▼ had the greatest change in the number of employees for one year.

Company A's average number of employees for the three years is Select... ▼ that of Company C.

Company B's percent decrease in the number of employees from 2009 to 2010 is Select... ▼ .

As with the Table Analysis questions, we've added the circled numbers so we can point out the different things that you'll see on your screen for a Graphics Interpretation question. Here's what each circled number represents:

1 The chart, graph, or image is always in the upper left of the screen. As shown here, the chart will take up a good deal of the screen. It will certainly be large and clear enough so that you can extract information from it. You can expect to see a variety of different types of charts or graphs including scatter plots, bar charts, line graphs, and circle (or pie) charts. For the most part, you'll see fairly standard types of graphs, however. Be sure to check out any labels on the axes as well as any sort of included legend.

2 These lines provide an explanation of the graph or chart. Mostly, you'll be told what the chart represents as well as what the individual lines, bars, or sectors may represent. Sometimes, you'll be given some additional information such as when measurements were made. For example, here you are told that the bars show the numbers of employees for each firm on December 31st of the year in question. This information is typically extraneous to answering the questions. The explanatory information always ends with the same line about selecting your answers from the drop-down menu.

These are the questions. Graphics Interpretation questions typically include two statements. You don't have to answer them in order, but you must answer them both to move on to the next question. Each statement is typically a single sentence with one drop-down menu. Each drop-down menu typically includes three to five answer choices. Choose that answer choice that makes the statement true.

Graphics Analysis questions mostly ask you to find relationships and trends for the data. You can also be asked to calculate percentage increases or decreases, averages, and medians.

Two-Part Analysis

Next up is the Two-Part Analysis question. In many ways, the Two-Part Analysis question is most similar to a standard math question. You'll typically be presented with a word problem that essentially has two variables in it. You'll need to pick an answer for each variable that makes some condition in the problem true.

Here's an example of a Two-Part Analysis question:

Two families buy new refrigerators using installment plans. Family A makes an initial payment of $750. Family B makes an initial payment of $1,200. Both families make five additional payments to pay off the balance. Both families pay the same amount for their refrigerators, including all taxes, fees, and finance charges. **1**

In the table below, identify a monthly payment, in dollars, for Family A and a monthly payment, in dollars, for Family B that are consistent with the installment plan described above. Make only one selection in each column. **2**

Family A	Family B	Monthly payment (in dollars)
○	○	50
○	○	80
○	○	120 **3**
○	○	160
○	○	250
○	○	300

As you might have surmised, we have once again added the circled numbers so we can described the different parts of the question. Here's what each circled number represents:

1 This first block of text is the actual problem. Here, you'll find the description of the two variables in the problem. You'll also find the condition that needs to be made true. As with any word problem, make sure that you read the information carefully. For these problems, you'll also want to make sure that you are clear about which information goes with the first variable and which information goes with the second.

2 This part of the problem tells you how to pick your answers. Mostly this part tells you to pick a value for column A and a value for column B based on the conditions of the problem. This part is mostly boilerplate text that varies slightly from problem to problem.

3 These are the answer choices. Two-Part Analysis questions generally have five or six answer choices. You choose only one answer choice for each column. It is possible that the same number is the answer for both columns. So, if that's what your calculations indicate, go ahead and choose the same number for both columns.

Most Two-Part Analysis questions can be solved using math that is no more sophisticated than simple arithmetic. There is one exception to that, however. While most Two-Part Analysis questions are math problems, you may see one that looks like a Critical Reasoning question. For these, you'll be give an argument and you'll need to do something like pick one answer that strengthens and one answer that weakens the argument. For these questions, just use the methods from our Critical Reasoning Chapter.

Multi-Source Reasoning

Finally, we come to the Multi-Source Reasoning question. Multi-Source Reasoning questions present information on tabs. The information can be text, charts, graphs, or a combination. In other words, GMAC can put almost anything on the tabs! The layout looks a little bit like Reading Comprehension because the tabbed information is on the left side of your screen while the right side shows the questions.

Here's an example of a Multi-Source Reasoning question:

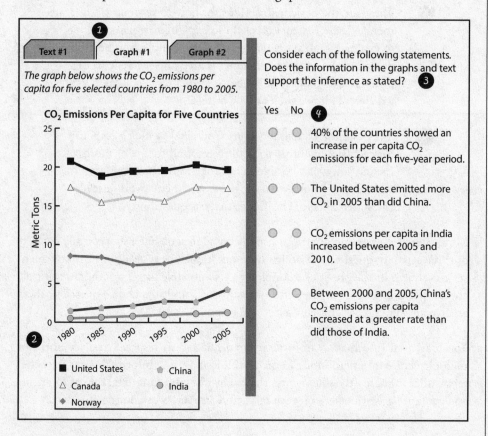

Again, we've added circled numbers to indicate the different parts of the question. Here's what each circled number represents:

1 The tabs appear across the top left of the screen. Some questions have two tabs and some, as in this example, have three. The tabs typically give you some sort of indication about what's on the tab. The currently selected tab is white while the unselected tabs are grey. GMAC can put almost anything on each tab including graphs, tables, charts, text, or some combination. It's a good idea to take a few seconds and get your bearings before attempting the questions. Make sure you know what is on each tab and how the information on one tab relates to information on the other tab or tabs.

2 The information for each tab appears on the left of the screen. In this case, the information is a graph. When you see a chart or graph, be sure to check out the axes. You'll also want to look for a legend or other information to help explain the information shown by the graph or chart. For tables, check out the column headings so as to better understand the table. Finally, don't neglect to read any supplied headings for the chart, graph, or table. Sometimes, that's all you need for the chart to make sense.

③ These are the basic instructions for how to respond to the statements. These instructions help to explain how you need to evaluate each statement. Here, for example, you need to determine whether the statements are valid inferences. In other cases, you may be asked to evaluate the statements for a different choice such as true or false.

④ These are the actual questions. You need to pick a response for each statement. If you fail to respond to one or more statements, you won't be able to advance to the next question in the section. In other words, these statements work just like the statements for the Table Analysis question type.

Multi-Source Reasoning questions usually come in sets. Each set typically consists of three separate questions. Two of those questions are typically in the statement style as shown in the previous example. It's also possible to get a standard multiple choice question as part of the set. For a standard multiple choice question, there are five answer choices and you select one response.

You may need information from more than one tab to respond to a statement or multiple choice question. Don't forget to think about the information on the other tabs while evaluating the statements. That's why it's important to take a few moments and get familiar with what's on each tab before starting work on the questions.

Part IV
GMAT Verbal
Practice Test

Chapter 6
Verbal
Practice Test

Okay, folks. Here's your chance to shine. This practice GMAT Verbal section contains 41 sentence correction, argument, and reading comprehension questions that are interspersed just as they'll appear on the real exam. To make this chapter as much like the real test as possible, sit down and answer them as best you can in 75 minutes. If you find yourself completely stumped on a question, guess and move on, just like you would on the real test. (Hey, it might be experimental.)

As you work on these problems, keep your pacing in mind. Remember that the first 10 questions count much more toward your final score than the last ten. The best way to use this section is to take it as you would a normal practice section, then to work through all the problems, untimed, for extra practice.

Unfortunately, this section can't match the experience of working at a computer because we haven't yet achieved the technology required for computer-adaptive books. But if you can answer most of these questions correctly during a standard time limit, you're on your way to a good score.

Note: In order to treat this practice exam as a real GMAT, complete these questions in order. Do NOT skip a question and return to it later.

The answers and explanations are in Chapter 7. When you're ready, turn to the next page and begin. Good luck!

1. Equestrian enthusiasts predict that the alleged abuse of anabolic steroids among horse trainers would subside if the testing of random animals is more vigorously enforced.

- ○ would subside if the testing of random animals is
- ○ would subside as long as the testing of the animals is more random and
- ○ will subside if random testing of the animals is
- ○ will subside if the animals were tested more randomly and
- ○ will have subsided when testing of the animals is more randomly and

2. Using steganography, the practice of hiding information in other information, encryption experts can conceal extensive messages in only a paragraph of ordinary text.

- ○ Using steganography, the practice of hiding information in other information, encryption experts can conceal extensive messages in only a paragraph of ordinary text.
- ○ Using the practice of hiding information in other information, which is called steganography, extensive messages can be concealed in only a paragraph of ordinary text by encryption experts.
- ○ Extensive messages can be concealed by encryption experts who use steganography, the practice of hiding information in other information, in only a paragraph of ordinary text.
- ○ Concealed in only a paragraph of ordinary text, encryption experts can use the practice of hiding information in other information, which is called steganography, for extensive messages.
- ○ The concealing of extensive messages in only a paragraph of ordinary text using steganography, which is the practice of hiding information in other information, is possible by encryption experts.

3. A survey of 1,200 residents of a certain state revealed that 34 percent found hunting to be morally wrong. Of those same 1,200 respondents, 59 percent said that they had never hunted before. From this information, the surveyors concluded that...

Which of the following best completes the passage above?

- ○ some respondents expressed their moral convictions more strongly than others
- ○ the people who expressed an objection to hunting had never hunted before
- ○ moral objection is not the only reason why people do not hunt
- ○ the people who had hunted before but stopped because of a moral objection outnumbered those who had never hunted but didn't find it morally wrong
- ○ some people hunt even though they are morally opposed to it

4. Many historians who have analyzed the exceedingly profound events in American history assert the electric light bulb of Edison's was the most groundbreaking invention of this or any century.

- ◯ the electric light bulb of Edison's
- ◯ it was when Edison invented the electric light bulb that
- ◯ that Edison's electric light bulb, which
- ◯ that it was Edison's electric light bulb that
- ◯ that it was Edison, who invented the light bulb, that

5. Dorsey received a dining room set from his grandmother, who had stored the furniture in a storage facility for more than a year. When he sat in one of the chairs, however, the wicker seat buckled and split. Dorsey attributed the break to the damp and musty conditions in the storage locker, which had caused the seat to rot.

Which of the following, if true, casts the most serious doubt on Dorsey's conclusion?

- ◯ The table, which was not made of wicker, did not appear to sustain any substantive damage.
- ◯ Dorsey broke through the seat of a brand-new identical chair that he bought to replace the broken one.
- ◯ The storage company had never received any complaints about rotted furniture in the past.
- ◯ Dorsey keeps a lot of his old furniture in his basement, which is also musty and damp.
- ◯ The furniture manufacturer refused to honor the chair's warranty because it felt the chair had been treated poorly.

Questions 6–9 refer to the following:

In her seminal work, *The Continuum Concept*, Jean Liedloff presents the controversial theory that Western methods of child rearing create the very problem these methods purport to eliminate—excessive dependency upon the caretaker. Liedloff contrasts her observations of modern American society with those of the Yequana tribe of the Amazon, with whom she lived on four separate occasions spanning several years.

Liedloff claims that all humans operate on a continuum and are genetically predisposed to thrive under certain conditions. We also compensate for treatment which does not coincide with these optimal conditions by adapting our behavior to stabilize our psyches. A baby who is in constant bodily contact with its caregiver receives physical stimulation that allows the child to feel secure and "right." In contrast, a child who is alone most of the time and left to "cry it out" does not receive the necessary physical contact. This creates a dependency in the child, who soon develops the grasping need for attention, even negative attention. Liedloff contends that some parents' fears that they will spoil their baby by holding it "too much" or by feeding it on demand are unreasonable and even detrimental to the child's mental health and social development.

Adults who have been deprived of their continuum needs as children often seek to stabilize themselves by engaging in self-defeating or destructive behavior, which replicates the treatment to which they have become accustomed. Victims of emotionally barren parents may tend to seek mates who are domineering and cold, making true intimacy virtually impossible. Others may feel a lingering sense of guilt induced by a caregiver who never seemed to accept the child's existence. This guilt makes it difficult for an adult to feel peaceful or happy unless he is in crisis either physically or emotionally; the unresolved feelings of shame from childhood do not allow the adult to live a pain-free life.

Liedloff's critics argue that this form of "attachment parenting" does not enforce the natural hierarchy of parent over child in the family relationship. They stress that without a clear dominance of parent over child and discipline requiring the child to bend to the will of the parents from the moment of birth, the child does not develop a sense of right versus wrong. Many of these critics espouse more scientific methods of raising children that rely on regularly scheduled feedings in infancy and careful control of the child's environment as the child grows older. Liedloff's response is that tight paren-

tal control over the child undermines its natural impulses toward socially acceptable behavior. Without choice, the child will not gain experience in making decisions and will be forced to look to an outside authority rather than use his own judgment. Upsetting the balance of the continuum by co-opting the child's natural ability to move toward independence and decision-making skills, she asserts, ultimately results in a lack of maturity and self-reliance in the adult.

6. The primary purpose of the passage as a whole is to
   ○ describe a strange phenomenon
   ○ clarify a vague notion
   ○ condemn an ill-informed opinion
   ○ refute a grievous misconception
   ○ support an alternative theory

7. According to the passage, Liedloff believes that adults whose sense of continuum is denied to them as children
   ○ are unable or unwilling to have children of their own
   ○ develop a strong sense of discipline and familial hierarchy
   ○ may suffer feelings of shame and inadequacy
   ○ seek mates whose strong sense of compassion can fill the void
   ○ are too self-absorbed and domineering to become adequate caregivers for their own children

8. Which of the following best describes the function of the passage's fourth paragraph?
   ○ It provides the reader the opportunity to see how both Liedloff and her critics rebut each other's opinions.
   ○ It resolves the argument between the two parenting schools by calling for further testing and research.
   ○ It undermines the passage's overall conclusion by suggesting that Liedloff's theories may be incomplete.
   ○ It stresses the need for all parents to establish their familial authority over their children.
   ○ It suggests that Liedloff would be willing to modify her theories and acknowledge the importance of more scientific methods.

9. Which of the following qualifies as an adult behavior that disturbs "the balance of the continuum" described in the final paragraph of the passage?

- ⬭ Prematurely encouraging interaction with other children who are slightly older
- ⬭ Imposing a strict sleeping regimen, regardless of the child's expressed desire to sleep
- ⬭ Resolving not to have children in order to stop the cycle of inadequate parenting
- ⬭ Providing the child with his own room as soon as is financially possible
- ⬭ Punishing a child who deliberately disobeys an order

10. A small marketing consortium wanted to get more young people to take up chess. Because chess is most enjoyable when two people of equal ability play one another, the group believed that few people play chess because it is so hard to find a suitable opponent.

Which of the following statements would most seriously undermine the consortium's viewpoint?

- ⬭ On average, a set of chess pieces costs much more than most other board games.
- ⬭ The chess industry received a lot of favorable publicity a few years ago when a computer defeated the world chess champion for the first time.
- ⬭ Tennis is most enjoyable when two equally matched opponents play each other, and the number of young tennis players has risen steadily.
- ⬭ Playing chess helps children develop analytical minds and learn to devise strategies to achieve long-term goals.
- ⬭ More than 50,000 chess sets were sold last year.

11. The transit authority of a certain city announced plans for a daily subway pass, which would cost $2.50 and afford a passenger unlimited access to the subway over a twenty-four-hour period. A consumer advocate was unimpressed with this offer because it benefited only tourists and did nothing for the average city commuter, who only rides the subway to and from work each business day.

If each of the statements above is true, which of the following conclusions can be drawn about the city's subway system?

- ⬭ The transit authority's special committee will weigh the merits of the day pass when it reconvenes.
- ⬭ The average commuter is dissatisfied with the price of the subway and is turning to other methods of transportation.
- ⬭ Discounting the day pass would put a strain on funds normally reserved for emergency measures.
- ⬭ The cost of one ride on the subway, regardless of the length of the ride or the time of day, is no more than $1.25.
- ⬭ A four-day pass at a cost of $10 would be equally useful to tourists.

12. The newest statistics released by the Labor Department indicate that jobless claims are down almost 1 percent, while real <u>wages, which had been expected to rise, have remained</u> steady.

- ◯ wages, which had been expected to rise, have remained
- ◯ wages, that had been expected to rise, remained
- ◯ wages that were expected to rise, instead are remaining
- ◯ wages, which did not rise expectedly, remained
- ◯ wages, which it had been expected would rise, instead are remaining

13. South Korea and Japan, which have the two most robust capitalist economies in northeastern Asia, have clawed their ways back from the brink of financial ruin and <u>now they take active roles in the success of both companies that are newer and smaller as well as</u> larger conglomerates.

- ◯ now they take active roles in the success of both companies that are newer and smaller as well as
- ◯ now take active roles in the success both of newer, smaller companies as well as that of
- ◯ they take active roles now in the success both of newer, smaller companies, as well as those of
- ◯ take active roles now in the successes of both companies that are newer and smaller as well as those of
- ◯ take active roles now in both the success of newer, smaller companies as well as

Questions 14–16 refer to the following:

No other country on earth has more profound lingual diversity than China, whose 1.3 billion inhabitants fall within eight major linguistic groups. Mainland academics may argue that all Chinese people are linked by the universal characters of written Chinese, but this assertion fails to address the simple fact that the eight localized spoken dialects, though related, are mutually incomprehensible.

Efforts to standardize spoken Chinese date back to 1913, when the Qing dynasty collapsed and the first Chinese republic was created. The delegates of this new representative government regarded a common language, or *guoyu*, as an ideological imperative, but regional loyalties threatened to scuttle the attempt from the start. Southern Chinese resented the thought that Mandarin, the language of the north and east that was spoken by the vast majority of Chinese, would be adopted as the official tongue at the expense of much of their own Cantonese terminology. In fact, it was the dialectic subtleties that helped widen the rift between the north and south when the northern Mandarin leader, Wang Zhao, attacked southern delegate Wang Rangbao after Zhao mistook a mundane utterance for an insult.

Further attempts to establish *guoyu* were revisited with rare fervor in the 1930s under the rule of Chiang Kai-shek, who went so far as to order that all literature not written in *guoyu* be confiscated and burned. When the Communists seized power in 1949, a common language fit perfectly with the party's plans for universal ideology according to Stalin's teachings. And still, the mutual enmity between the north and south persisted, as northerners rallied around the cry of "Force the south to follow the north!"

Modern China's government has succeeded in bringing about a universal language, now referred to as *putonghua*, which is now the standardized version of modern Chinese language that is taught in universities and spoken by government members in official addresses. *Putonghua* has become the language of the urban and educated, but it has yet to permeate the more rural areas of the country, where local dialects predominate. Even those who can speak *putonghua* have such thick regional accents as to make it impossible for a Mandarin farmer in Beijing to understand his southern counterpart in Shanghai. Further, the Taiwanese and Cantonese languages have undergone a new resurgence as part of the counterculture at universities and along China's southern coastline. Chinese have made laudable inroads toward unifying their lingua franca, but China's size, coupled with its increasing growth rate, suggests that local tongues will persevere for a long time to come.

14. According to the passage, the most consistent obstacle that the prospect of a unified language has encountered is
    ○ political uncertainty
    ○ government censorship
    ○ widespread ignorance
    ○ regional pride
    ○ a lack of nationalized education

15. As a result of the events of the twentieth century in China as described in the second and third paragraphs of the passage, the author would probably agree with which of the following statements?
    ○ *Putonghua* will persist in Chinese culture because its characters are far more universal than those of *guoyu* ever were.
    ○ In very populous countries, government edict is not always strong enough to resist the will of the people.
    ○ The resurgence of counterculture is a constant phenomenon, but the individual events seldom have the staying power to become anything more than passing fads.
    ○ Mandarin may yet become China's national language because most Chinese speak it already.
    ○ A government cannot call itself a representative democracy as long as it sanctions the destruction of literature.

16. According to the passage, each of the following has influenced the adoption of a universal language in China EXCEPT

    ◯ Chiang Kai-shek
    ◯ members of the Qing dynasty's royal family
    ◯ Communists
    ◯ resistance from Cantonese speakers
    ◯ the modern Chinese government

17. In an exhaustive study that explains how humans distinguish different scents, Dr. Linda Quidd asserts that the nerve lining of a mouse's nose contains roughly the same number of olfactory receptors <u>that a human nose does</u>.

    ◯ that a human nose does
    ◯ that human noses do
    ◯ as that of a human's nose
    ◯ as those of a human
    ◯ as human noses do

Questions 18–19 are based on the following:

Terry, a high school senior from State A, expressed an interest in attending Fullem State College, which was located in State B. After a little research, Terry's parents discovered that Fullem State College offered residents of State B a substantial discount from its normal tuition cost. Therefore, the parents decided to move to State B.

18. Which of the following, if true, is the most important reason why the parents might reconsider their decision?

- ○ Most scholarships are given to applicants who establish financial need.
- ○ To qualify for the lower tuition, applicants must prove that they have lived in State B for at least three years.
- ○ There are many colleges in State A that offer tuition discounts.
- ○ State B is several hundred miles from State A, and moving there would be difficult.
- ○ Regular tuition at Fullem State College is lower than that of most state colleges.

19. Which of the following, if true, would strengthen the parents' conclusion?

- ○ State B offers a large tax credit to families who send their children to colleges within State B.
- ○ Terry's sister, Leslie, graduated from Fullem State College five years ago.
- ○ The housing market in State B is unpredictable.
- ○ More than two-thirds of all students who attend Fullem State College do not need financial aid.
- ○ If the lower-tuition plan at Fullem State College is successful this year, it is likely that the program will be expanded in subsequent years.

20. According to a recent survey, today's college students are inclined to involve themselves in political issues only if they would be expecting to financially gain.

- ○ only if they would be expecting to financially gain
- ○ if they would expect only to gain financially
- ○ only if their expectations can be gained financially
- ○ if financial gain could only be expected by them
- ○ only if they can expect to gain financially

21. In most cases, the price of a commodity is directly proportionate to its scarcity in the marketplace; however, there is one notable exception. Worldwide diamond production doubled between 1986 and 1996; in that time, however, the average price of a diamond increased by more than 15 percent.

Which of the following, if true, would explain the diamond's rise in price despite its abundance?

- ○ The price of precious gems such as sapphires and opals is at an all-time high.
- ○ The number of contractors whose sole job is the cutting and polishing of raw diamond ore has doubled.
- ○ Newly established stable governments in African nations have encouraged foreign investment and helped diamond mines flourish.
- ○ Per capita diamond consumption is much higher in North America than it is in Asia.
- ○ A powerful cartel that controls more than 90 percent of the world's diamonds releases them into the market depending on conditions in the world economy.

Questions 22–24 refer to the following:

Inspired by a wave of uncertainty about currencies in several emerging markets in recent years, many investment banks are beginning to market their versions of a new investment tool designed to predict when a currency's value will decline sharply. Many academics and economists have combined their efforts to create these "risk indicators" in order to predict when financial turmoil in a nascent capitalist market is forthcoming.

Creators of this new model define a currency crisis as a drop of at least 10 percent in a currency's real value. Working with a list of all of the currency crises that have occurred within the past ten years, researchers suggest a number of market or economic variables that may have helped bring the crashes about. Such factors include a country's exchange-rate overvaluation, slowing economic growth, or a rising debt burden. Statisticians then use sophisticated econometrics to look for relationships between these factors and the currency dips they may have caused.

Representatives of the International Monetary Fund (IMF) question whether these new models are any improvement over the techniques that are currently in place. The risk indicators, the IMF argues, are too dependent on the benefit of hindsight and cannot account for any new economic phenomena that may arise. The IMF has also accused some of the investment banks of "data mining," whereby analysts configure the information they cull from various sources until they finally verify the conclusion they have conditioned themselves to seek.

Further skepticism has been fueled by a comparison study of the risk indicator models, which was convened by Andrew Berg and Catherine Pattillo, a pair of IMF economists. After funneling economic data through each of the three most prominent models, Berg and Pattillo determined that none would have accurately predicted Asia's currency freefall that began when Thailand's baht was dislodged from its American dollar standard in July 1997. In fact, two models would have sounded a more severe alarm toward the Philippines, which has not undergone a currency crisis, than for either South Korea or Thailand, whose respective recoveries may never be complete.

22. The passage is chiefly concerned with
○ warning that attempting to predict currencies fluctuations is a useless enterprise
○ advocating the indispensable role of the IMF in stabilizing the currencies of countries to which capitalism is relatively new
○ expressing doubts as to the reliability of some new attempts to predict financial phenomena
○ contrasting new and sophisticated financial models with older methods that are more concerned with careful research
○ recommending that better investor models be created before one isolated contagion leads to worldwide recession

23. Which of the following does the passage suggest about South Korea?
○ It has received financial consultation and support from the IMF.
○ Its currency recently devalued by more than 10 percent.
○ Its economy is currently growing slower than that of the Philippines.
○ The new risk indicators would have detected its economic downturn had they been in place several years ago.
○ Its currency is closely tied to the American dollar.

24. Which of the following, if it happened soon after this article was published, would undermine the skepticism toward the viability of the "risk indicator" models?
○ The value of the Filipino peso plummeted.
○ Berg and Pattillo resigned from the IMF.
○ The South Korean economy showed signs of slowing down further.
○ Thailand restored its connection to the American dollar.
○ The IMF changed its definition of a currency crisis to an 8 percent drop in value.

25. Public safety activists, <u>being concerned about the rise in the number of car accidents and the average person's attention span being shrunk gradually</u>, feel that the introduction of the "netcar," a vehicle equipped with access to the Internet, is a terrible mistake.

- ○ being concerned about the rise in the number of car accidents and the average person's attention span being shrunk gradually
- ○ concerning themselves about rising car accidents and shrinking attention spans among average people
- ○ because they are concerned about the rising of the number of car accidents, also the shrinking of the attention span of the average person
- ○ concerned about the rise in the number of car accidents and the gradual shrinkage of the average person's attention span
- ○ given that they had been concerned about the rise in the number of car accidents and the gradual shrinkage of the average person's attention span as well

26. Antismoking lobbyists have tried to label smoking as a societal concern that must be curbed by government legislation. A problem can't be labeled a social problem, however, unless it harms others without their consent. Governments are powerless to regulate a harmful activity if those who do not indulge in that activity are not at risk.

Which of the following strategies would most likely achieve the lobbyists' goal?

- ○ Quoting legislation that has been drafted to punish drunk drivers
- ○ Calling for higher "luxury taxes" on tobacco products
- ○ Citing the number of cancer-related deaths in the past ten years
- ○ Compiling statistics about the health hazard of secondhand smoke to non-smokers
- ○ Boycotting all items produced by tobacco companies and their wholly owned subsidiaries

27. Many of America's political allies have demanded that the United States repeal the <u>Helms-Burton law of 1996, tightening the embargo on all Cuban products and, according to opponents of it, violating</u> several international treaties.

- ○ Helms-Burton law of 1996, tightening the embargo on all Cuban products and, according to opponents of it, violating
- ○ Helms-Burton law of 1996, whose tightening of the embargo on all Cuban products violates, according to its opponents,
- ○ Helms-Burton law of 1996, which tightens the embargo on all Cuban products and which, according to its opponents, violates
- ○ embargo's tightening by the Helms-Burton law of 1996 on all Cuban products and the violating, according to opponents of it, of
- ○ tightening the embargo of the Helms-Burton law of 1996 on all Cuban products and, according to its opponents, violating

28. To encourage each student athlete to remain at one institution throughout his or her four years of eligibility, the intercollegiate rules committee drafted a new rule mandating that students who transfer to a different college wait a year before representing that new college in athletics. The mother of one such athlete thought the rule was unfair because the time off would cause her son's skills to atrophy and thus damage his chance to pursue a professional career.

The mother assumes that

- ○ she would have advised her son not to transfer if she had known about the rule
- ○ all professional athletes owe their success to the playing experience they received in college
- ○ the rules committee is made up of former college athletes who understand how difficult it is to balance scholarship with athletics
- ○ it is uncommon for someone with no collegiate experience to thrive at the p rofessional level
- ○ her son has no place else to play during his one-year suspension

29. To determine whether there are deposits of frozen water on the moon, research scientists at NASA launched two unmanned satellites that orbited the moon's atmosphere, <u>analyzing</u> radar echoes from the lunar surface.

○ analyzing
○ as an analysis technique of
○ to the analysis of
○ to analyze
○ a technique for analyzing

30. The new legislation governing presidential campaign contributions allows political parties to raise money only through a <u>process with high standards in contrast to</u> a group of fundraising events that are unregulated and unsanctioned.

○ process with high standards in contrast to
○ process that has been standardized highly and not within
○ highly standardized process rather than at
○ high process of standards instead of
○ process of high standards rather than that of

31. Interest in a 3,200-acre parcel of barren land in Welsh County has been virtually nonexistent because it is not zoned for commercial use. A real estate developer, though, has created a business plan to convert the property into a low-grade airport that, when completed, would drive the value of the surrounding properties lower. Many local residents, therefore, are trying to pool their assets and buy the property outright.

Last week, the Welsh County town council voted to repeal the restriction in the town charter that prohibits all commercial development on parcels of land smaller than 5,000 acres.

The statements above, if true, best support which of the following conclusions?

○ The people who have property adjacent to the land in question will seek out other real estate developers who might want to use the land for other more aesthetically pleasing uses.
○ The Welsh County town council does not always act solely in the financial interest of town's residents.
○ Though short-term property values will probably drop, the community will ultimately benefit when young families arrive to take advantage of the bargains.
○ If residents can persuade the town council to reconsider its decision, their property values will rise.
○ The original zoning laws in Welsh County were enacted because of pressure from the area's wealthiest residents.

32. The visual phenomenon known as refraction alters the appearance of objects as they are seen through water. All objects look larger than they actually are, but darker objects appear much more magnified than lighter objects. Hence, a darkly colored pebble on the floor of a swimming pool looks much larger than a white pebble, as long as the two are placed an equal distance from the eye of the viewer.

The conclusion above would be more properly drawn if it were made clear that the

- ○ darkly colored pebble is assumed to be greater in size than the white pebble
- ○ darkly colored pebble is assumed to be the same size as the white pebble
- ○ darkly colored pebble is assumed to be smaller in size than the white pebble
- ○ pool floor is light in color
- ○ pool floor is dark in color

33. The mass-marketing of companies that specialize in DNA testing has inspired fears that the DNA testing process will become too commonplace, resulting in emotional trauma to those who are ill-equipped to cope with the results, and greatly increasing the number of lawsuits that are brought against hospitals and adoption agencies.

- ○ greatly increasing the number of lawsuits that are brought
- ○ greatly increase the number of lawsuits brought
- ○ it would greatly increase the number of lawsuits that would be brought
- ○ it would greatly increase the bringing of a number of lawsuits
- ○ greatly increasing the number of those who would bring lawsuits

34. During periods of extreme economic volatility, it is easy to mistake an increase in overall stock prices as the start of another bull market.

- ○ an increase in overall stock prices as the start of another bull market
- ○ the overall increasing of stock prices as the starting of another bull market
- ○ overall increasing stock prices for another bull market that is starting
- ○ an overall increase in stock prices for the start of another bull market
- ○ an increasing of stock prices as a starting bull market

Questions 35–38 refer to the following:

Public health officials are becoming concerned about chlorine, a chemical that is added to many municipal water supplies to reduce bacterial growth. New evidence shows that the rate of first-trimester miscarriages is increased significantly when pregnant women drink five or more glasses of chlorinated water per day. When the chlorine in the water reacts with plant material acids the chemical trihalomethane is formed. Trihalomethane is believed to be the cause of the miscarriages, and it is also linked to increased cancer risk in animals. Lead, which has been shown to cause brain damage in small children, is another main contaminant of urban water systems, as it seeps from old pipes into the water flowing through them. Many water supplies are also contaminated with toxic bacteria, cysts, or algae. Increasing concerns about the effects of harmful contaminants have caused an increase in the number of alternate methods of water filtration that are available to the general public.

There are six major systems, each with its advantages and considerable drawbacks. Steam distillation, in which water is boiled and the steam is collected and cooled, produces water without contaminants. However, energy must be used to heat the water, the resulting water tastes flat, and some organic compounds may boil with the steam and contaminate the water. Carbon filtration removes chlorine from water and leaves it with a better taste, but it cannot remove minerals or heavy metals. In addition, the filter is no longer effective if it becomes clogged, and the carbon can trap and breed harmful bacteria. The ion exchange method uses charged particles in a filter which are exchanged with charged particles in the water to remove minerals and toxic metals. This method has a corrosive effect on pipes, and it does not remove organic molecules. It also increases the levels of sodium, iron, and lead in the water. Ultraviolet light is simple and can kill microorganisms, but it has no effect on chemicals or minerals in the water. Reverse osmosis removes minerals, toxic-heavy metals, and bacteria by forcing the water through a semipermeable membrane. This method is extremely slow, wastes large amounts of water, and corrodes the most durable of pipes.

Of the many different types of water filtration systems available, a combination KDF/carbon block system may be the most effective. The KDF system, which stands for kinetic degradation fluxion, forces water through a chamber containing a mixture of copper and zinc. In the chamber, the copper becomes a cathode and zinc an anode; the electrochemical reaction that takes place removes chlorine, chloramine, iron, hydrogen sulfide, and many other harmful substances from the water. The water is then forced through a solid carbon block filter, which removes more impurities, such as bacteria and algae, from the water. Many KDF/carbon block filtration systems also contain a ceramic pre-filter, which removes other bacteria such as *Escherichia coli, Streptococcus sp.*, and fecal coliform, as well as cysts such as *Cryptosporidium sp.* and *Giardia sp.* As a by-product of filtration, the KDF/carbon block system puts small amounts of copper and zinc into the water that are not harmful to humans.

35. Which of the following best describes the organization of the passage?
   ○ Several methods are described and ranked in terms of desirability.
   ○ A general theory is offered and refuted by several counterexamples.
   ○ A current process is assailed, and several alternatives are presented as possible replacements.
   ○ An old solution is revived as a possible remedy to a new problem.
   ○ A paradox is presented, and several examples are used to reconcile it.

36. Each of the following is a disadvantage of the ion exchange method of water filtration EXCEPT
   ○ higher sodium levels in the water
   ○ damaged pipes
   ○ unaffected contaminants of an organic nature
   ○ dangerous copper and zinc contamination
   ○ an increase of lead

37. According to the passage, which of the following can be inferred about the KDF system?

  ◯ It prevents the formation of trihalomethane in the water supply.
  ◯ It would work much better if used in concert with a semipermeable membrane.
  ◯ The electrochemical reaction causes most of the copper and zinc that are originally introduced into the water to dissolve.
  ◯ Without the additional ceramic pre-filter, it is no more effective than the combined effect of ion exchange and ultraviolet light.
  ◯ Its ability to remove iron from water is superior to that of ion exchange.

38. According to the passage, the author's opinion of the best water filtration system would probably change if which of the following were true?

  ◯ If the KDF system is used indefinitely, the levels of copper and zinc that it introduces into the water supply will eventually become toxic.
  ◯ All new residential dwellings are fitted with pipes made of durable plastic that lead cannot seep through.
  ◯ Ultraviolet light is one-tenth as expensive as each of the other techniques mentioned.
  ◯ Subsequent studies have revealed that there is no relation between trihalomethane and cancer.
  ◯ KDF is available only in urban areas with tax bases that withstand the cost of installing such a system.

39. Mesoporous metals are not indestructible, but their durability is such that they are able to withstand any delivered blow of a force of less than 12 newtons.

  ◯ their durability is such that they are able to withstand any delivered blow of
  ◯ they are of such durability, they have the ability to withstand any blow delivered with
  ◯ there is so much durability that they can withstand any blow that is delivered by
  ◯ they have such durability as to withstand any delivered blow of
  ◯ they are so durable that they can withstand any blow delivered with

40. In each of the past four years, the percent increase of the profits of Japan's five largest semiconductor firms has been less than that of the year before. This trend marks a severe departure from the industry's peak in 1993, when revenues of each of these five firms grew at an average annual rate of 47 percent since the beginning of the decade. Clearly, the trade-deficit law enacted by the Japanese government in 1993 has had an adverse effect on the industry, which accounts for a large portion of the Japanese gross domestic product.

The conclusion of the argument above cannot be true unless which of the following is true?

○ Japan's gross domestic product has also shrunk since 1993.

○ The original goal of most trade-deficit laws is to protect domestic products from cheaper imports, yet not every one achieves this goal.

○ The five companies mentioned have encountered new pressure from smaller companies that hold patents on newer semiconductor technology.

○ Profits of semiconductor companies would have kept climbing steadily if the government had not passed its 1993 trade-deficit bill.

○ Many other sectors of Japanese commerce, such as its auto industry, have also suffered declining profits since 1993.

41. Some State Department officials hope to end the border skirmish by bargaining with the new dictator, others by proposing imposing stiff economic sanctions on the country's exports, and still others by demanding that NATO launch a full-scale invasion.

○ by proposing imposing stiff economic sanctions on the country's exports, and still others by demanding

○ by proposing the imposition of stiff economic sanctions on the country's exports, and still others demand

○ propose imposing stiff economic sanctions on the country's exports, and still others are demanding

○ are proposing the stiff imposition of economic sanctions on the country's exports, and still others are demanding

○ propose the stiff imposition of economic sanctions on the country's exports, and still others demand

That's it. Pencils down. Did you answer the questions in order and make sure to register a response for each question in the time allotted?

Turn to the next chapter for the answers and explanations to see how you did. Next, go back to the ones you missed and take a second shot at them. Then read the explanations to all the questions, even the ones you answered correctly. Remember, just because you got a question right doesn't mean you understand everything about it.

Keep practicing, and don't forget to take the GMATPrep® tests to experience a full computer-based GMAT.

Chapter 7
Verbal
Practice Test:
Answers and
Explanations

VERBAL PRACTICE TEST ANSWER KEY

1.	C	22.	C
2.	A	23.	B
3.	C	24.	A
4.	D	25.	D
5.	B	26.	D
6.	E	27.	C
7.	C	28.	E
8.	A	29.	A
9.	B	30.	C
10.	C	31.	B
11.	D	32.	B
12.	A	33.	B
13.	B	34.	D
14.	D	35.	C
15.	B	36.	D
16.	B	37.	A
17.	C	38.	A
18.	B	39.	E
19.	A	40.	D
20.	E	41.	E
21.	E		

VERBAL PRACTICE TEST EXPLANATIONS

1. **C**   The sentence is incorrect as written because it misuses the subjunctive tense (the abuse *would* subside if testing *were enforced*). Choice (B) also has this problem and is long and wordy. Choice (D) brings in *were*, but forgets about the *would*; it also tries to trick you because it looks parallel (*more randomly* and *more vigorously*). Choice (E) unnecessarily introduces the future perfect tense (*will have subsided*) and is also very wordy.

2. **A**   This sentence is fine because *Using steganography* correctly modifies *encryption experts*. Also, the phrase *in only a paragraph of ordinary text* should modify *extensive messages*. Choice (B) has a misplaced modifier because it suggests that messages use steganography. In (C), the phrase *in only a paragraph of ordinary text* should modify where the messages are hidden, not steganography; it's also constructed passively. Choice (D) has a misplaced modifier here because the experts weren't concealed in the text. Choice (E) is constructed passively, and *the concealing* is not the right subject of the sentence.

3. **C**   This is an inference question, involving fun with numbers. If 59 percent of the residents said they had never hunted before, and only 34 percent expressed a moral objection, at least 25 percent of the respondents had some other reason. Choice (A) is wrong because we don't know how strongly the views were expressed; all we have is the numbers. It's possible that someone had tried hunting and later found it morally wrong, so (B) is out. As confusing as (D) is, it's actually false. Do a little math: 34 percent think hunting is wrong, and 59 percent said they had never hunted. Choice (E) is also certainly possible, but we don't know if this is *definitely* true.

4. **D**   The idiom is *assert...that*, so you can eliminate (A) and (B). The idiom tested here is it *was...that was*. Because the was part of *that was* is not underlined, you need *it was* in the underlined portion. Choice (C) is a sentence fragment, and (E) incorrectly suggests that Edison was the invention instead of his light bulb.

5. **B**   A weaken-the-argument question. If Dorsey broke a brand-new chair as well, then it's possible that the chairs could support his grandmother but can't hold anyone who is heavier. Choice (A) is out because the table and chairs aren't comparable—we don't know if Dorsey sat on the table as well. Choice (C) might be true, but that doesn't mean there isn't a problem now (there's a first time for everything). Choice (D) doesn't address whether the chair rotted in the storage facility, and neither does (E); his grandmother could have been at fault.

6. **E**   In the first sentence of the passage, the author calls Liedloff's theory *controversial*, and it's also different from the Western methods that Liedloff asserts are causing more problems than they solve. The majority of the rest of the passage lists supporting points of Liedloff's thesis.

7. **C**   Begin reading at the beginning of the third paragraph, where the passage talks about *adults who have been deprived of their continuum*. Later in this paragraph, the author mentions that some of these adults *may feel a lingering sense of guilt*, and the use of *shame* in (C) is an accurate paraphrase.

8. **A**   The beginning of the fourth and last paragraph begins with *Liedloff's critics*, and then we see a reference to *Liedloff's response* later in the paragraph. Though most of the passage is devoted to examining Liedloff's ideas, the difference of opinion is never resolved. Nor do we get the impression that Liedloff's work is incorrect or incomplete; we just know that some people disagree with her.

9. **B**   *Upsetting the balance of the continuum* appears in the passage's last sentence, and it refers to *co-opting the child's natural ability to move toward independence*. Thus, depriving a kid's continuum involves imposing your own schedule on him, and (B) is the best example of this.

10. **C**   Because tennis and chess both require a suitable opponent and tennis is flourishing, there must be some other reason why kids don't play chess. Choice (A) is a knock against chess, but it doesn't address the premise about finding someone to play with; neither does (B). Whether chess is a useful activity is not relevant, so (D) is out. Choice (E) is bad for two reasons: (1) We have no data to compare, so we don't know if the number is rising or falling, and (2) we don't know that all sets that were purchased are being used.

11. **D**   If the cost of one ride were more than $1.25, the day pass would benefit *anyone* who rode the subway at least twice a day. Because the pass does not benefit daily commuters, each trip must cost less than $1.25. Choice (A) is completely irrelevant, so we can't infer it. We can't infer (B) either; just because this new pass offers no benefit doesn't mean that commuters are unhappy. Choice (C) is wrong because we don't know how the transit authority allots its money. Many people fall for (E), but it's not necessarily true; a $10 pass benefits only those tourists who stay in town at least four days.

12. **A**   Don't get bogged down by the *that* vs. *which* conundrum. Instead, look at the verbs. The sentence is in the present tense (*jobless claims* **are** *down*), so *remain* must be in the present tense also. Eliminate (B) and (D), which are in the past tense. Choice (A) uses *have remained*, which is consistent, and it properly sets off *which had been expected to rise* with commas; (C) doesn't do that. Choice (E) has all sorts of problems, not the least of which is its excessive wordiness.

13. **B**   If you have another subject in the underlined portion of the sentence, it becomes a run-on sentence. Therefore, you don't want the pronoun *they* to appear in your final answer; eliminate (A) and (C). The key to the rest of this question is the placement of *both*. The construction in (D) is flawed because it's possible that there are only two newer and smaller companies and that the government supports *both* of them. *Both* is also misplaced in (E), making the construction not parallel. Choice (B) sounds a bit awkward, but it is perfectly parallel (*the success of…as well as that of*); *that* is a pronoun for *success*.

14. **D**   The passage first mentions *localized spoken dialects* at the end of the first paragraph, and the theme persists throughout. *Regional loyalties* are mentioned in paragraph two (second sentence), and *mutual enmity between the north and south* occurred after the Communists arrived (last sentence of the third paragraph).

15. **B** The passage talks about several government plans to impose a universal language on its 1.3 billion people—the first republic in 1913, Chiang Kai-shek, and then the Communists. Even the modern government has tried (with a bit more success), but the new language hasn't reached the rural counties, and other languages have become part of the counterculture (last two sentences of passage).

16. **B** Read carefully here. The Qing dynasty is mentioned in the second paragraph, but the first attempts to create a universal language didn't happen until after the family had been overthrown. It's possible that the new language was a reaction against dynastic rule, but we don't know that for sure. Every other answer choice has had an influence, including (D); Cantonese speakers have kept both *guoyu* and *putonghua* from becoming universal.

17. **C** The idiom is *same…as*, so eliminate (A) and (B). Now it gets a little tricky because you have to keep track of the things you're comparing. The sentence compares the nerve lining of a mouse's nose to the nerve lining of a human's nose. So you need the pronoun *that*. Choice (D) is wrong because *those* is plural (a human only has one nerve lining), and (E) doesn't refer to the nerve lining.

18. **B** If (B) were true, Terry's parents wouldn't be able to get the discount. Therefore, moving to State B wouldn't do them any good. Choice (A) doesn't factor in because we don't know if Terry needs the money or not. Choice (C) might be true, but Terry wants to go to Fullem State. Choice (D) is an attractive choice, but even though it might be a real hassle to move to State B, the move might be worth it if the family can save substantial money on Terry's education. Choice (E) might also be true, but out-of-state tuition might still be too high for Terry's family.

19. **A** Getting a big tax credit is an excellent alternate reason to move to State B, especially if Terry wants to attend Fullem State. Choice (B) doesn't address whether moving to State B is a good idea. Lots of people pick (C), but *unpredictable* doesn't necessarily mean *bad*; this is a common trick that the test writers use. A question will include a word that conjures a negative connotation when it isn't necessarily negative at all. *Unpredictable* means you don't know what will happen, but it could work out great. The housing market could skyrocket, for example. Get rid of (D), because the other students don't matter to Terry. He might still need the money. And (E) is out because an expanded program next year doesn't do Terry any good now.

20. **E** *To financially gain* is a split infinitive, so eliminate (A). The first part of the sentence is in the present tense, so the rest should be as well. You can eliminate (B) because *would expect* doesn't agree. Choices (C) and (D) are passively constructed, and *only* is misplaced in (D) as well. Choice (E) is in the active tense, there's no split infinitive, and *only* is in the right place.

21. **E** It doesn't matter how many diamonds are produced if a cartel restricts their entry into the market. Keeping them scarce for consumers keeps the price up. The other gems in (A) are irrelevant, and (B) and (D) don't explain how diamonds defy economic principles. Choice (C) also doesn't explain why the price rose.

22. **C**   The main idea of the passage is the discussion of these new "risk indicators" that can help people predict a fall in the value of a currency (or a *financial phenomenon*) and the author's overall opinion is that they aren't that reliable. Choice (A) expresses a similar point, but it's too extreme (*a useless enterprise?*).

23. **B**   You have to look in two different places to answer this question, but the logic follows. The last paragraph implies that South Korea has endured a currency crisis because it is in the process of recovery (last sentence of passage). The first sentence of paragraph two defines a currency crisis as a 10-percent dip in a currency's value.

24. **A**   We're still looking at the last paragraph, which talks about *further skepticism*. Berg and Pattillo found that two of the models predicted problems in the Philippines, yet there were no problems as of yet. If the Filipino peso were to plummet, the risk indicators would seem more accurate.

25. **D**   The underlined portion must describe the activists, who are *concerned*. The construction also needs to be parallel (concerned about the *rise* and the *shrinkage*). Choice (A) contains *being*, so it's out right away. Choice (B) is wrong because car accidents aren't rising; the *number* of accidents is rising. The use of *they* and *also* is awkward and unnecessary in (C). Apart from the wordiness of (E) and the unnecessary use of *had been*, the use of *as well* is awkward and redundant.

26. **D**   The argument's premise is that you can't penalize smokers unless they harm non-smokers. The lobbyists can make their point by attempting to prove that smokers do put non-smokers in danger. Lots of people like to choose (A), but we don't know if smokers and drunk drivers are comparable—that's what the lobbyists must establish. Choices (B), (C), and (E) don't address the harm to those who don't smoke.

27. **C**   You can eliminate (D) and (E) right away, because people want to repeal the *law*, not the *tightening*. Choice (C) is the best choice because it uses *which* properly, and it also uses parallel construction. Choice (A) makes it look like the political allies are doing the tightening and violating. Also, the pronoun *it* is ambiguous. Choice (B) is wrong because you should use *who* or *whose* only when you're referring to a person. *Whose* incorrectly refers to the law.

28. **E**   If it were possible for her son to play someplace else and keep his skills sharp, she wouldn't have to worry about her son losing his talent. Choice (A) is wrong because what she *would have* done is not as important as what she is doing now—challenging the rule. Choice (B) is too extreme, and (C) is wrong because the makeup of the rules committee is out of the scope. Choice (D) may be true, but it's not impossible. This kid might be a star!

29. **A**   You should use *analyzing* at the beginning of the phrase, because that's what the satellites did. Because NASA launched two satellites, it's incorrect to refer to them as a *technique*; eliminate (B) and (E). Choice (C) is incorrect because *to the analysis* is not idiomatic. And you can cross off (D) because to *analyze* is not complete. It would have been better if the sentence had said *used to analyze*.

30. **C** This one is really tricky. (In fact, it just plain stinks.) The key is the word *at*, which is the preposition you need for parallel construction (*raise money **through**…rather than **at***). Also, *highly standardized* appropriately modifies (describes) *process*.

31. **B** Here's another inference question. The land in question is smaller than 5,000 acres, so it is about to become available for commercial use. Because this will upset a lot of residents, it must be true that the town council has other motives in mind. (Note the nice wishy-washy tone: *does not always act*.) We don't know how the residents will respond, so (A) is out. Choice (D) is also a popular wrong choice, but we can't assume that property values will rise. We can assume that they won't fall because of the new airport. Choices (C) and (E) go into topics about which the passage tells us absolutely nothing.

32. **B** This is an obliquely worded assumption question. The conclusion is that a dark pebble will look larger than a white pebble, so it must be assumed that the two pebbles are the same size. Choices (A) and (C) are eliminated because refraction would have nothing to do with the situation if the dark pebble actually were larger than the white pebble. (It would of course look bigger—it *is* bigger!) Conversely, a larger white pebble might counteract the illusion and make the two appear to be the same size. Choices (D) and (E) are wrong because the color of the pool floor affects each pebble equally, so the color doesn't matter.

33. **B** This question also revolves around parallel verb choice. If you focus your attention on the second half of the sentence, the secondary subject is *the DNA testing process*. The process will *become too commonplace…and greatly increase the number*. The verb *resulting* is a red herring, because it appears in the appositive clause between the commas and has no direct bearing on the parallel construction. Therefore, *increasing* is incorrect; eliminate (A) and (E). Also, the phrase it *would* is unnecessary and not parallel, so you can eliminate (C) and (D).

34. **D** The proper idiom is *mistake…for*, and there's a subtle two/three split (*for* vs. *as*) among the answer choices. Choices (A), (B), and (E) use *as*, so they're out. Choice (C) has awkward, non-parallel construction, and *overall increasing stock prices* is not idiomatic.

35. **C** The first paragraph discusses the new concerns about an established method of purifying water (chlorine). The remainder of the passage bombards us with many alternative ideas and the pros and cons of each. Choice (A) is close, but the six new ideas are never actually ranked.

36. **D** Go back and read all about ion exchange, which is first mentioned in the middle (sixth sentence) of paragraph two. Each of the answer choices is mentioned in the subsequent sentences except (D). Use of copper and zinc doesn't come up until the last paragraph, which is about the KDF process. It's a classic case of misdirection.

37. **A** This one requires a little reading in two different places. The last paragraph tells us that the KDF system *removes chlorine* from the water (third sentence of last paragraph). Earlier in the passage, we learn that chlorine *reacts with plant material acids* and *trihalomethane is formed* (third sentence of paragraph one). Because the KDF system gets rid of chlorine, trihalomethane can't be formed.

Even though the passage's author asserts that KDF *may be the most effective* (first sentence of last paragraph), we still don't know anything about direct comparisons with any of the other alternatives mentioned.

38.   **A**   The author is clearly a big fan of the KDF system, which works by introducing *copper and zinc into the water* (last sentence of passage). The author states that these metals are *not harmful to humans*. If we later learned, though, that unlimited use of KDF creates toxic levels of copper and zinc, then the KDF system isn't nearly as effective as the author thinks. She might change her mind.

39.   **E**   Look at the last word of each answer choice. The difference is between the prepositions *of*, *with*, and *by*. In this case, it is idiomatic to use *delivered **with** a force of less than 12 newtons*, so you can eliminate everything except (B) and (E). Choice (E) uses the proper idiom *so durable that*, and (B) is wrong because the idiom it wants to use is *such…that*. Because *that* doesn't appear in the sentence, it's unidiomatic.

40.   **D**   An assumption question. The author of this argument says that the semiconductor companies were doing just fine until the new law in 1993. Therefore, it must be assumed that without the law, these companies would have maintained growth. If the companies would have faltered anyway, then the law clearly isn't to blame. Choices (A) and (C) follow this last line of reasoning; if the GDP is also shrinking or new companies are adding new pressure, then maybe the law didn't bring on the problems. Because this weakens the conclusion, it can't be an assumption. The original goal of the law in choice (B) is out of the argument's scope, as are the other sectors of Japanese commerce mentioned in (E).

41.   **E**   Here's a great sample question about parallelism. The non-underlined portion establishes the form that the rest of the sentence must take: (1) The sentence is in the present tense (*officials hope to end*), and (2) *by bargaining* indicates that we're going to use *-ing* words. The key is recognizing that *propose* needs to agree with *hope*, not *bargaining*. Therefore, (A) and (B) have to go. Choice (C) is not parallel because *propose* doesn't match *are demanding*. The words *are proposing* and *are demanding* are parallel in (D), but neither is parallel with the original verb, *hope*. Choice (E) is parallel, and the three verbs—*hope, propose,* and *demand*—are all in the same form.

Part V
Appendix

Appendix A
Grammar
Odds and Ends

Well, here we are at the end of the book. Before you finally put this book down and move on with your life, here are some miscellaneous thoughts about proper grammar to look for on sentence correction questions and when you write your essays.

You won't get called on many of these in conversations with your friends (unless your friends are a bunch of pedantic know-it-alls), but they'll come in handy during the GMAT application process.

A FEW MORE TEST TRAPS

The following four items are common tricks the test writers use to create wrong answer choices. Once you're familiar with them, you'll see how often they show up on the GMAT.

Mixing Up Word Order

This is a catch-all problem that the test writers like. It's mostly related to the rule for misplaced modifiers: A word that modifies another should be next to it. You can really mess up a sentence just by putting the same words in different places and creating awkward sentence construction.

Based on accounts of **various** political theorists…

Based on **various** accounts of political theorists…

The meaning of the sentence depends on the placement of various; in the first phrase, various modifies political theorists, and the second phrase suggests that the accounts vary.

GMAT writers like to change the word order around to create wrong answer choices, especially when the entire sentence is underlined. When you see a disparity like this one, compare the two answer choices to each other and decide which one best conveys the meaning of the original sentence.

Verbosity, Loquaciousness, Prolixity

The best writing conveys the most using the smallest number of words. Why say something in eight words when you can do it in four?

> Most of the time, the shorter answer choices are better than the longer ones. When in doubt, keep it short and sweet.

Here's a question in which the number of words in the answer choice is a compelling factor:

> Although he had decided to become an actor
> <u>while being very young</u>, Donald DiMarco didn't act
> in his first major motion picture until he reached
> the age of seventy-eight.
>
> ◯ while being very young
> ◯ while in his youth
> ◯ at the time that he was being young
> ◯ in the time of his youth
> ◯ in his youth

You can eliminate (A) and (C) because they contain being, and you're left with (B), (D), and (E). Because (E) expresses the exact point that the other two do and uses fewer words, it's the best answer. Sometimes the test writers just like to test your proficiency with economy of words (and your essay readers will thank you for expressing your ideas as succinctly as possible).

Note: This is *not* an instruction to look at all five choices and pick the shortest one. There is absolutely no guarantee that the shortest answer is the best answer. It's more of a guideline than a rule. If you've narrowed your choices down to two and you have to make an educated guess before you move on to the next question, pick the shorter choice.

Being Repetitious and Redundant by Repeating Things Again

Redundancy is related to verbosity, and it's a sickness from which many average writers suffer. The test writers know this, and they like to write answer choices that don't seem redundant at first.

Some examples of redundant phrases include:

Redundant	Remedied
free gift	gift (when is a gift not free?)
surrounded on all sides	surrounded
as many as six inches wide or wider	at least six inches wide
and my father was also there	and my father was there
the same exact thing	the same thing
whether or not	whether
used for mining purposes	used for mining
the reason why	the reason
demand that she should go	demand that she go

A question that contains redundant answer choices might look something like this:

> An individual investor must develop the discipline not to sell blue-chip stocks when plummeting prices <u>have fallen to reach</u> their short-term lows.
>
> ◯ have fallen to reach
> ◯ are falling to reach
> ◯ have fallen or reached
> ◯ have fallen or are reaching
> ◯ reach

The non-underlined portion of the sentence already contains *plummeting*, so there is no reason to use any form of the verb *fall* in the answer choices. Therefore, you can eliminate all of the choices but (E).

The Subjunctive Mood

If you grew up in an English-speaking household and studied a foreign language in high school, you probably learned about the subjunctive mood in your second language before you acknowledged it in your first. The subjunctive mood has two purposes in English. The first is to express the conditional tense, and it usually involves *would* and *were*:

I **would** not water-ski naked if I **were** you.

If he **were** to grow another four inches, he **would** have to buy new pants.

Note that the verb is always *were*, regardless of the subject.

Wrong: If I **was** a rich man …

Right: If I **were** a rich man …

The second use of the subjunctive is to express a demand or request, and this construction follows two strict rules—*that* always comes right after the verb, and the second verb is always in the simple present tense:

Her father demanded **that** she **return** home by 8 p.m.

Grandma requested **that** the window **be** closed.

Wrong answers on questions that involve the subjunctive tense usually involve the word *should* (note the redundancy list on the previous page):

Despite the thousands of protests from devoted fans who <u>demanded that he should</u> shave off his new moustache, Freddie Mercury insisted on keeping it.

- ◯ demanded that he should
- ◯ were demanding him that he
- ◯ demanded that he
- ◯ had demanded him to
- ◯ demanded for him to

If you follow the basic construction rules for this form of the subjunctive, you'll see that (C) is the best choice.

OTHER GRAMMAR STUFF YOU SHOULD KNOW

These points don't appear as often on sentence correction questions, but you should keep them in mind as you write your essays. They're simple and rather obvious, but it never hurts to brush up on the little things.

Singular Pronouns

What's wrong with this sentence?

> Each of the 50 states have an official flag, bird, and flower.

Some students think this sentence sounds fine because the plural noun *states* agrees with *have*. As we discussed in Chapter 2, though, *of the 50 states* is a prepositional phrase. The subject is *Each*, which is a singular pronoun. The sentence should look like this:

> Each [of the 50 states] **has** an official flag, bird, and flower.

To maintain a strong sense of subject-verb agreement, you should know that each of the following pronouns is singular:

another	everybody
any	neither
anything	no one
each	nobody
either	none (not one)
every	

To make this easier to visualize, think of this:

> If you can place the word *one* after a pronoun, it's a singular pronoun that takes a singular verb tense.

> Neither (one) of the astrophysicists **is** able to perfect time travel.

Also: *The number of* suggests a definite number of things, so it takes a singular verb. *A number of*, on the other hand, is less clear, so it takes a plural verb:

The number of people who can access the Internet at home is rising dramatically.

A number of people who have resisted using the Internet **are** finally caving in.

The Insidious "They"

Remember Sting's song lyrics at the beginning of Chapter 1? In conversational English, it has become commonplace to use the pronoun they instead of *he* or *she*, because of basic convenience. Therefore, we end up saying things like this:

Before taking a test, it's important for every person to do **their** homework.

Yeesh. That's some really rotten grammar; *person* is a singular noun, and *their* is a plural pronoun.

The test writers know that we use *they* incorrectly all the time in our daily conversation, so it likes to set traps using *they*:

<u>Each American, regardless of their ethnic background, is</u> protected under the rights explicitly expressed in the Constitution.

- ○ Each American, regardless of their ethnic background, is
- ○ The ethnic backgrounds of each American is regarded as
- ○ All Americans, regardless of their ethnic background they have, are
- ○ Each American, regardless of his or her ethnic background, is
- ○ The ethnic background of all Americans is regarded to be

The correct answer is (D), because each is a singular pronoun that takes *is* as a verb. A might appear correct at first glance, but *their* doesn't agree with *each*. Choice (E) has idiom trouble, because *regard to be* is not idiomatic. Choice (B) is incorrect because the subject and object don't agree, and (C) is incorrect because it's impossible for all Americans to share the same ethnic background.

Make the Subjects and Objects Agree

That's the point of this next bit: Make sure the objects reflect their actual numbers. Okay, that didn't come out right. Let this sentence explain it better:

Celia and Ella brought their husband to the wedding.

This sentence is incorrectly worded because it looks as though the two women have the same husband. It's unlikely that a GMAT sentence would advocate bigamy, so the correct sentence should be written like this:

Celia and Ella brought their husbands to the wedding.

Subject and Object Pronouns

Pronouns that perform the action in a sentence (subject pronouns) are different from those that receive the action (object pronouns):

	Subject	Object
First-person singular	I	me
Second-person singular	you	you
Third-person singular	he/she/it	him/her/it
First-person plural	we	us
Second-person plural	you	you
Third-person plural	they	them

The pronoun you use depends on the word's role in the sentence. Most people have no problem with the singular pronouns; the problems arise when multiple nouns are used.

Between you and I, my parents are starting to act strangely.

Although the pronouns appear in the beginning of the sentence, they are objects of the preposition *between*. If you separate the two, you'll realize that *between you* makes sense, but *between* I does not. Therefore, the correct sentence reads:

Between you and **me**, my parents are starting to act strangely.

In some conversations you're inclined to use the pronoun and the noun right next to each other. If you're ever unsure of which pronoun to use, take out the noun and see if it makes sense:

We revolutionaries need to stick together.

We [ ] need to stick together.

There's nobody here but us bank robbers.

There's nobody here but **us** [ ].

Also, when making comparisons, make sure the pronouns are in the same form as the nouns:

WRONG: He is taller than **me**.

RIGHT: He is taller than **I** [am].

And if your name is Sheila and someone calls asking for you, you should say "This is *she*" instead of "This is *her*."

Semicolons

Semicolons are used for more than just the winking eyes on your emoticon. The only time to use a semicolon is when you want to link two complete sentences.

Joan paused for a moment as she considered her options; it still wasn't too late to run back to her car and forget about the blind date.

Weird Plurals

As you match up your subjects and your verbs, be sure to remember that each of the following words, even though it sounds singular, is actually plural. We often misuse these words in conversation, but it's important to get them right in your writing.

Data is the plural form of *datum*:

Wrong: The data is sufficient to answer the question.

Right: The data **are** sufficient to answer the question.

Media is the plural form of *medium*:

Wrong: The media has always portrayed the president too positively.

Right: The media **have** always portrayed the president too positively.

Criteria is the plural form of *criterion*:

Wrong: What is your criteria for the perfect date?

Right: What **are** your criteria for the perfect date?

Alumni is the plural form of *alumnus* (a male graduate of a school); *Alumnae* is the plural of *alumna* (a female graduate of a school):

> **Wrong:** My brother is an alumni of Notre Dame.

> **Right:** My brother is an **alumnus** of Notre Dame.

WHEN TO USE WHICH WORD

Have you ever had a prolonged debate over the proper use of a word? Do you want to become more popular at your next cocktail party or family gathering? Then this section is for you. The following are a few words that are common on sentence correction questions.

Between vs. Among

If a sentence compares two items, use *between*. If you're dealing with three or more items, use *among*:

> In a presidential election, most Americans choose **between** the Democratic candidate and the Republican candidate.

> **Among** the five candidates at the New Hampshire primary, Senator Batard is clearly the front-runner.

Note: You'll see *among* on the GMAT, but you won't see *amongst*. The two words are absolutely interchangeable when you're writing a sentence, but *amongst* isn't used as much in normal discourse because it's antiquated. Avoid using it when you write your essays; stick with *among*.

-er vs. -est

When you're comparing two things, add *-er* to the end of the adjective to form the *comparative* degree:

> Texas is much larger than Oklahoma.

If you're comparing three or more objects, add -est to the adjective to form the *superlative* degree:

> Maine is easily the largest of all six New England states.

Further vs. Farther

Lots of people think these words are interchangeable, but there is a distinction. Use *farther* to indicate a greater tangible distance, and use *further* to indicate that intangible progress has been made:

> I don't intend to pursue this matter any **further**.

> Forrest Gump ran **farther** than any other man had ever run.

Fewer vs. Less

The use of either of these words depends on whether the nouns in the sentence are countable. If the nouns are countable (such as books, people, or kneecaps), use *fewer*:

> There are **fewer** people in the state of South Dakota than there are in New York City.

If you have an uncountable quantity (such as time, soup, or money), use *less*:

> When my wife had our first child, we found that we had a lot **less** time to ourselves.

All together, now:

> There is a lot **less** traffic during rush hour now because fewer people drive their cars to work.

Note: The only time that *less* is involved with countable objects is when fractions, percents, or other numbers are involved. (It's an arcane rule that doesn't come up on the GMAT very often, but it might if you get a really hard question.)

> **Less** than one-quarter of all high school students can find Argentina on a map.

> The production of East Timor amounts to **less** than 1 percent of the world's GDP.

Note the distinction between these two sentences:

> There are **fewer** than 1,000 species of frog left in the Amazon river basin.

> The number of species of frog left in the Amazon river basin is **less** than 1,000.

Its vs. It's

Never confuse these two because their meanings are very different. *Its* is the possessive of *it*, and *it's* is the contracted form of *it is*:

It's never too late to learn to play the piano.

The baby elephant never strayed far from **its** mother.

Note: Words that sound the same but have different meanings are called homonyms. The most common examples of homonyms that are frequently confused are *your* vs. *you're* and *their* vs. *they're*. You won't have to distinguish these on sentence correction questions, but you'll lose your readers' respect if you mess them up on your essays.

Your mother said that **you're** expected to be home by 7:30.

They're too far away to hear what **their** mother wants.

Lie vs. Lay

One meaning of the word *lie* is straightforward; it means to say something that is false:

The witness should never **lie** to the jury.

The judge believed that Wu **lied** under oath.

The confusion arises when you consider the other meaning of *lie*, which is to recline. *Lay*, on the other hand, means to put something down. The confusion occurs because the past tense of *lie* is *lay*:

Present tense: After church, my dad usually **lies** down on the couch.

Past tense: After church, my dad **lay** down on the couch.

Many vs. Much

The rule here is just like the rule for fewer vs. less. If the nouns that are being compared are countable, use *many*; otherwise, use *much*:

There is too **much** traffic on this highway because too **many** people drive to work.

More vs. Most

The rules for these words are just like those that pertain to *-er* vs. *-est*. *More* and *most* are just irregular forms of comparative words; use *more* for two items, and use *most* for three-plus items:

Nicole has **more** stock options than Heather does.

Of all the companies in the Fortune 500, Microsoft is worth the **most** money.

The same rule holds true for each of these adjectives that have irregular forms when used as comparative or superlatives:

Adjective	Comparative	Superlative
bad	worse	worst
good	better	best
little	less	least
far	farther, further	farthest, furthest

Note: There are also several words that have no comparative or superlative form because the simple form of that word expresses the point to the highest possible degree. For example, it's impossible for something to be *more unique* than something else. Either it's unique (which means there's nothing else like it), or it's not. Words like this include *perfect, fatal, empty, wrong, dead, blind, alone,* and *pregnant.*

That vs. Which

You're not likely to be forced to make this distinction on the GMAT. If something is wrong with an answer choice, there will probably be a much more egregious flaw other than it used *that* instead of *which*. The rule is: *That* is restrictive, which means that it helps to identify what it is that we're talking about, it *restricts* us to a particular thing. "The car **that** is in the garage..." means that we're identifying a particular car—the one in the garage as opposed to the one on the street, say. *Which* is non-restrictive, which means that we already understand what it is we're talking about, and that we're merely getting some additional information about it. "The car, **which** is in the garage..." means that we already know what car we're talking about—there's only one car—and we are learning the additional information that it happens to be in the garage. Usually, *which* will be set off by a comma, and *that* will not be.

Here are some additional examples:

> Bananas, **which** are high in potassium, are considered an ideal food for dieting.

> The bananas **that** I left in the refrigerator have gone bad.

Also, the pronoun *which* always refers to the most recent noun in the sentence (usually the one right before the comma):

> **Wrong:** I bought a car and a dress, which had only 3,000 miles on it.

> **Right:** I bought a dress and a car, which had only 3,000 miles on it.

Who vs. Whom

> Lou: So I pick up the ball, and I throw it to who?

> Bud: Now that's the first thing you've said right.

> Lou: I don't even know what I'm talking about!

Lou was right; he doesn't know what he's talking about. You don't throw to *who*, you throw to *whom*!

Lots of people are unsure about when to use *who* or *whom*, but it's really very simple. *Who* is a subject pronoun that indicates that you don't know the person committing the action:

> **Who** left this empty milk carton in the refrigerator?

Whom is an object pronoun that receives action:

> To **whom** am I speaking?

Note that *whom* usually comes right after a preposition (*to* whom, *at* whom, and so on). The simplest way to remember which pronoun to use is this:

> If you answer the question with he, use *who*. If you answer the question with *him*, use *whom*.

Let's answer the previous two questions as an example:

Q: **Who** left this empty milk carton in the refrigerator?

A: **He** did.

Q: To **whom** am I speaking?

A: You're speaking to **him**.

Get it? If you stick to that rule, you can't go wrong.

Appendix B
Grammar
Glossary

Here are several grammar terms that you might come across either in this book or while on some other grammatical pursuit. This is by no means an exhaustive list, but it's all you need to know for the GMAT (and then some). Don't spend a lot of time memorizing these because you won't be tested on the terms themselves on the GMAT. They will be helpful to know as you study, though.

active voice	When the grammatical subject of a sentence performs the action of the verb. (Example: The girl threw the boomerang.) The GMAT generally prefers the active voice to the passive voice. (Example: The boomerang was thrown by the girl.) See also: *passive voice*.
adjective	A word used to modify (or describe) a noun or pronoun.
adverb	A word usually used to modify a verb but also to modify an adjective or another adverb.
antecedent	The noun to which a pronoun refers.
apples to oranges	A term (related to parallel construction) that relates to the importance of avoiding comparisons of unlike things (nouns to verbs). Comparing like things would be apples to apples (noun to nouns).
article	The words *a*, *an*, and *the*. *A* and *an* are indefinite articles, and *the* is the definite article.
clause	A group of words that contains a subject and a verb. See: independent clause; dependent clause, subordinate clause.
collective noun	The name given to a group or collection of objects.
conjugation	The systematic arrangement of all the forms of a verb.
conjunction	A word used to join other words or groups of words, such as *and, but*, and *so*.
dependent clause	A group of words that has a subject and verb but is not a complete sentence. It needs to be attached to an independent clause to be part of a sentence. (Also known as a *subordinate clause*.)
direct object	The noun in a sentence that receives the action.
future perfect tense	The verb tense that denotes action that will be completed at some definite time in the future. (Example: By the year 3000, the Red Sox *will have won* the World Series many times.)
future tense	The verb tense that denotes future time. (Example: The Red Sox *will win* the World Series next year.)
gerund	The result of adding *-ing* to a verb, thus creating a term used as a noun. (Example: *Winning* the World Series would be a great thing for the Red Sox to do.)

independent clause	A group of words that expresses a complete thought and thus can exist as a simple sentence.
indirect object	The object for which something else is done. (Example: Carlos gave the book to *me*. *Book* is the direct object, and *me* is the indirect object.)
infinitive	The verb form in which the verb is preceded by the preposition *to*. (Example: I want to win the Publishers Clearinghouse Sweepstakes.)
misplaced modifier	A modifying word or phrase that is in the wrong place in a sentence and thus seems to modify the wrong word.
modifier	A word or group of words that describes another word.
noun	A person, place, or thing.
participle	A verb form that is used as an adjective. (Example: This book is *exciting*.)
parts of speech	Words that are classified depending on what they do in a sentence (nouns, verbs, adjectives, and so on).
passive voice	When the grammatical subject of a sentence receives the action of the verb. (Example: The cat was chased by my dog, Spot.) In that example the subject is *cat* but the cat isn't performing the action of the verb—it's not doing the chasing. Instead it's receiving the action of the verb—being chased. The GMAT generally prefers the active voice. (Example: My dog, Spot, chased the cat.) See also: *active voice*.
past perfect tense	The verb tense used to convey the thought that two events happened in the past and one happened before the other. Verbs are usually accompanied by *had*. (Example: Apes *had conquered* the world when the Red Sox finally won a World Series.)
past tense	The verb tense that denotes an event that happened before right now. (Example: The Red Sox *won* the World Series in 1918.)
person	A reference to the speaker in a sentence. The first person is the person speaking (I); the second person is the person spoken to (you); and the third person is the person spoken of (he, she, it).
phrase	A group of words that lacks either a noun or a verb (and thus is not a clause nor a sentence).
possessive	The case that shows ownership, usually denoted by *'s* at the end of a singular noun.

preposition	A word that shows the relation between its object and some other word in the sentence. Many idiom questions involve using the proper preposition. (Example: Scholars attribute many clever quotations *to* Winston Churchill. *To* is the proper preposition.)
prepositional phrase	A modifying phrase containing a preposition and an object. (Example: The runner ran on the track. The prepositional phrase *on the track* describes where the runner ran; *on* is the preposition; and *track* is the object of the preposition.)
present perfect tense	The verb tense used to convey action that is completed before the sentence was said. Verbs are usually accompanied by *has* or *have*. (Example: This cable channel *has shown* the same awful movie 15 times this week.)
present tense	The verb tense that denotes what is happening right now.
pronoun	A word used in place of a noun for the sake of brevity or to avoid repetition.
proper noun	A noun (like a name) that designates a particular person, place, or thing and is usually capitalized.
run-on sentence	A sentence in which two independent clauses are linked together without the use of a conjunction or semicolon between them. (Example: The candidate won the election, the students went crazy celebrating on campus.)
split infinitive	An improper verb usage in which the infinitive form is interrupted by another word. (Example: The female astronaut wanted *to* boldly *go* where no woman had gone before.)
subject	The part of a sentence that drives the action.
subjunctive mood	A verb form used to express: (1) hypothetical situations that are contrary to fact (Example: If the Red Sox *were* to win the World Series, Boston would burn down); and (2) wishes and demands (Example: Tyrone demanded *that* the Red Sox *win* the World Series before he died).
subordinate clause	A clause (also known as a *dependent clause*) that cannot serve as a sentence all by itself and needs to be linked to a main clause (or *independent clause*).
superlative degree	A term used when more than two items are compared. This is usually denoted by the suffix *-est* after an adjective. (Example: Rosa scored the *highest* on the GMAT of anyone in her class because she did all of the practice questions and drills in the book.)
verb	A term that denotes the action in a sentence.

Appendix C
Idiom List

Here's a list of some of the idioms that have appeared in sentence correction questions on actual GMATs in recent years. Of course, this is not an exhaustive list of all the idioms you'll have to know; that's why there are a few empty sheets at the end of this list. Whenever you encounter an idiom that you've never seen before, add it to this list and memorize it.

A

able to, ability to

> I am no longer *able* to run ten miles as fast as I used to.

> Sloths have the *ability* to sleep while hanging from their toes.

accede to

> Once defeated, the military dictator had to *accede* to NATO's demands.

access to

> After the home team lost, reporters were not given *access to* the coach's office.

according to

> *According to* the etiquette expert, it is very rude to stick out your pinkie as you drink tea.

account for

> The Brazilian rain forest *accounts for* 40 percent of all species of tree frog.

accuse of

> I *accused* my little brother of stealing my favorite football jersey.

acquaint with

> When I moved to London, I had to *acquaint* myself *with* English social customs.

agree with

> I don't *agree with* your viewpoint.

allow for

> When you budget your money, you should *allow for* emergency expenses.

amount to

> When the trial was canceled, all the lawyer's preparation *amounted* to nothing.

appear to

> The natives of this island don't *appear to* be very friendly.

apply to

> Traffic laws don't *apply to* international diplomats.

argue over

> The newly married couple didn't *argue over* money very often.

as [adjective] as

Your cat isn't *as* friendly *as* my cat.

associate with

My mother told me never to *associate with* people I don't know.

assure that

I *assure* you *that* my sister is the ideal person for this job.

at a disadvantage

Our desperate financial situation put us *at a disadvantage* while we were negotiating.

attempt to

I will *attempt to* write my B-School essays after I finish dinner.

attend to, attention to

New parents must *attend to* their child's cries.

The book editor was known for her *attention to* detail.

attest to

I can *attest to* the fact that John has never been to Indonesia.

attribute to

Many clever quotes are *attributed to* Oscar Wilde.

available to

Before you make a decision, be sure you know all the options that are *available to* you.

B

based on

The award-winning movie was *based on* a book that virtually no one read.

because of

Because of her broken leg, she was unable to ski for two months.

believe to be

These artifacts are *believed to be* remnants of the Ming dynasty.

between [A] and [B]

There are 14 rest stops on the highway *between* Baltimore *and* Washington, D.C.

C

call for

> Desperate times *call for* desperate measures.

choice of

> Given the *choice of* liver or ice cream, I would select the latter.

choose from [nouns]

> Business school candidates can *choose from* hundreds of accredited programs.

choose to [verb]

> Many people *choose to* attend business school after they have worked for only two years.

claim to

> My uncle *claims to* have eaten 200 hot dogs in half an hour.

collaborate with

> The actor *collaborated with* two ghost writers on his autobiography.

conclude that

> After years of research, the scientist *concluded that* baked beans do not cause baldness.

consequence of

> Bankruptcy is usually a *consequence of* poor money management.

consider

> Dr. Melnitz is *considered* the world's foremost authority on medieval manuscripts.

> **Note:** Although the test writers do not like you to use *consider to be*, it's perfectly fine to use it in ordinary English. This is just one of the ways in which GMAT English differs from normal English.

consist of

> The heart *consists of* four chambers that pump blood throughout the body.

consistent with

> Her new findings are *consistent with* contemporary theories.

continue to

> If you *continue to* make noise back there, I'll turn this car around and we'll go home.

contrast with

> His low-key speaking style *contrasted with* his partner's more passionate oratory.

contribute to

> Would you care to *contribute* your time to the church's tutoring program?

convert to

> The alchemist Rumpelstiltskin can *convert* lead *to* gold.

cost of [something]

> The *cost of* sending your child to college has tripled in the last decade.

cost to [someone]

> After the war, the *cost to* the surviving inhabitants of the small village was devastating.

credit with

> Dr. Jonas Salk is *credited with* the discovery of the polio vaccine.

D

date from

> This ancient parchment *dates from* the Revolutionary War.

deal with

> I'll *deal with* that problem later.

debate over

> My parents always *debate over* which movie the family will see.

decide to (not decide *on*)

> After a lot of deep thought, Latisha *decided to* take the job offer in Moscow.

defend against

> The small startup *defended* itself *against* the hostile takeover.

define as

> Perjury is *defined as* the act of lying while under oath.

delighted by

> The woman was *delighted by* her daughter's impending solo flight.

demonstrate that

> This evidence will *demonstrate that* dogs can do algebra.

depend on

> Whether I go to the ball game *depends on* the weather.

depict as

> In recent textbooks, Columbus has been *depicted as* a genocidal maniac.

descend from

> On the Fourth of July, lots of firecrackers *descend from* the sky.

different from

> The customs of the countries of the Far East are *different from* ours.

difficult to

> It is *difficult to* determine whether mice can sing to each other.

distinguish [A] from [B]

Can you *distinguish* indigo *from* violet?

draw on

Surgeons *draw on* years of experience when they try new procedures.

due to

The company's shortfall was *due to* lessening global demand for its products.

E

[in an] effort to

In an *effort to* end the war, the general called for a cease-fire.

either...or

I will *either* read the paper *or* go to the movies.

enamored with

When my family met my new girlfriend, everyone was *enamored with* her.

encourage to

Recent college graduates are *encouraged to* work for five years before applying to business school.

-er than

My biceps are strong*er than* your biceps.

estimate to be

The estate of Count von Hammerbanger is *estimated to be* in the billions.

expose to

Parents are worried that television *exposes* their children *to* too much violence.

extend to

I *extended* my arm *to* the dog and let it lick my palm.

extent of

No one knows the *extent of* the queen's fortune.

F

fear that

I *fear that* robots will take over the world in 100 years.

fluctuations in

There have been many *fluctuations in* the new company's growth pattern.

forbid to (not forbid *from*)

> Native South Koreans are *forbidden to* attend gambling casinos within Korea.

force to

> My parents *forced* me *to* attend military school, even though I didn't want to go.

frequency of

> The *frequency of* electrical fires on the subway is truly alarming.

from [A] to [B]

> Every house *from* Allentown *to* Bethlehem lost power during the blackout.

H

hypothesize that

> Some nutritionists *hypothesize that* too many dairy products can cause cancer.

I

in contrast to

> *In contrast to* my opponent, I believe that town funds should be used to build a new library.

in danger of

> People who ignore speed limits put themselves *in danger of* causing an accident.

in order to

> You have to break a few eggs *in order to* make an omelet.

in violation of

> By mistreating the prisoners, the general was *in violation of* the rules laid out by the Geneva Convention.

inclined to (also *disinclined* to)

> Young children who watch television are *inclined to* become very lazy adults.

infected with

> People who are *infected with* a deadly virus must be isolated from other patients.

instead of

> Today I will eat a salad *instead of* my usual meal of meat and potatoes.

introduce to

> My mother almost fainted when she was *introduced to* Frank Sinatra.

isolate from

> People who are infected with a deadly virus must be *isolated from* other patients.

J

just as...so too

> *Just as* I have crossed over to the Dark Side, *so too* will you, my son.

L

less than

> On average, college students have *less* money *than* their parents.

likely to (also *unlikely* to)

> Whenever I eat Brussels sprouts, I'm *likely to* throw up.

liken to

> The clerk *likened* the man's complaining to the barking of a small dog.

M

mistake for

> My brother is often *mistaken for* Jack Black.

model after

> The Rotunda at the University of Virginia is *modeled after* the Pantheon in Rome.

more than

> The Chinese eat *more* rice *than* any other people do.

move away from

> The police officer told the intruder to **move away from** the door.

N

[a] native of

> The famous opera singer is a *native of* Italy.

native to

> Koala bears are *native to* Australia.

neither...nor

> *Neither* rain *nor* sleet shall keep me from the swift completion of my appointed rounds.

not [A] but [B]

> The opposite of love is *not* hate *but* indifference.

not only ... but also

> My sister is *not only* brilliant *but also* quite charming.

not so much...as

> The reason for the soaring stock market is *not so much* ignorance *as* it is optimism.

O

on account of

> *On account of* the brutal winter, the farmer's corn production suffered greatly.

opportunity for [noun]

> Before I take this job, what is my *opportunity for* advancement?

opportunity to [verb]

> I'd like to take this *opportunity to* thank all the little people who made this award possible.

opposed to

> Pacifists are *opposed to* any form of fighting or aggression.

opposite of

> The *opposite of* love is not hate, but indifference.

P

permit to

> Children are not *permitted to* attend an R-rated movie without their parents.

persuade to

> I finally *persuaded* my parents *to* let me attend the rock concert.

predisposed to

> Baby turtles are *predisposed to* fend for themselves early in life.

pressure to

> The United Nations was *pressured to* impose sanctions on the country.

prevent from

> Safety latches *prevent* small children *from* playing with cleaning products.

prized by

> Rhinoceros horn is *prized by* some cultures as a potent aphrodisiac.

prohibit from

> In New York City, smokers are *prohibited from* smoking inside any public building.

protect against

> Chemical treatment can help *protect* your car *against* rust and corrosion.

provide with

> The technical college *provides* each new student *with* a brand-new laptop.

Q

question whether

> I'm beginning to *question whether* saltines have any nutritional value.

R

range from [A] to [B]

> Scores on the GMAT *range from* 200 to 800.

rather than

> I'd *rather* swim in the ocean *than* sit on the beach.

regard as

> In Asian cities, waving crazily for a taxicab is *regarded as* a rude gesture.

replace with

> The five-star restaurant *replaced* its homemade desserts *with* frozen ones.

require to

> Grandma always *requires* us *to* remove our shoes before we come in the house.

required of

> What exactly is *required of* the applicants for this job?

[the] responsibility to

> I have the *responsibility to* care for my dog.

responsible for

> I am *responsible for* my dog's welfare.

result from

> Success usually *results from* hard work.

result in

> Hard work usually *results in* success.

rule that (subjunctive)

> The principal has *ruled that* all students can call her by her first name, Maria.

S

[the] same as

> Your hat is the *same as* mine.

see as

> The dictator *saw* the uprising *as* a threat to his authority.

send to

> I *sent* a birthday card *to* my grandmother.

sense of

> Dogs have an acute *sense of* smell.

so [adjective] as to [verb]

> Her debts are *so* extreme *as to* threaten the future of the company.

so…that

> His debts are *so* extreme *that* the company may soon go bankrupt.

spend on

> I *spend* more than $10,000 per year *on* eating out.

subject to

> Members of Congress are *subject to* the same laws as are ordinary Americans.

substitute [A] for [B]

> In an effort to lower my cholesterol, I *substituted* margarine *for* butter in my diet.

suffer from

> I *suffer from* the heartbreak of psoriasis.

superior to

> My grandfather's spaghetti sauce is *superior to* that store-bought brand.

supplant by

> After the massive cutbacks at the plant, my uncle was *supplanted by* a large robot.

suspicious of

> I'm *suspicious of* people who don't shake hands firmly.

T

target at

> The shoe company *targeted* its advertising *at* high school–age kids.

the -er…, the -er

> *The* bigg*er* they are, *the* hard*er* they fall.

think of…as

> I've grown to *think of* my best friend *as* the brother I never had.

threaten to

> After ten hours of negotiations, both parties *threatened to* walk out of the room.

train to

> I *trained* my puppy *to* bring me the newspaper every morning.

transmit to

> The submarine *transmitted* the coded message *to* all the ships in the area.

try to (not try *and*)

> If you *try to* hold your breath for more than a minute, your face will turn blue.

type of

> This is the *type of* situation that I usually try to avoid.

U

use as

> My wife hates it when I *use* the lamp *as* a hat stand.

[the] use of

> *The use of* nuclear weapons in World War II was condemned by many nations.

V

view as

> The dictator *viewed* the uprising *as* a threat to his authority.

vote for

> Rather than *vote for* the Democrat or Republican, I voted for the Libertarian.

W

[the] way to [verb] is to [verb]

> *The way* to deal with my father-in-law *is to* nod enthusiastically at everything he says.

willing to (also *unwilling* to)

> Most teachers are *willing to* meet with their students after school and give extra help.

worry about

> Economists *worry* too much *about* America's trade deficit.

About the Author

Doug French has been a GMAT instructor and course developer with The Princeton Review since 1992, and he has been training GMAT instructors since 1995. He has taught classes for the GMAT, SAT, LSAT, and GRE in the U.S., Europe, and Asia, and he can teach you any math topic from simple addition to BC calculus.

Doug also writes fiction, draws cartoons, and does voice-overs. He lives with his family in New York City, which is known to be the best city in the world (except during the summer, when it becomes really pungent).

NOTES

NOTES

NOTES

NOTES

NOTES

NOTES

NOTES